# BETWEEN WAR AND
# THE STATE

# BETWEEN WAR AND THE STATE

Civil Society in South Vietnam, 1954–1975

**Van Nguyen-Marshall**

SOUTHEAST ASIA PROGRAM PUBLICATIONS

AN IMPRINT OF CORNELL UNIVERSITY PRESS   ITHACA AND LONDON

First published 2023 by Cornell University Press

Library of Congress Cataloging–in–Publication Data

Names: Nguyen-Marshall, Van, 1967– author.
Title: Between war and the state : civil society in South Vietnam,
    1954–1975 / Van Nguyen-Marshall.
Description: Ithaca : Southeast Asia Program Publications, an imprint of
    Cornell University Press, 2023. | Includes bibliographical references
    and index.
Identifiers: LCCN 2022051732 (print) | LCCN 2022051733 (ebook) |
    ISBN 9781501770579 (hardcover) | ISBN 9781501770586 (paperback) |
    ISBN 9781501770593 (pdf) | ISBN 9781501770609 (epub)
Subjects: LCSH: Civil society—Vietnam (Republic) | Associations,
    institutions, etc.—Vietnam (Republic) | Vietnam War, 1961–1975—
    Social aspects. | Social action—Vietnam (Republic) | Political
    participation—Vietnam (Republic) | Vietnam (Republic)—Social
    conditions.
Classification: LCC HN700.5.A8 N47195 2023  (print) | LCC HN700.5.A8
    (ebook) | DDC 306.209597—dc23/eng/20230210
LC record available at https://lccn.loc.gov/2022051732
LC ebook record available at https://lccn.loc.gov/2022051733

In memory of my parents, Nguyễn Văn Toan and Trần Thị Thanh,
who showed me what resilience looks like

# Contents

# Acknowledgments

It is hard to know where to begin. I began researching this book more than a decade ago, and the debt I incurred along the way is weighty. I will start by thanking the Canadian Social Sciences and Humanities Research Council for funding much of the research. This funding allowed me to conduct research in Vietnam and in the United States.

I am grateful to the Vietnam Academy of Social Sciences and the Southern Institute for Social Sciences in Ho Chi Minh City for facilitating and hosting my many research visits. Their support was critical in obtaining access to archives and libraries and conducting interviews. I am truly grateful for their help. The archivists and staff at the National Archives II, as well as the General Sciences Library in Ho Chi Minh City, provided invaluable assistance. I thank them for putting up with my many requests. I am also grateful to Cornell University Library for its open-door policy, which gave me access to Cornell's rich and valuable collection of Republican-era periodicals and publications. I thank the staff at the Olin Library, Kroch Asian Library, and Division of Rare and Manuscript Collections for their friendly and professional assistance.

A sincere thank you to the folks at Cornell University Press and Southeast Asia Program Publications, especially Sarah Grossman for taking a chance on this project and for her stewardship during the manuscript-to-book process. Jacqulyn Teoh handled all my queries with patience and clarity. A special thank you to the two reviewers, whose comments and suggestions were insightful and constructive. Their input made this book better. Any remaining shortcomings are the result of my inability to fully follow their suggestions.

The photographs in this volume came from Harry Hallman, Ngy Thanh, and the Vietnam Center and Sam Johnson Vietnam Archive at Texas Tech University. I thank them for granting me permission to use these photographs. The map was expertly created by Toronto cartographer Jeff Allen.

Chapters 5 and 6 were previously published in the *Journal of Vietnamese Studies* and *War and Society*, respectively. I am thankful for the opportunity to publish my work in these esteemed journals and for their permission to republish these pieces here. Both chapters have been revised and contain additional information.

My research assistants during different legs of the project were immensely helpful. I wish to thank Derek Lipman, Nguyễn Thu Vân, Michelle Nguyen, and specially Nguyễn Ngọc Anh, who helped me track down important figures in South Vietnam's civil society.

Many people shared their stories and life experiences with me. Their willingness to do so gave this book more depth and color. I am deeply grateful for their generosity and trust in me: Ông Bạch Công An, Ông Đoàn Thanh Liêm, Ông Hoàng Đức Nhã, Ông Huỳnh Tấn Mẫm, Bà Huỳnh Thị Ngọc Tuyết, Ông Lâm Thành Qúy, Ông Nguyễn Huỳnh Tân, Ông Nguyễn Kinh Châu, Bà Nguyễn Thị Oanh, Ông Nguyễn Tường Cẩm, Bà Nguyễn Vân Hạnh, Ông Nguyễn Văn Nghị, Ông Ngy Thanh, Father Phan Khắc Từ, Thích Đồng Bổn, Thích Tâm Đức, Thu-Hương Nguyễn-Võ, Ông Trần Khánh Tuyết, Ông Trần Quang Lâm, Bà Trần Thị Nên, Ông Trần Trí, Ông Trần Văn Sơn, Bà Triều Giang Nancy Bui, Ông Trịnh Cung, Bà Trùng Dương (Nguyễn Thị Thái), and Ông Uyên Thao.

I express special thanks to Ông Ngy Thanh, Bà Trùng Dương, and Ông Uyên Thao, who took a strong interest in my work and have been an inspiration. I also want to thank my close friends in Hanoi who opened their homes to me and my family: Ông Bà Nguyễn Văn Kự, Nguyễn Thanh Liêm and family, Nguyễn Thanh Hà and family, Nguyễn Thị Nhung, and Hoàng Hòa Tùng.

As the citations throughout this book show, my understanding of Vietnam and the Vietnam War rely heavily on the painstaking research and brilliant analyses of numerous other scholars. I thank the following in particular for their friendship, for sharing their research with me, and for giving me feedback and encouragement: Olga Dror, Sean Fear, Judith Henchy, Alec Holcombe, Ann Marie Leshkowich, Hy Van Luong, David Marr, Edward Miller, Michael Montesano, Nathalie Huỳnh Châu Nguyễn, Thu-Huong Nguyen-Vo, Helle Rydstrom, Geoffrey Stewart, Mitchell Tan, Angie Ngoc Tran, Nu-Anh Tran, Jay Veith, Alex Vo-Thai, Tuong Vu, Alexander Woodside, and Peter Zinoman. I want to mention the late Lisa Welch Drummond in particular. Her friendship deeply influenced me as a person and as a scholar. My colleagues at Trent also deserve an acknowledgment for their ongoing support and friendship, especially Jennine Hurl-Eamon, Carolyn Kay, Antonio Cazorla Sanchez, David Sheinin, Caroline Durand, Trisha Pearce, Dana Capell, and Finis Dunaway.

On the home front, my friends and extended family have been my rock of support, especially during the COVID-19 pandemic. My friends Dawn Lyons and Paula Sarson continue to be there for me through thick and thin. I cannot ask for better family-in-laws than the Marshalls. My father-in-law, Robert E. Marshall, has always taken an interest in my work. I am truly blessed with the support of my seven siblings—Khanh, Nguyệt, Đạt, Thủy, Hương, Hằng, and Hà—and their families. My brother Đạt was enormously helpful because he introduced me to friends and associates who participated in South Vietnam's civil society.

My husband and children will be relieved that this book is now completed. My husband has read too many iterations of it, and his questions and comments pushed me to clarify my argument. I could not have done this without his support and love. Thank you to my daughter, Vĩnh Xuân, for her unfailing belief in me and her encouragement. Chester, who came into our lives at the tail end of this project, provided me with reasons to grow and develop in ways that I did not anticipate. I am grateful to the three of them for giving me a rich, loving home life.

# Abbreviations

| | |
|---|---|
| AFL-CIO | American Federation of Labor–Congress of Industrial Organizations |
| ARVN | Army of Vietnam (main military force of the RVN) |
| ASVN | Associated State of Vietnam |
| CARE | Cooperative for American Remittances to Europe |
| CIA | Central Intelligence Agency (US) |
| CORDS | Civil Operations Revolutionary Development Support (US) |
| COSVN | Central Office of South Vietnam |
| CRS | Catholic Relief Service |
| DRV | Democratic Republic of Vietnam (North Vietnam) |
| ICP | Indochinese Communist Party |
| IRC | International Rescue Committee |
| IVS | International Voluntary Service |
| MAFS | mutual-aid and friendly societies |
| NGO | nongovernmental organization |
| NLF | National Liberation Front |
| NYVS | National Youth Voluntary Service |
| PAVN | People's Army of Vietnam (main military force of the DRV) |
| PLAF | People's Liberation Armed Forces (military force of the NLF) |
| PPI | Popular Polytechnic Institute (Trường Bách Khoa Bình Dân) |
| PRP | People's Revolutionary Party (southern branch of the Lao Động Party) |
| RVN | Republic of Vietnam (South Vietnam from 1955 to 1975) |
| SRV | Socialist Republic of Vietnam |
| SSU | Saigon Student Union (Tổng Hội Sinh Viên Sài Gòn) |
| SVN | State of Vietnam |
| SYSS | School of Youth for Social Service (Trường Thanh Niên Phụng Sự Xã Hội) |
| UBC | Unified Buddhist Congregation (Giáo hội Phật giáo Việt Nam Thống nhất) |
| UNDP | United Nations Development Program |
| USAID | United States Agency for International Development |
| USIA | United States Information Agency |
| USOM | United States Operations Mission |

VCL      Vietnam Confederation of Labor
VCW      Vietnam Confederation of [Catholic] Workers
WASS     Women's Association for Social Service (Hội Phụ nữ Việt Nam
         Phụng Sự Xã Hội)
WSM      Women's Solidarity Movement (Phong Trào Phụ Nữ Liên Đới)
YCW      Young Christian Workers (Thanh Lao Công)

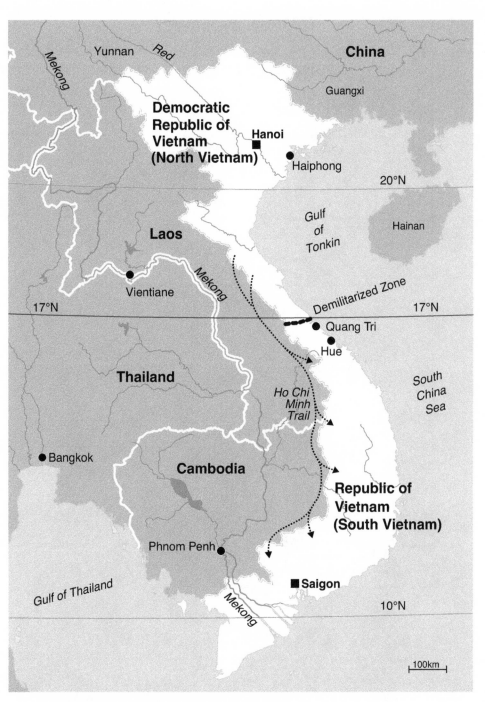

Vietnam, 1954–1975. Map created by Jeff Allen.

# THEORY AND SCOPE

In January 1956, less than three months after the proclamation of the Republic of Vietnam (RVN, or South Vietnam), Ngô Đình Diệm's government turned its attention toward surveilling civil society. Interior minister Nguyễn Hữu Châu requested an inventory of all voluntary organizations south of the seventeenth parallel. That survey revealed the existence of more than four hundred voluntary associations, ranging from labor unions and philanthropic groups to student associations and cultural clubs.[1] According to the classifications used by the officials who compiled the inventory, there were 150 labor unions, 148 mutual-aid and friendly societies, 94 religious groups, 18 arts and culture organizations, and 17 philanthropic associations. Significantly, only thirty-five were operating with government permission. The officials flagged five organizations that were suspected of harboring communists or supporters of other political rivals.[2] Also alarming to the interior minister was the lack of information the government had about these four hundred organizations beyond their names and their founders. This prompted the minister to instruct city mayors and provincial heads to be more vigilant in enforcing state regulations when dealing with voluntary organizations and to make sure only registered organizations could operate.

The new government's concern about voluntary groups—an important component of civil society—is revealing on two counts. First, the government was aware of civil society's potential power and was therefore eager to control this social realm. As subsequent chapters show, while South Vietnamese authorities wanted to harness the energy of voluntary associations to enhance state-building endeavors and supplement the state's social welfare provisions,

1

government officials were also wary of civil society's potential to challenge the state and create dissent. Second, Nguyễn Hữu Châu's inquiry reveals that South Vietnam's public life was robust. People's associational activities were significant enough to attract state attention and surveillance. Over the next two decades, essentially the life span of the RVN, voluntary organizations continued to grow and South Vietnamese citizens continued to participate in associational life. Many groups attended to the specific needs of their members, while others aspired to improve living conditions for their communities and to shape the life of the nation.

While there is no lack of books on Vietnam and its wars, few have examined South Vietnam's civil society, and to my knowledge, none has made this important arena of social interaction in the Republican period its focus.[3] This book examines South Vietnam's extensive associational life and covers an array of groups, from mutual-aid societies and charities to professional and rights organizations. By examining people's voluntary public activities, this book offers a unique glimpse into South Vietnam, a society grappling with postcolonial changes, territorial division, nation building, civil war, and foreign intervention. The underlying motivation of this book is to understand the wartime experiences of the South Vietnamese people in a way that does not reduce them to mere victims of violence. While many Vietnamese on both sides endured profound suffering and loss, they were not passive victims defined only by wartime adversities. The activities of voluntary organizations provide tangible evidence of how some residents of South Vietnam, mainly in the urban centers, articulated and responded to the dramatic events that shaped the history of the RVN (1955–1975).

Because of its origin, its dependence on US aid, and its eventual defeat, South Vietnam has been overlooked by historians both inside and outside Vietnam. The general view was that South Vietnam did not have a legal basis for governance or existence. Its establishment was supposed to be transitory, and the decision to divide the country was made without consulting the population in either the north or the south. Consequently, South Vietnam was often considered inconsequential in historical narratives of the Vietnam War (circa 1960–1975), or it has been depicted as a shell of a state without a constituency and without a nation.[4] Any historical attention it received tended to focus on the corrupt and incompetent political and military leaders, who were dismissed as puppets of the United States.[5]

In the last twenty years, the scholarship on South Vietnam has been growing because of better access to archival material and because of the recognition that little is known about its people, particularly their motivations, aspirations, and actions. There is now consensus among historians that while the US played a critical role in establishing the RVN and in executing the war, the Vietnamese people were crucial actors who had a hand in shaping the fate of their short-lived state.

By using Vietnamese-language sources and paying attention to the decisions and actions of Vietnamese actors, research has provided a more nuanced treatment of South Vietnam and deepened our understanding of Vietnamese history and the Vietnam War. For the most part, these works focus on the South Vietnamese political establishment, the South Vietnamese military, and the communist-led insurgency and its supporters.[6] A few offer glimpses into South Vietnamese society, shedding light on diverse and important subjects such as South Vietnam's antiwar movement, education system, and student activism.[7] This book contributes to this growing body of literature by examining the South Vietnamese people's voluntary social and civic activities. In addition to insights about wartime South Vietnam, the book explores state-society interactions, particularly how civil society navigated the demands of the war, the state, and competing political forces.

# Civil Society, Associational Life, and the Public Sphere

By the standard definition, voluntary associations are those organizations that individuals join freely, without coercion. They are the manifestation of civil society, commonly conceived as "the constellation of associational forms that occupy the terrain between individuals and the state."[8] Another component of civil society is the public sphere, idealized as the site where critical, informed engagement about the common good transpires.[9] There is still significant debate about the definition and nature of civil society and its components.

The general assumption is that civil society is relatively free from state control and is "an arena occupied by a fluid and loosely bundled assemblage of interests at various stages of institutionalization; civil society is, by nature, plural."[10] Because it is plural and relatively unrestrained, civil society is sometimes conceptualized as inherently antistate, and its activities are perceived as contrary to the state's interest. Some scholars, policymakers, and activists therefore believe that civil society can foster democratic development and protect society against authoritarianism. The experiences in Latin America, postcommunist eastern Europe, and sub-Saharan Africa seemed to support this positive view of civil society. In these places, voluntary and religious organizations played an instrumental role in spearheading democratic development.[11] By virtue of being components of civil society, associational activities and the public sphere have also been theorized as being autonomous and supportive of democratization.

Within this positive assessment of civil society's potential is the notion that not all associational activities fit within the realm of civil society. General criteria that determine whether an organization is a constituent of civil society include

independence from the state, civility toward those with different views, and willingness to "work and interact with the state."[12] According to these measures, some
groups fall outside of civil society, including organizations—such as the Ku Klux
Klan—that use violence against those with opposing views and revolutionary
organizations that do not recognize the legitimacy of the state and seek its overthrow. Some definitions also imply that civil society aspires to work for the collective good rather than selfish or parochial interests. In this schema, self-help and
kin-based organizations would not be considered components of civil society.[13] In
other words, the quality of a group's activities is a significant consideration in this
positive conceptualization of civil society. These standards are important for theorists who consider civil society the basis for democracy, because to foster an open
and democratic society, civil society needs to be "forward-looking and open to
rational communication with groups different from themselves."[14]

There are theorists, however, who define civil society more broadly to include
groups that do not explicitly set out to perform civic duties but focus instead on
members' shared interests. Robert Putnam, for example, evinces that voluntary
associations, including those formed to serve narrow interests, have the capacity
to build social trust, networks, and norms—known collectively as social capital—
which in turn promotes and maintains economic development and effective governance.[15] Influenced by Alexis de Tocqueville's work that connected the vibrancy
of American associational life to the country's democratic tradition, Putnam suggests that voluntary tradition builds a foundation for trust and cooperation and
develops "the 'I' into the 'we.'"[16] In other words, associated participation encour-
ages people to adopt a collective perspective, and the social capital that accrues
from associational life can contribute to building a strong civil society.

Countering this positive assessment of civil society's potential are scholars who
contend that civil society has not always been independent, equal, or open. For
example, Mary Ryan's study of religious benevolent associations in nineteenth-
century US cities illustrates that while associational life can build trust and cooperation, it is also instrumental in reinforcing elite dominance and privilege.[17]
Similarly, Pierre Bourdieu shows that social capital has greater potential to reify
hierarchical social relations than to promote horizontal social solidarity. According to Bourdieu, social capital is deeply implicated in the stratified economic and
social structure because one needs adequate means and connections to accumulate social capital.[18]

Foremost among the sober critics of civil society's emancipatory potential was
Antonio Gramsci, who perceived civil society as neither separate nor independent
from the state. For Gramsci and other advocates of this school of thought, civil
society is an important component of a society's superstructure wherein the state
and the elite maintain hegemony through influence, inducement, and manipula-

tion.[19] The other constituent of the superstructure is the political society, which the state dominates through the use (or threat) of violence and force. Civil society in this view includes a wide variety of associative forms that "are non-production-related, non-government and non-familial, ranging from recreational groups to trades unions, churches, and political parties."[20] These sociocultural institutions underpin and support the capitalist economy in many modern societies. As such, it cannot be assumed that civil society exists in opposition to the state; in fact, it should be expected that some sectors of civil society, such as the economic and political elite, will share some of the same interests and goals as the state and will cooperate with the state to achieve their common objectives. In addition, the elite depend on the state to protect their hegemony with an "armor of coercion."[21]

On the surface, Gramsci's view of civil society appears bleak, holding little promise for civil society to act independently, defend society's interests, or oppose the state. Diving even a little below the surface, though, reveals that the dynamics within civil society offer many possible trajectories that could lead to a vast array of fates for any given society and its political system. Gramsci suggests that neither civil society nor the state is unified or uniform in its interests and views. As a result, many competing interests operate in civil society, with a complex and unpredictable constellation of alliances. The state itself "is engaged in a struggle with other actors to dominate popular ideas, values, and norms."[22] Because it is a domain of contestation, plurality, and coalition making, elite hegemony is never complete. The contestation may lead the state to intervene directly to reassert hegemony if the threat to its stability appears imminent. Meanwhile, the plurality and conflict within civil society also present opportunities and space for "counter-hegemonic narratives" to be articulated and mobilized.[23] Moreover, because the state's moral authority depends on maintaining a functioning civil society, it may be necessary for the state, even an authoritarian state, to compromise at times.[24]

Similar limitations have been noted with regard to the democratizing potential of the public sphere. According to Jürgen Habermas, the bourgeois public sphere first emerged in eighteenth-century Europe as an arena of open and free debate. Because of its ability to keep the state in check, the public sphere was considered an important element in democratization.[25] However, as critics have pointed out, the nature of this idealized public sphere was restrictive, making it inaccessible to marginalized peoples such as women and the working class.[26] Historians of non-Western societies have discovered that the public sphere did not necessarily promote democracy and can in fact coexist with authoritarian rule, as in the cases of French colonial Vietnam and pre–World War II Japan.[27] To explain the apparent contradiction, Elizabeth Berry explains that Japan's public sphere was not "the space where popular sovereignty was claimed but where leadership was scrutinized and disciplined by criticism."[28] In other words, to understand the public sphere in societies outside of Western democracies, one needs to "detach the public sphere from the telos of democracy."[29] Shawn McHale similarly argues that the public sphere in French colonial Vietnam was not linked to democratization but was a hierarchical domain where "particularistic interests contested their views."[30]

Informed by theories about the nature and potential of civil society, this book examines the associational life and public sphere of South Vietnam. In the RVN, many competing forces were at work to influence public life. The authoritarian governments of Ngô Đình Diệm (1954–1963), various military juntas (1963–1967), and Nguyễn Văn Thiệu (1967–1975) defined the limits of associational and public activities. The RVN's police force closely monitored those suspected of supporting communists or other political opponents. The US government and foreign aid organizations also played a role in associational life by dispensing aid and advice in an attempt to win favor and influence. In addition, the Lao Động Party and its southern organizations, the National Liberation Front (NLF) and People's Revolutionary Party (PRP), infiltrated some key organizations in an effort to proselytize members. Along with the multiple forces influencing South Vietnam's civil society, the exigencies of war circumscribed the content and form of associational life. The war created massive numbers of refugees, orphans, and wounded, and assisting these wartime victims became the focus of many organizations. The interplay of these forces made civil society a highly contested domain, wherein diverse groups and participants vied for influence and advantage. Voluntary organizations had to learn how to navigate these dominant forces and circumstances, adjusting their activities, goals, and membership to ensure their survival.

## Methodology and Scope

This book examines an array of voluntary associations and their activities in South Vietnam. The groups discussed include mutual-aid associations, cultural clubs, professional societies, charitable organizations, community development groups, women's associations, student organizations, and rights movements. Where possible, I utilized accounts from personal interviews and memoirs of participants.[31] However, for the most part, I relied on archival and textual evidence. As such, my discussion focuses on officially registered and active organizations that left written records, such as registration applications, club charters, correspondence with government officials, and state surveillance reports. Although voluntary associations were required to apply to the government for permission to operate, many did so without official sanction. Moreover, many small and ad hoc groups operated throughout South Vietnam, particularly in small towns and villages, and left few documentary traces. Given the lack of primary sources, this book concentrates more on formal urban organizations and less on informal rural associations.

By examining urbanites' public life, the book challenges the persistent stereotype that South Vietnam was a place without society or agency. Its robust associational life points to the existence of an active civil society that managed to survive despite war, government repression, and economic hardship. The diversity of South Vietnam's civil society suggests significant plurality in people's outlooks, attitudes, and aspirations. Their public activities also illuminate their concerns, hopes, and values. The desire to accumulate social capital probably motivated many to join organizations, but others became members of clubs that offered economic, social, or spiritual support. Some joined associations that promoted progressive change, while others participated to maintain traditional social ties and customs. Whatever their motivations, people were not passive; they were actively trying to improve the social situations of themselves or others.

Each chapter of the book focuses on a particular example of civil society. It is not meant to be a survey, and it does not claim to be an examination of all important associations or all facets of civil society. My intention is to present a diverse sample to display the plurality of public life. Though discrete and different, these various forms of associational activities operated in similar circumstances of sociopolitical turmoil and warfare.

Chapter 1 provides a brief narrative of the origin of South Vietnam and the historical context of the Vietnam War. Chapter 2 examines mutual-aid and friendly societies, a form of social group that has long roots in Vietnam. Like those found elsewhere, South Vietnamese mutual-aid organizations were established to look after members' special interests and were based on shared identities or activities, such as place of origin, recreational interests, or employment.[32]

More outward-looking, altruistic organizations and social welfare projects were also prevalent in the RVN, and these are discussed in chapter 3. Volunteers established many charitable and welfare endeavors to provide emergency and long-term aid. This was a gendered sphere of activity where women were highly visible. Class, religion, and politics were also important factors that influenced people's access to participation.

Some voluntary groups saw the need to work for more sustained change, and chapter 4 focuses on three development efforts that aspired to do just that. Though different in nature and approach, the Popular Culture Association (Hội Bách Khoa Bình Dân, 1954–1975), the Buddhist School of Youth for Social Service (Trường Thanh Niên Phụng Sự Xã Hội, 1965–1975), and the New Life Development Project (Kế Hoạch Xây Đời Mới, 1965–1971) were ambitious social development projects initiated and operated by Vietnamese volunteers with the goal of contributing to nation building.

Youths and their associational activities in the 1960s and 1970s are the focus of chapter 5. Like student organizations in the US in the 1960s, South Vietnamese youth groups were vocal, dynamic, and dedicated to their various causes. While antiwar, left-leaning student activists were grabbing headlines, anticommunist students were also politically and socially engaged. Between these two extremes were self-identified apolitical groups that participated in social relief and community development. Despite their different political viewpoints and approaches, students were united in their enthusiasm for social involvement and their desire to shape the fate of their country.

Chapter 6 takes an in-depth look at the newspaper *Sóng Thần* and its civic activities. Established by a group of citizens concerned about government corruption, the newspaper saw itself as the champion of the people. One of its major social endeavors was organizing the retrieval and burial of thousands of corpses left along Highway 1 during the 1972 Easter offensive.

The last chapter focuses on several rights movements that emerged in the 1970s to fight for prison reform, human rights, freedom of the press, and an end to corruption. The wide array of social and political activities covered in this chapter illustrates that South Vietnam's public sphere was pluralistic and its civil society robust, albeit beleaguered at times by state control and the demands of warfare.

# THE HISTORICAL AND POLITICAL LANDSCAPE

The Republic of Vietnam (RVN) lasted a mere two decades. The backstory of its birth, however, dates to the mid-nineteenth century, when France began colonizing Vietnam, known then as Đại Nam (Greater South).[1] This chapter provides an overview of the origin and evolution of the RVN. The narrative, though condensed and brief, provides the context for a better appreciation of the conditions in which South Vietnamese civil society operated.

In 1802 Nguyễn Phúc Anh, who became known as the Gia Long emperor (reigning from 1802 to 1820), established the Nguyễn dynasty to rule over the territory that would become modern Vietnam. The Chinese Qing court formally recognized this new vassal kingdom as Việt Nam, but the second Nguyễn emperor, Minh Mạng, named it Đại Nam in 1838.[2] With its establishment, the Nguyễn dynasty ended nearly three centuries of civil wars between various Viet clans that had been vying for control.

Ruling over their new Đại Nam kingdom, Gia Long and succeeding Nguyễn monarchs deployed a multiplicity of philosophies, beliefs, and social practices to legitimize the clan's claim to power and to centralize control. Among the rich cache of political, religious, and social philosophies available to the ruling house were Chinese Confucianism, Mahayana Buddhism, Cham Hinduism, and a Khmer-inflected Theravada Buddhist tradition. Ethnic and religious diversity was especially prominent in the southern parts of the kingdom. Prior to the seventeenth century, the south was inhabited by Cham and Khmer peoples who had established their own respective kingdoms; they fought against each other and against the Viet people living north of them. Known as the Inner Realm

(Đàng Trong), the southern region under the Nguyễn monarchs was an outward-facing society that engaged not only in agriculture but also in maritime trade. In contrast, the northern Outer Realm (Đàng Ngoài) was dominated by Viet ethnic people who lived in tightly knit villages and amassed their wealth mostly from farming.[3]

To assert more control over the disparate populations in the kingdom, Minh Mạng applied techniques and practices based on those of the Qing court in China.[4] Drawing on Chinese examples was not new for the Vietnamese. The Chinese empire had ruled the northernmost part of what would become Vietnam for about one thousand years in the first millennium (111 BCE–939 CE). Even after the Vietnamese established their own independent polity, they remained within the Chinese-dominated cultural world and maintained strong diplomatic and trading ties with China as a Chinese vassal state.

Along with efforts to centralize control over the population, the Minh Mạng court took harsh measures against Christianity and missionaries. The ruling Nguyễn monarchs considered Christianity's monotheism and sanction against ancestor worship a serious threat to the social, political, and ethical foundation of Đại Nam.[5] Minh Mạng's anti-Christian stance and the severe punishments meted out to Christians, which were affirmed by subsequent emperors, provided France with a pretext to attack and begin annexing Đại Nam's southern provinces in 1858.

## French Colonialism and Vietnamese Responses

By the mid-nineteenth century, France was eager to obtain a foothold in Asia, where other Western states had already established colonies. Since the northern region of Đại Nam offered a possible trade route to China, France made control of the Nguyễn kingdom its goal. Citing the persecution of Christian missionaries as justification, France attacked the southern region of Đại Nam and captured Saigon in 1859. By 1883, France controlled all of Đại Nam, which was administered as three different *pays* (countries): Tonkin (north), Annam (central), and Cochin China (south). Cambodia and a group of associated kingdoms that later became modern Laos were soon incorporated to make French Indochina.

Early Vietnamese armed resistance to French rule, such as the Save the King (Cần Vương) movement of 1885–1896, was unsuccessful.[6] By the turn of the twentieth century, some nationalist leaders sought to reform Vietnamese society and prepare it for independence. Reformists saw the futility of taking up arms against the colonialists, given that France was vastly superior both technologically and militarily. They were also convinced that Vietnam's sociocultural practices, still heavily influenced by China, needed to be abandoned to make Vietnam modern. As a result, scholar Phan Chu Trinh called for abolition of the imperial civil service examinations, which were written in Chinese script and based on Confucian classics, philosophy, and literature. Phan Chu Trinh and other reformers considered this system a detriment to modernizing Vietnam, as it did not promote modern or Western knowledge, nor did it encourage innovation.[7]

In addition to their criticism of Vietnam's traditional society, reformers condemned France for not living up to its republican ideals and failing to fulfill its *mission civilisatrice* in the colony. Specifically, Vietnamese reformers, many of whom embraced republicanism, wanted the indigenous education system to be developed and modernized.[8] To address this situation, reformers promoted private voluntary endeavors to provide modern education for Vietnamese students. One such initiative was the Go East (Đông Du) program, established in 1905 to send students to Japan, where they could benefit from living and studying in a modern society. This program was organized and funded by a group of patriots, including Phan Bội Châu, Cường Để, and Nguyễn Thành, who formed the Modernization Society (Duy Tân Hội). By 1907, the Modernization Society had raised enough funds to send at least one hundred students to Japan.[9]

Around the same time, other reformers, most prominently Phan Chu Trinh and Lương Văn Can, established the Eastern Capital Free School (Đông Kinh Nghĩa Thục), which provided free schooling for Vietnamese students. Operating on donations and volunteerism, the school offered eight levels of education, from primary to high school, with a modern curriculum that included math and science. The school also offered language classes in French, Chinese, and a Vietnamese romanized alphabet (Quốc Ngữ), which was being promoted to replace Chinese and Sino-Vietnamese scripts.[10] In addition to providing an academic education, the school tried to foster pride in Vietnamese history and culture while stoking anti-French sentiments. It was not surprising that French authorities closed the school in 1908 and jailed many of the teachers and founders.

By the mid-1920s and into the 1930s, the anticolonial critique expanded to highlight more explicitly socioeconomic issues and their impact on the masses. A new generation of Vietnamese intelligentsia, many of whom had gone through the Franco-Vietnamese education system, used the emerging public sphere to call attention to the lack of progress in people's living conditions after several decades of French rule.[11] In fact, the situation seemed worse. Landlessness and tenancy were on the rise, while land accumulation for rice and rubber plantations enriched only a small minority in society. Tax policies and state monopolies on salt, alcohol, and opium were considered unfair and onerous. The Great Depression (1929–1933) impoverished people further and highlighted the colonial government's uneven

economic investments and development policies. Economic hardship and disparity provoked rebuke from the intelligentsia and rebellion from the peasants.

During these decades, political and religious organizations emerged to direct
people's grievances and aspirations. Multiple rebellions broke out in Tonkin and
Annam, which were economically poorer than Cochin China. In 1930 one of
the most notable uprisings took place. Comprising some 125 different protest
actions, the Nghệ-Tĩnh rebellion erupted in the Annam provinces of Nghệ An
and Hà Tĩnh.[12] Some of the demonstrations were instigated by communist cadres, while others were led by peasants who were infuriated by high taxes, official
corruption, and the state's alcohol monopoly.[13] To quell the rebellion, French authorities used brutal force, including aerial bombings and the burning of entire
villages.

In the south, two important politico-religious mass movements took root. The
Cao Đài religion was founded in 1926 in Tây Ninh, and the Hòa Hảo Buddhist
sect was established in 1939 in Châu Đốc province. Famous for its syncretic faith
and veneration of diverse spiritual, political, and literary personages, Cao Đàism
proclaimed to offer the world a spiritual path to redemption. Hòa Hảo Buddhism,
which evolved from a millenarian Buddhist sect of the nineteenth century (Bửu
Sơn Kỳ Hương), was founded by Huỳnh Phú Sổ, a young mystic thought to possess healing powers. Referred to as "Venerable Teacher" by his followers, Sổ's
message of egalitarianism, charity, and simple living resonated with the impoverished peasants of the Mekong Delta. These two religions offered spiritual sus-
tenance and social support. Both Cao Đài and Hòa Hảo built on peasants'
traditional custom of forming mutual-aid societies to help members cope with
economic insecurity, debt, and seasonal migration.[14] Underlining these religions'
spiritual and social messages were strong critiques of colonialism and the promotion of an independent state. Their timely sociopolitical message and their
accurate reading of people's spiritual and social needs made both Cao Đài and
Hòa Hảo immensely popular. They attracted such large followings that the
French colonial government felt the need to clamp down on their activities. As
later sections show, by the mid-1940s, both religions were playing important roles
in nationalist politics.

Along with these politico-religious movements, secular political parties were
active in anticolonial agitation. The Vietnam Nationalist Party (Việt Nam Quốc
Dân Đảng), which modeled itself on China's Nationalist Party (Guomindang),
was founded in 1927 by a group of teachers, journalists, civil servants, and merchants who wanted Vietnam to be independent, united, and developed.[15] In 1930
the Vietnam Nationalist Party instigated a munity at Yên Bái garrison, which
French authorities quickly put down. As a result, many of the party's leaders were
either executed or imprisoned.[16]

In 1930 another important political movement emerged: the Indochinese Communist Party (ICP). Among its founders was Nguyễn Sinh Cung, who was known by a number of aliases, including Nguyễn Ái Quốc and later Hồ Chí Minh. This revolutionary spent much of his early adulthood—from 1911 to 1941—in Britain, the United States, France, the Soviet Union, and China. Politically astute and charismatic, he united three different communist groups and became their leader.[17] Hồ Chí Minh continued to lead the party into the postcolonial period and became an important unifying symbol for communists and revolutionaries during the Vietnam War. The ICP's analysis of the situation in Indochina emphasized the burdens of high rent, usury, and unfair taxation.[18] The ICP and other nationalist movements did not attract mass support before World War II, and French repression limited their ability to propagate their messages and to organize. The colonialists' brutal response to anticolonial activities deterred many potential members from joining. Nationalists therefore had to operate underground, in remote areas, or abroad.

# The End of French Colonial Rule and the Division of Vietnam

Vietnamese nationalists got a break when World War II impinged on French control in Indochina. The disruptions of the war provided important opportunities for Vietnamese nationalists to organize and to challenge French rule. Unlike the situation in other Southeast Asian colonies, where the Japanese removed Western colonial authorities and took complete control, the French in Indochina were allowed to remain in power. This less antagonistic relationship stemmed from the fact that France had capitulated to Nazi Germany in June 1940 and the new French government was now a German ally. In return for France's continued authority in Indochina, Governor-General Jean Decoux had to allow Japanese troops to be stationed there and had to supply rice, fuel, fiber, and other raw materials to support Japan's war effort.

In response to France's alliance with the Axis and the introduction of another imperial power into the colony, the ICP established the League for Vietnam's Independence (Việt Nam Độc Lập Đồng Minh Hội, or Viet Minh for short) in May 1941. This organization was meant to be a coalition of Vietnamese nationalists of all political views. However, the ICP held key positions in the Viet Minh and directed its activities, and it made great efforts to obfuscate its role.[19] Significantly, the Viet Minh's platform called for national independence rather than a socialist revolution, in the hope of making its movement attractive to more nationalists. By the end of World War II, the ICP had attracted fewer than five thousand members.[20] By contrast, the Viet Minh, with its broad goal of national independence, drew large numbers of nationalists and patriots who were eager to fight both the French and the Japanese.

When it became clear that Germany was losing the war in March 1945, Japan turned against its French ally, disarming and imprisoning French soldiers and officials. The Japanese handed power to Emperor Bảo Đại, who established the Empire of Vietnam. Because Japan still controlled military affairs, contemporary critics, particularly communists, dismissed this as fake independence. Nevertheless, many noncommunist nationalists saw Japan's coup as a step toward independence and were hopeful.[21] Despite the lack of complete autonomy, Bảo Đại and his government began to build the foundation for a new polity and sought to restore the food supply to Tonkin, where famine had killed a million people.

The famine, which peaked in the winter of 1944–1945, was caused by multiple factors. The most important causes were the colonial authorities' requisition of rice and other crops for Japan's war effort, Allied bombing of the transportation system, and a lack of political will to alleviate the severe food shortage.[22] Grassroots efforts to help the famine victims were bolstered when Bảo Đại came to power. From March to May 1945, voluntary organizations in Tonkin raised more than 780,000 piastres. In Cochin China twenty organizations were established, and within a month they had raised 1.7 million piastres to buy rice to ship to the north.[23] These relief campaigns were instrumental in building community connections, especially as the Vietnamese were working toward self-rule.

Bảo Đại's empire, however, was short-lived. When Japan surrendered on August 15, 1945, the Viet Minh quickly gained control of Vietnam.[24] Aiming to consolidate its power before the Allies arrived to accept Japan's surrender, the Viet Minh launched an insurrection on August 19. Japanese troops did not intervene when Viet Minh cadres took control of important government offices and installations, and no other groups opposed the Viet Minh either. News of the insurrection ignited uprisings throughout Vietnam. Although local insurrections were carried out in the name of the Viet Minh, there was little central leadership, communist or otherwise.[25]

Even though Bảo Đại had a larger military force than the Viet Minh, the emperor abdicated and turned power over to the Viet Minh provisional government.[26] Bảo Đại's peaceful abdication and the ceremonial transfer of power endowed the Viet Minh with "essential national legitimacy."[27] On September 2, 1945, the Viet Minh established the Democratic Republic of Vietnam (DRV), with Hồ Chí Minh as the provisional president. In return for the emperor's abdication and support, the DRV provisional government comprised many noncommunist nationalists, including Bảo Đại as an adviser.[28]

France, however, was not ready to give up Indochina. Once French forces were released from prison and rearmed by the British, they began to attack Vietnamese nationalists in Saigon.[29] Despite Hồ Chí Minh's diplomatic efforts to secure a cease-fire agreement, war broke out in December 1946. This war of independence, known as the First Indochina War, pitted the DRV's newly formed and poorly armed Defense Force of about 100,000 troops against France's fully equipped Expeditionary Corps. Until the Chinese Communist Party won its civil war in 1949, the DRV had virtually no foreign support. Consequently, DRV troops were instructed to pursue guerrilla tactics rather than face the French directly on the battlefield.[30] Despite their military superiority, the French could not dislodge DRV forces from the mountains and rural areas, where they had fled when the French took control of the major cities and towns.

By the start of the war, the Viet Minh's image as a broad-based, nonpartisan independence movement had come into question. It was becoming clear to noncommunist nationalists that the ICP dominated the Viet Minh, even though the ICP had supposedly been disbanded in 1945. In fact, in the heady days following formation of the DRV, communists began to attack their political rivals, including Trotskyists, revolutionary nationalists, and so-called reactionary politicians and intellectuals.[31] Assassinations of noncommunist Viet Minh members, especially those belonging to groups such as the Đại Việt, Hòa Hảo, and Cao Đài, continued throughout the First Indochina War.[32]

Disenchanted by what they saw as communist betrayal, many noncommunist nationalists threw their lot in with the newly created Associated State of Vietnam (ASVN). In 1949 France established semiautonomous states for Vietnam, Cambodia, and Laos to attract support from the Indochinese population. To underscore their continued dependence on France and their colonial provenance, all three states were members of the French Union. Bảo Đại was invited to be the head of state for the ASVN. The Bảo Đại government, led by Prime Minister Trần Trọng Kim, had some measure of independence, but France still controlled financial, military, and legal matters.[33] Despite its semi-independent status, the ASVN (along with the Associated States of Cambodia and Laos) was recognized by the US and Britain in February 1950. A month earlier, the Soviet Union and the People's Republic of China had done the same for the DRV.[34] Thus, by 1949, there were already two states competing for control of Vietnam, each with its own powerful foreign supporters.

By 1954, after eight years of war, both sides were ready to negotiate an end to the fighting. However, before the talks took place in Geneva, the DRV won a major victory on the battlefield. DRV general Võ Nguyên Giáp led an attack on Dien Bien Phu, a French outpost in the northwest near the border with Laos.

Võ Nguyên Giáp and his troops, supported by over a quarter million civilian porters and workers, laid siege to the French base for nearly two months, until the French forces surrendered.[35] This was exactly what the DRV leadership wanted: a decisive victory that would give them an advantage at the negotiating table. However, the Geneva Accords did not give the DRV control of all of Vietnam. Instead, they stipulated that the country would be temporarily divided at the seventeenth parallel, with the DRV controlling the north and the ASVN administering the south. A referendum would be held in two years to unify the country and determine its political nature. Because noncommunist nationalists and supporters of the ASVN did not want a communist party in power, they had lobbied vigorously for this arrangement.

The United States, deeply concerned about the growing communist influence in Asia, had been increasing its aid for France's agenda in Vietnam throughout the post–World War II period. By 1954, the United States was covering 80 percent of France's war-related expenditures. Not surprisingly, during the Geneva talks, the United States was squarely behind the proposal to divide Vietnam. As neither the Soviet Union nor the People's Republic of China wanted to start another major conflict with the United States, both communist powers urged the DRV to accept the terms. Representing the DRV at the conference, Hồ Chí Minh reluctantly agreed to a temporary division at the seventeenth parallel.

The Geneva agreement allowed the Vietnamese people to live under the regime of their choice during the period of division. It stipulated that residents of Vietnam had three hundred days to relocate to the region of their choosing. Nearly 900,000 northerners moved south, taking advantage of the free transportation provided by France and the United States. About 76 percent of the refugees were Roman Catholic and 23 percent were Buddhist.[36] Moving north were about 173,000 Viet Minh troops and 86,000 military families, party cadres, and prisoners of war.[37] There were multiple reasons why people left the north and moved to the south. Some were escaping poverty, while others feared communist repression. Civil servants, landowners, and those with links to the French, in particular, had reason to leave. News of radical land reforms and the persecution of landlords in areas controlled by the Viet Minh convinced the political and economic elite, even those who were nationalists, to leave their homes and take a chance in the south.[38] Approximately 90,000 migrants were members of the professional and business class.[39] Many intellectuals also left, not only to avoid repression but also because important academic institutions relocated to the south. Among the schools that moved were the elite Chu Văn An (formerly known as Trường Bưởi), Trường Vương, Nguyễn Trãi, and College of Law.[40]

Numerous Catholic northerners also left to avoid religious discrimination. Although the majority of Vietnam's population (80–85 percent) were Mahay-

ana Buddhists, Roman Catholicism had flourished under French rule. The colonial state supported the activities of the Catholic Church and its missionaries,
in part because Catholic institutions and organizations provided health care,
education, and social support for adherents and nonadherents alike.[41] These social
services gave some substance to the *mission civilisatrice* rhetoric France used to
justify colonization. This symbiotic relationship between the colonial regime
and the Catholic Church contributed to the stereotype of Catholics as ardent
supporters of colonialism. In addition to their close association with French authorities, Catholic clergy were considered potential rivals by the communists.
Many Catholic priests commanded not only religious but also sociopolitical authority in their parishes. The tension between the Catholic population and the
communists drove many Catholics from the north.

The United States and the ASVN did their best to encourage migration to the
south to demonstrate the unpopularity of communism. Moreover, migration to
the south would allow the ASVN to influence a larger share of the population
when the unification referendum took place in two years. To this end, the US
Central Intelligence Agency (CIA) produced propaganda that sought to deepen
people's fears and anxieties about communism. In addition to providing free
transportation to the south, the United States provided funds and support to
build temporary refugee shelters and facilitate resettlement there. The DRV was
not passive in this process, and its government was similarly keen to keep its
population in place. Moreover, it was willing to employ predominantly punitive
tactics to convince the population to stay, such as the use of military force, administrative delays, and intimidation.[42]

Despite the Geneva Accords' requirement that a unification referendum be
held in two years, this was not done, and the division remained in place until
1975. Ngô Đình Diệm, prime minister of the ASVN, argued that since his government had not signed the agreement, it was not bound by its terms.

Immediately upon Vietnam's division, both halves embarked on nation-
building efforts in their respective territories. Like numerous former colonies in
Asia and Africa in the wake of World War II, both North and South Vietnam faced
significant challenges as they endeavored to establish a framework for governance
as well as to generate national cohesion and a sense of shared identity.[43] These postcolonial states also had to contend with socioeconomic problems associated with
colonialism, such as economic underdevelopment, dependency, and class disparity.
For the two Vietnams, there was the added problem of competing claims for legitimacy. Both North and South Vietnam claimed to be the rightful government of
Vietnam as a whole, and both set about building their respective nations.

In the DRV, the Indochinese Communist Party—now known as the Lao
Động (Workers) Party—initiated a number of campaigns to transform society

in accordance with communist ideals. The party aimed to establish a modern, industrialized society in step with the Soviet Union and the People's Republic of China. Land reform began in 1953; collectivization of agricultural production and resources followed in 1958. In urban centers, businesses and enterprises were nationalized. The party-state also took control of the media, arts, and culture, providing strict guidance and censorship for publication and production. With its extensive control over politics, economy, and society, the DRV was able to mobilize and direct the people's efforts in a comprehensive and effective manner when war began again in the early 1960s. Like the DRV, the political leaders of South Vietnam sought to build a nation-state. Though embracing a different ideology from their northern counterparts, southern leaders were similarly inspired to build an independent, modern, and industrialized nation.

## Building a Nation-State in the South

At the time of the Geneva Conference, Bảo Đại had just appointed Ngô Đình Diệm prime minister of the ASVN. Like Hồ Chí Minh, Diệm had been a strong advocate of national independence and had participated in nationalist politics since the 1930s. He came from an influential mandarin Catholic family; his father had served as a high-ranking official in the imperial court. In 1933, when Diệm was thirty-two, Bảo Đại recruited him into the imperial government and gave him the most important cabinet position: minister of the interior.[44] However, he resigned after a few months when he realized that meaningful reforms were not achievable under French rule. After his resignation, Diệm continued to work for Vietnam's independence inside and outside the country. Throughout the 1940s, Diệm and his brother Ngô Đình Nhu participated in a number of nationalist organizations. Because of his reputation as an impeccable nationalist, Diệm was tapped by many Vietnamese groups for leadership roles. Even Hồ Chí Minh offered him a cabinet post in the DRV in late 1945, but Diệm turned him down. Diệm was a republican who rejected communism on ethical and moral grounds. Diệm and his brother Nhu would later embrace personalism, a philosophy associated with French scholar Emmanuel Mounier that proposed a middle path between communism and capitalism.[45] Diệm also had personal reasons to refuse Hồ's offer. In 1945 communist cadres had captured and executed Diệm's eldest brother and the brother's son. The pair were buried alive for alleged counterrevolutionary activities.[46]

In 1950 Diệm went to the United States, where he lobbied influential American political figures, State Department officials, academics, and religious leaders on behalf of Vietnam's future. Among his diverse group of admirers were

US senators John Kennedy and Mike Mansfield, political scientist Wesley Fishel, and founder of the Office of Strategic Services William Donovan. Diệm impressed these men with his political commitment to a noncommunist Vietnam, but more so with his enthusiasm for modernizing and developing Vietnam with US aid and technology.[47] Thus, there was little surprise when Bảo Đại asked Diệm to be prime minister in 1954 (the third such invitation from Bảo Đại since 1945).[48]

One of Diệm's first tasks as prime minister was to assert the independence of the ASVN. He withdrew the ASVN from the French Union and changed its name to the State of Vietnam (SVN). He also abolished the French monetary unit the piastre in favor of the Vietnamese dong and took command of administrative responsibilities that had formerly been under French authority, such as border control, customs, and immigration.[49]

More challenging was Diệm's effort to consolidate government control over the territory of South Vietnam. Historically, southern Vietnam had always been socioculturally diverse, and it continued to be so in the twentieth century. The population was composed of many different ethnic, linguistic, religious, and political groups. Winning over the people's loyalty would prove to be a challenge, especially since the SVN did not have a monopoly of political or military power. Three major organizations held significant influence at this time: Cao Đài, Hòa Hảo, and Bình Xuyên.

The Cao Đài and Hòa Hảo religious movements had accrued significant political and military power during World War II by allying first with Japan and then with France in 1947.[50] As a result of these strategic alliances, Cao Đài's army was fifteen thousand strong and controlled important economic interests in Tây Ninh province by the summer of 1954.[51] During the same period, the Hòa Hảo amassed a following of more than one million people and a military force of twenty thousand troops.[52]

The third power holder in the south was the Bình Xuyên, which was created in 1945 when diverse armed groups came together while participating in Viet Minh-led anticolonial activities in the Saigon-Cholon area. By 1947, the Bình Xuyên had grown to about two thousand troops.[53] The organization controlled the police force in Saigon and the lucrative gambling, prostitution, and drug businesses in the Saigon–Cho Lon region. As Diệm attempted to consolidate power in the summer of 1954, these three organizations controlled one-third of the population and territory in South Vietnam.[54]

By the fall of 1955, Diệm had essentially neutralized the threats from these three groups. He used a combination of bribery, coercion, and military force to defeat them. Factionalism within their ranks made it easier for Diệm to convince rival blocs to defect to the government side and thus weaken their organizations. US military aid and support also played a critical role. In February 1955 the

United States began providing aid, training, advice, and equipment directly to the Vietnamese National Army (as opposed to doing so through the French). Diệm's success over these armed organizations led to increased US aid. By 1961, US aid for military and economic assistance would amount to US\$2 billion.[55]

Another obstacle for Diệm was the communists cadres left behind. The Lao Động Party had instructed about ten thousand of its fighters to stay in the south and not regroup in the DRV, as stipulated by the Geneva Accords.[56] These embedded communists would be responsible for future political agitation and mobilization among the southern population. To deal with this threat, Diệm began a campaign to expose and arrest communists and their sympathizers on July 20, 1955. Diệm's Denounce Communists (Tố Cộng) campaign lasted five years and led to 1,000 to 5,000 executions and between 25,000 and 190,000 arrests.[57] However, not all those killed or arrested were communists. Some were noncommunist former members of the Viet Minh, and some were merely sympathizers. While the campaign effectively eliminated many communist cells, it also eroded Diệm's reputation and alienated many people because of its indiscriminate and heavy-handed approach.

In addition to neutralizing threats from political and military opponents, Diệm sought to centralize power by removing Bảo Đại as the head of state. On October 23, 1955, Diệm held a referendum, asking voters to choose between Bảo Đại and him. Through blatant manipulation, Diệm received 98 percent of the vote, taking the role of chief of state. Three days later, Diệm announced the establishment of the Republic of Vietnam and his position as its president.

By the end of 1955, Diệm had built the foundation for a modern state and succeeded in consolidating political power. Though this constituted an important aspect of nation building, another vital element was still missing.[58] The people's sense of identification with and commitment to this new state remained tenuous. The influx of nearly 900,000 northern refugees into the south's already heterogeneous population made achieving social cohesion even more difficult. Efforts to resettle refugees and help them establish suitable livelihoods put great pressure on the economy, even with the substantial US financial aid at the government's disposal. Even though more than half (58 percent) of the refugees had been settled by 1955, there were still significant issues related to social integration.[59] While the majority of the refugees were ethnic Vietnamese, there were distinctive accents, clothing, vocabulary, and customs among the Viet people from different regions. Even the Catholics of the north had different ecclesiastical practices than their Catholic counterparts in the south.[60] There was also a perception among southerners that the government favored the northern refugees, particularly the Catholics, at the expense of the local population. In addition to their initial stipend of 700 dong per person and rations, refugees received housing subsidies.[61] It was no wonder that many southerners felt aggrieved, particularly if they were struggling to survive.

Not all refugees from the DRV were of the Viet ethnic majority. Approximately forty-five thousand were ethnic Chinese, and fifteen hundred were from various ethnic minorities of the highlands.[62] People of Chinese ancestry made up Vietnam's second largest ethnic population, accounting for about one million people in the RVN by 1965. Beginning in 1956, in an effort to integrate the ethnic Chinese—both those newly arrived and local residents—Diệm promulgated a number of policies that essentially compelled them to become citizens of the RVN and adopt Viet cultural practices.[63] The government explained that these policies were meant to provide the ethnic Chinese with citizenship rights and ensure their inclusion in the new nation. Not surprisingly, there was strong resistance from the Chinese community.[64] Although the majority of the Chinese population gradually submitted to these Vietnamization policies by becoming citizens of the RVN, ethnic Chinese in South Vietnam continued to maintain their customs and collective identity. Chapter 2 shows that ethnic Chinese voluntary organizations were still active into the 1970s.

Integrating the northern refugees and the ethnic Chinese population was not the only focus of Diệm's nation-building endeavor. To create a sense of belonging and loyalty among the masses, Diệm looked to education. Like many nation-building projects throughout history, the RVN's considered education a cornerstone. This emphasis on learning was not an aberration; education was central to Vietnamese society, which had been deeply influenced by Chinese literary and bureaucratic culture. During the French colonial period, Vietnamese reformers promoted modern education to prepare the people for self-government, and during the brief life span of the Empire of Vietnam (March–August 1945), the government focused on developing and reforming education. Prime Minister Trần Trọng Kim emphasized the need for technical training and advocated use of the Vietnamese romanized alphabet as the language of instruction. His minister of education Vietnamized secondary public schools, and these reforms helped pave the way for the mass education that developed in both the DRV and the RVN.[65] Similarly, when Diệm came to power, he prioritized the nationalization of schools and universities; he made Vietnamese the national language for education and for all official matters.[66] The government also invested in education, built more schools and institutions of higher learning, increased teacher training programs, and established cultural institutions.

The Vietnamese government's concerns about education matched those of US officials and academics who were becoming more involved in Vietnam. In the early 1950s US policymakers, technocrats, and development workers saw education—specifically, a system based on the American model—as the panacea for the lack of development and progress in societies such as Vietnam. From the perspectives of US officials and aid personnel, education that emphasized scientific and technical knowledge along with English-language proficiency could modernize society, boost economic development, promote political stability, and defend against insurgency.[67]

Consequently, the United States began to provide financial aid directly to Bảo Đại's government to fund technical and vocational schools. US aid for education continued into the post-1954 period, supporting new vocational training institutions, primary and secondary schools, and teacher training programs. In South Vietnam, the US Operations Mission (USOM) spearheaded these efforts, which included addressing the severe shortage of classrooms, particularly for high school students. As a result, from 1955 to 1960, enrollment more than doubled for elementary students and more than tripled for secondary students.[68] Jessica Elkind notes that many of "these construction projects depended on cooperative arrangements or self-help initiatives, on which the local community or provincial officials and USOM worked together and supplied equal amounts of funding."[69] In other words, Vietnamese government officials and local communities were active in expanding and reforming education to suit the perceived needs of society. As subsequent chapters show, many Vietnamese voluntary organizations worked to make education more accessible to a wider population, especially the poor.

## Insurgency and Civil Unrest

By 1959, the RVN government's efforts to eliminate communist agitators in the south led to a critical milestone in the history of the Vietnam War. The Denounce Communists campaign had significantly reduced the number of communists remaining in South Vietnam; moreover, these repressive actions severely limited the activities of those communists who had managed to survive. Fearing the complete elimination of southern communists, party leaders Lê Duẩn and Lê Đức Thọ lobbied the leadership in Hanoi to arm southern cadres and allow them to engage in military activities. Until 1959, the Lao Động Party had focused on reconstructing and developing the DRV, rather than promoting revolution and war in the south. This "North First" policy meant that southern cadres were not permitted to engage in violent revolutionary or military activities in the south; their main tasks were to mobilize support among the people and carry out political agitation. The Politburo did not want to commit resources to a war in the south before the DRV was ready. The First Indochina War had demanded great sacrifices from the people and had resulted in the loss of at least 350,000 Vietnamese lives, both military and civilian.[70]

Lê Duẩn and Lê Đức Thọ, however, convinced the Politburo that the dire situation in the south required a change in policy. As a result, in January 1959 Resolution 15 was passed, permitting southern communists to use force for self-defense. The party also instructed the DRV's People's Army of Vietnam (PAVN) to establish Unit 559, which would be tasked with resurrecting, expanding, and maintaining the supply trail that ran from north to south along Vietnam's mountainous western border with Laos and Cambodia. Known in the West as the Ho Chi Minh Trail, this supply route had been used with success during the First Indochina War. This land route was vital to the communist war effort, especially when mines and bombing made transport by sea more dangerous. By late 1961, nearly five thousand PAVN troops had been sent south by land and sea; by 1962, full regiments of the PAVN, along with weapons and supplies, made their way to South Vietnam.[71]

To organize and coordinate the activities of southern communists, the Lao Động Party created the National Liberation Front (NLF; Mặt Trận Dân Tộc Giải Phóng Miền Nam) in 1960. Modeled after the Viet Minh, this new organization would recruit noncommunist critics of Diệm's government. It took a concerted effort to hide the communists' role in the NLF from the public and from noncommunist members.[72] The NLF's "Ten-Point Manifesto" called for the establishment of a democratic, pluralistic, and neutral government that would unify and develop Vietnam.[73] No mention was made of capitalist exploitation, socialist revolution, or Marxism-Leninism. However, as Pierre Asselin notes, in "reality, the organization was intended to harness Vietnamese patriotism and nationalism . . . in the furtherance of Party ambition below the 17th parallel."[74]

The following year, the party established a military force in South Vietnam called the People's Liberation Armed Forces (PLAF). This force of twenty-five thousand soldiers was supplemented by eighty thousand local guerrilla and self-defense troops.[75] Though often depicted as the military wing of the NLF, the PLAF was in fact a component of North Vietnam's main military force, the PAVN.[76] In a similar attempt to disguise the Lao Động Party's dominance over southern revolutionary activities, in late 1961 the party renamed its Southern Committee the People's Revolutionary Party (PRP). In reality, the PRP was the southern branch of the Lao Động Party and was controlled, along with other revolutionary organizations in South Vietnam, by the Central Office of South Vietnam (COSVN), which received its directives from Hanoi.

By the time the NLF was founded, Diệm had alienated many sectors of the political elite, intellectuals, and peasants. He was accused of being nepotistic, autocratic, and repressive. Many intellectuals and professionals criticized his family's dominance in government and politics; they particularly resented the power commanded by Diệm's brother Nhu, who was not an elected official. Nhu led a semisecret organization called the Revolutionary Personalist Workers' Party (Cần Lao Nhân Vị Cách Mạng Đảng). Known commonly as Cần Lao, this organization recruited most of its members from the civil and military services to propagate the state's agenda and to scrutinize political opponents.[77] By 1960, Diệm and Nhu had provoked criticism across the political spectrum, from liberal democrats to right-wing anticommunist groups. The latter feared that Diệm's indiscriminate use of force against the Left and his autocratic methods in general would fuel support for the NLF. Some members of the armed forces also opposed him, leading to an attempted coup in November 1960 and an attack on the presidential palace in February 1962.[78]

Diệm's rural policies also created deep resentment among the people. The government's land reform policy in 1955, for example, provided land to very few tenants or landless people but antagonized many landowners. Later initiatives—the land development of 1956, agrovilles of 1959, and strategic hamlets of 1961—all required people to move to or live in state-designated locations; they were carried out in haste and relied on coercion.[79] Diệm had intended for these projects to solve what he called the "Three Enemies": communism, underdevelopment, and disunity. Although the slogan was used to mobilize support for these top-down projects, it articulated real concerns. As Tuong Vu and Sean Fear point out, the RVN, like many former colonies throughout Asia and Africa, "faced extraordinary challenges including widespread illiteracy, deep social divisions, economic dependency, and political instability."[80]

The land development project, in particular, was supposed to bring economic benefits because people would be cultivating new land. The program was also intended to afford people the opportunity to work collectively to build the necessary infrastructure and cultivate a sense of community. According to Diệm, settling new land typically "called for qualities of initiative, a communal sense, ability to organize, mutual assistance, discipline, recognition of merit, self-policing, and defense against robbers and brigands."[81] In the same manner, the fortified agrovilles and strategic hamlets were meant to protect the villagers from NLF infiltration, in addition to encouraging a sense of unity, an ethic of self-help, and the habit of civic responsibility. Though based on lofty aspirations, these programs were carried out in a heavy-handed manner, and there was no effective communication about the ideals behind them. Although the strategic hamlets initially hampered the NLF's access to villagers, by late 1962, the NLF had found ways to infiltrate and attack the fortified hamlets.[82]

Despite the lackluster results of the strategic hamlet program, it continued until Diệm was overthrown in a coup on November 1, 1963. By this time, Diệm's popularity had reached an all-time low. Diệm and Nhu's mishandling of the Buddhist protest movement in the preceding summer tilted the scales. The Buddhist uprising was a culmination of built-up grievances arising from religious discrimination, Diệm's authoritarianism, and growing US involvement. Underlying these issues, as Edward Miller argues, were competing notions of Vietnamese nationalism.[83] Buddhist leaders, inspired by the Buddhist revival movement at the turn of the twentieth century, were promoting the idea of a Buddhist-centered nation-state, which Diệm did not support. As chapters 3 and 4 show, advocates of Buddhist revivalism encouraged Buddhists—both laity and clergy—to engage with the wider world. As a result, many Buddhist organizations and social action programs were established in the RVN.

The tension between the state and the Buddhist community boiled over when the Buddhist flag was banned from public display during the Buddhist Vesak celebration on May 8, 1963. Several days earlier, the Catholic flag had been prominently displayed during a Catholic celebration, and this blatant act of discrimination drew Buddhist protesters into the streets of Huế, where they were met with police brutality. Nine of the young protesters died.[84] As Buddhist grievances with the Diệm government grew, senior Buddhist monk Thích Quang Đức immolated himself in downtown Saigon. This touchstone event and subsequent demonstrations did not induce the state to negotiate a compromise with the Buddhists. Instead, Diệm ordered the police to raid pagodas and arrest Buddhist monks. Diệm's heavy-handed response did irreparable damage to his reputation and his relationship with the Buddhist community.

Many US officials already considered Diệm and Nhu a liability, and they now had greater reason to argue for Diệm's removal. In the fall of 1963 the US embassy in Saigon gave the green light to a group of generals who carried out a coup. Diệm and Nhu were executed the next day. Their deaths ended what would later be known as the First Republic (1955–1963).

Replacing Diệm was a group of military generals who jostled for power, creating an unstable political situation. This period of military rule (1963–1967) was characterized by many coups and countercoups, with some governments lasting for only a few months. For example, the Trần Văn Hương's government lasted from November 1964 to January 1965, and Phan Huy Quát was prime minister from February to June 1965. The instability caused by the intense rivalry among the generals led to widespread public discontent in South Vietnam. Symptomatic of the general dissatisfaction with the political situation, a Buddhist uprising erupted in May 1966. Although it began in Huế, demonstrations soon spread to other cities, and the Buddhists were joined by other groups, including Catholics, labor unions, and students. Among their grievances, the protesters wanted an end to military rule and US intervention.[85]

Facing domestic and US pressure, Nguyễn Cao Kỳ, who had been prime minister since June 1965, relented and allowed the creation of a new constitution. In September and October 1967 elections were held for the National Assembly and the presidency. Despite these changes, the Second Republic was inaugurated with two military men in control. Lieutenant General Nguyễn Văn Thiệu and Air Vice Marshal Nguyễn Cao Kỳ were elected president and vice president respectively. Thiệu, with a different running mate, would go on to win a second term in a controversial election in 1971 (see chapter 7).

Although the Second Republic was more politically stable, in that there were no coups, the military situation was growing more precarious. Since 1965, both the DRV and the United States had increased their armed presence in South Vietnam. But even before the introduction of US and North Vietnamese military forces, South Vietnamese society had been feeling the impact of the ongoing war between republicans and communists. The rural population was hardest hit, as the warring forces contested for villages' loyalty. Neither side looked kindly on anyone suspected of collaborating with the other side. The state resorted to torture and imprisonment, while the NLF often used summary executions to intimidate and get cooperation from villagers. The fighting, the destruction, and the lack of security led many people to leave their rural homes and seek refuge in towns and cities. By 1965, around one-eighth of the 16.1 million people in South Vietnam had already been displaced.[86]

The droves of rural refugees fleeing their war-torn villages put great pressure on the infrastructure and services of towns and cities. Refugee camps were established throughout South Vietnam, but they were not enough. Some were just shantytowns without sanitary services.[87] As a result, many made do, using whatever they could find to build shelters. According to a contemporary observer in Saigon, the "flattened Coke or beer can appeared to be the number one building supply item in Saigon. Tins were cut, hammered flat, and then nailed together to provide sheets of metal used for walls and roofs."[88] These makeshift shelters highlighted the stark disparity between the elite and the poor in South Vietnam. Military and government officials, professionals, and the economic elite lived in elegant villas with many modern amenities, while the urban poor and refugees struggled to survive. This dire situation prompted many people to participate in charity and social work.

For the most part, urban residents were shielded from direct contact with the war, but they were still affected. Urbanites were exposed to terrorism, a tactic used by the NLF to disrupt life. Common bombing targets were restaurants, cafés, and hotels that catered to Americans and wealthy Vietnamese. Like the elite of the French period, the upper class in the RVN tended to be comfortable in a Western cultural milieu; many could speak some French or English and had the benefit of a Western education either in Vietnam or abroad. The NLF also assassinated prominent anticommunist individuals to deter others from speaking out or getting involved in anticommunist activities.[89] After 1965, the violence intensified when US combat troops arrived in South Vietnam.

# Americanization of the War

August 1964 marked an important point in the history of the Vietnam War. Military engagement in the Gulf of Tonkin between a North Vietnamese torpedo boat and the destroyer USS *Maddox* on August 2, as well as an alleged North Vietnamese attack on US warships on August 4, opened the way for the deployment of US troops in Southeast Asia. Following these incidents, the United States launched retaliatory air strikes on the DRV, and in March 1965 it sent combat troops to South Vietnam. The first deployment consisted of two marine battalions, and the number of troops quickly rose from there. At the peak of US military involvement, there were approximately half a million American troops fighting on Vietnamese soil.

By 1965, the DRV's troops in South Vietnam had also increased. Under the leadership of party general secretary Lê Duẩn, the DRV planned a major military offensive in the wake of Diệm's overthrow. To this end, complete regiments of the PAVN were sent south, and the transport of weapons and supplies quadrupled in 1964.[90] Lê Duẩn's plan for a major offensive was not realized until 1968, when the PAVN and PLAF jointly launched a surprise attack on 105 cities and towns throughout South Vietnam during celebrations of the Lunar New Year (Tet).[91] Known as the Tet Offensive, this brought the war into the cities and, for the first time, exposed many urbanites to violence beyond the occasional NLF terrorist attacks.

Communist forces did not maintain control of the places they attacked or instigate an uprising against Thiệu's government, as the offensive's architects had hoped. Nevertheless, the shock of the attack had a significant bearing on the course of the war. In particular, the insurgents' ability to breach and occupy the exterior of the US embassy compound caused great alarm in the United States. For many Americans, the Tet offensive revealed the extent to which their government had been deceiving them. President Lyndon Johnson had assured Americans that US troops were winning the war, yet the televised and photographic images of the offensive told another story. Americans responded to this new narrative with increased demands for the withdrawal of US troops from Vietnam. Consequently, Johnson announced he would not run for reelection in 1968, acknowledging his mistakes in handling the war.

With mounting antiwar sentiments throughout the United States, it became politically difficult for Washington to continue fighting. US leaders began peace talks with the DRV in May 1968 in Paris. The negotiations met many roadblocks, however, and dragged on for nearly five years. Both sides continued to mount offensives while pursuing peace talks, a tactic the North Vietnamese called "talking while fighting."[92]

The pressure to achieve a diplomatic resolution increased when Richard Nixon was elected president in 1968 on a platform of "peace with honor." However, while continuing to hold peace talks, Nixon escalated US military action in Vietnam and expanded it into neutral Cambodia. From 1969 to 1970 the US Air Force carried out Operation Menu, which covertly bombed the border region of Cambodia and Vietnam. In 1970, when the US-allied General Lon Nol took power in a coup d'état in Cambodia, the United States expanded its bombing campaigns to support his regime against Cambodian communists. In addition, US military forces and the Army of Vietnam (ARVN) jointly invaded Cambodia in an attempt to destroy the Vietnamese communists' southern headquarters and their supply bases.

The DRV likewise continued its aggression in the hope of gaining an advantage on the battlefield and at the negotiating table. DRV leaders believed a decisive win could cripple Thiệu's government and provide leverage at the Paris talks.[93] With this goal in mind, the DRV mounted an invasion of South Vietnam in March 1972, commonly known as the Easter offensive. By the time of the Easter offensive, most US troops had already left Vietnam. Since 1968, the United States had been transferring military responsibilities to the ARVN and steadily withdrawing US combat troops. At the beginning of 1972 there were only 139,000 US troops left, with another 70,000 scheduled to be withdrawn by May.[94]

The Easter offensive was therefore an important test for Vietnamization; it was the first engagement of this magnitude carried out by the ARVN mainly on its own. Although many ARVN soldiers fought bravely and showed strong resolve, it was clear that the ARVN was still heavily dependent on the United States, particularly US airpower. Despite regaining much of the territory lost during the Easter offensive, many ARVN soldiers were pessimistic about their ability to withstand communist forces once the US pullout was complete.[95]

To retaliate for the Easter attack, the United States launched Operation Linebacker in May, sending B-52 bombers deep into North Vietnam and mining Haiphong harbor. Peace talks resumed following these violent offensives and counteroffensives, but they stalled again in late 1972. The US response to this newest roadblock was another bombing campaign, Operation Linebacker II. For twelve days, December 18–29, the US Air Force conducted close to two thousand sorties and dropped more than twenty thousand tons of bombs on the DRV. Unlike in previous campaigns, this time, much of the bomb load was dropped on the cities of Hanoi and Haiphong. Mines were also laid in important North Vietnamese ports.[96]

Shortly after the December bombing, an agreement was finally reached. The main provisions of the peace treaty, signed on January 27, 1973, included a cease-fire from all sides, the complete withdrawal of US and allied forces, and the formation of a National Council of National Reconciliation and Concord composed of the Saigon government, the NLF and the communist-led provisional revolutionary government, and a neutral group. To the chagrin of Thiệu and non-communists in South Vietnam, PAVN forces south of the seventeenth parallel did not have to regroup to the north.[97] And after the Easter offensive, the DRV had 100,000 troops in South Vietnam.[98] The South Vietnamese government was deeply upset by the treaty, which Thiệu considered a cut-and-run maneuver by the United States. Nixon assured Thiệu that the Americans would send support if the DRV broke the agreement. Unfortunately for Thiệu and the RVN, the Watergate scandal nullified Nixon's promise.

Not surprisingly, the Paris peace provisions were quickly broken. With little incentive to abide by the treaty, the RVN attempted to regain as much territory from communist forces as it could before the last US troops left.[99] Communist troops were ordered to respect the peace treaty, but they responded in kind to ARVN incursions. For their part, DRV leaders had decided to make plans for the war's final stage as early as March 1973.[100] When it became clear in the spring of 1974 that the US would not come to the aid of South Vietnam, DRV leaders ordered their forces to begin the last general offensive to "liberate" South Vietnam. Helped by the RVN's severe economic problems, low troop morale, and Thiệu's poor military decisions, the DRV was able to accomplish its goal by April 30 of the following year.

That day marked the conclusion of the war and the end of the RVN. Despite its short duration, the RVN made an indelible impact on people's lives and on history. For historians, South Vietnam continues to be a topic of debate and controversy. For the South Vietnamese, this was their home. Without the benefit of historical hindsight, the people of South Vietnam did their best to make it a better place for themselves, their kin, and their community.

# SOCIABILITY AND ASSOCIATIONAL LIFE IN SOUTH VIETNAM

Over the two decades of the RVN's existence, voluntary associations played an important role in the lives of many people. This chapter focuses on mutual-aid and friendly societies (MAFS; *hội tương tế ái hữu*), a form of voluntary organization that exists in many societies and has deep roots in Vietnam. In both rural and urban settings, mutual-aid organizations help people deal with the vagaries of life by offering social support, opportunities to forge group connections, and financial assistance. In early industrializing cities in France and Argentina, for example, mutual-benefit groups provided workers with protection in times of illness or death.[1] In rural areas, mutual-aid societies may take the form of labor exchange and rotating credit organizations.

In general, these associations operate on the basis of formally established reciprocity. Typically, mutual-aid groups are established with specific mechanisms and arrangements formulated to protect or advance the needs of their members. Not all mutual-aid groups, however, prioritize tangible exchanges. Some function as a vehicle for moral and social support, providing members with opportunities to share social, recreational, or spiritual interests. Societies undergoing major sociopolitical shifts tend to see a proliferation of mutual-aid societies, as was the case in postapartheid South Africa and postsocialist Tanzania.[2] While there is a great deal of variation, the common denominator for most mutual-aid groups is that they focus on meeting the needs of members rather than those of society at large.

Because of these groups' priorities, some scholars do not consider MAFS a constitutive element of civil society. The prevailing assumption among many theorists is that civic engagement is a defining aspect of civil society. MAFS therefore appear parochial not only in their mandates but also in their tendency to form associations based on kinship, locality, and religion. MAFS lack not only a civic outlook but also horizontal ties, both of which are important for building social trust and engagement.[3]

Other scholars find the strict definition of civil society too narrow and Western-centric. Robert Weller favors the term "alternative civility" rather than "civil society" in his study of Taiwanese voluntary groups and their civic work.[4] He suggests that kinship, lineage, religious, and other informal and localized organizations have the potential to be mobilized for civic engagement and democratization. Though particularistic in their orientation, these organizations are still capable of building social ties and trust. As Weller notes, rotating credit associations could not function without "a high level of horizontal trust."[5] Hy Van Luong contributes to this debate with his research on the reemergence of voluntary organizations in Vietnam in the reform (đổi mới) period beginning in the mid-1980s. During this time, Vietnam moved toward a market economy as the state curtailed its role in the provision of social, educational, and health services. These changes were critical factors in fueling the proliferation of voluntary associations, especially MAFS based on kinship, communal ties, and identity. Luong argues convincingly that in the late 1990s these so-called traditional forms of organizations—rather than urban-based, bourgeois civil society groups—were exerting the "strongest and most effective pressure on the state."[6] Moreover, these groups voiced their concerns and grievances "through open confrontation and occasionally adversarial open dialogue," rather than through subtle or passive approaches.[7]

Luong's research also indicates that kinship and mutual-aid organizations can play a positive role in economic development. His findings show that in the northern and central regions of Vietnam, where there were "denser community-based networks and polyadic relations," people relied on these ties to access, at a lower cost, the resources, information, and support they needed to improve their livelihoods.[8] In the south, where there were fewer such organizations, economic growth was less robust. It is clear from both Weller's and Luong's work that although mutual-aid associations do not generally profess an orientation toward civic engagement, the social ties and trust they generate are useful for economic development and can be mobilized for broad collective action.

Mutual-aid and friendly societies have a long history in Vietnamese society. Evidence suggests that they performed a useful role for many sectors of the population in both the French colonial and postcolonial periods. When Vietnam was divided in 1954 following the Geneva Accords, MAFS continued to proliferate in the south. By examining a sample of these organizations, this chapter provides insight into South Vietnamese society, the sociopolitical changes that unfolded there, and how people grappled with these changes. While the South Vietnamese MAFS may not have met the criteria for elements of civil society, they operated on trust, organizational procedure, and rules of governance—important ingredients for a functioning economy and society. For the most part, MAFS also created the horizontal ties that are important for both economic and political development.

## Mutual Aid before 1954

Evidence suggests that MAFS predated the French colonial period in Vietnam by several centuries. Some of this evidence comes from village covenants (*hương ước*), which were governing bylaws dating back to the fifteenth century for some northern villages.[9] Standard in many village covenants were regulations for MAFS, such as rice- or money-lending societies. The enshrinement of these regulations in village governance documents strongly suggests the prevalence and importance of MAFS in Vietnamese society before French colonial rule.

During the Nguyễn dynasty (1802–1945), a variety of MAFS existed in northern villages. Nguyễn Từ Chi distinguishes two types of MAFS in the Nguyễn period: *phe* and *hội*.[10] While both were voluntary organizations, the *phe* had more connections to the village administration. For example, the *phe tư văn* (literati association), which existed in many northern villages, assumed social, moral, and ritual roles in village life. Open only to scholars, this elite organization sometimes exerted political pressure on the village administration.[11] Other types of *phe* included those based on residency—neighborhood, road, or alley. These *phe* generally had a strong focus on socializing and feasting.

The *hội* were associations founded by individuals without any connections to the village government. They were highly specialized in function and reflected the particular needs of their membership. For example, there were associations for petty traders, rotating credit societies, organizations that helped pay wedding and funeral expenses, and Lunar New Year feasting clubs. Also popular were sports and cultural associations, such as the martial arts club and the traditional *chèo* musical theater association.[12] Elderly Buddhist women had their pagoda societies (Hôi Chu Bà), which were extensive throughout the northern region.[13] Club members helped maintain the pagoda and performed prayers during ceremonies. In addition to these religious activities, the Hội Chu Bà organized social gatherings, followed established procedures for selecting group leaders, and collected membership dues.[14] Interestingly, the women's pagoda groups lasted into the twenty-first century. In fact, in North Vietnam—and later in the Socialist Republic of Vietnam (SRV)—the Hội Chu Bà was the only voluntary association permitted to operate with relative independence from the state from the 1950s through 1990s.[15]

The practice and ethics of mutual aid were supported by the existence of granaries, institutions that stored rice to regulate grain prices, provided low-interest loans to the poor, and fed the hungry in the event of a food crisis.[16] Under the rule of the Nguyễn monarchs, some granaries were administered by the imperial government, while others were controlled by the provinces and communes. At the commune level, the granaries relied on the voluntary participation of local officials and elite families who administered and stocked the facility. Under French control, the granary system ceased to exist at the national and provincial levels, but some granaries continued to operate at the commune and village levels into the 1920s.[17]

During the French colonial period, voluntary associations were allowed to operate with some restrictions. Groups had to apply for permission and were required to refrain from participating in political debates and activities. Many mutual-aid organizations, especially funeral and ceremonial societies, operated during this period. The Mutual-Aid Society for Northerners (Hội Bắc Việt Tương-Tế) is a good example. Established in 1924 in Saigon, this society's main purpose was to help members compete with Chinese and Indian merchants. The group had an executive committee of six people and a management committee of thirteen.[18] In addition to its pragmatic function, the organization maintained a cemetery. The shared cemetery and the associated funereal rituals likely helped cement relations within the organization.[19]

Other types of MAFS concentrated on supporting members during times of financial difficulty. The Great Kindness Society (Hội Quang Huệ) of Cao Bàng province, for instance, proposed to build a granary to help members who were experiencing difficulties such as a house fire or crop failure. Although the society also aided the poor in the community, its main concern was the welfare of members.[20] Some MAFS during the French era made this focus clear in their names. In Nam Định and Phú Thọ provinces, there were two MAFS with the same name: Self-Benefit Society (Hội Tự Ích). Because of their protective nature and predominantly inward perspective, MAFS were often criticized. The urban Vietnamese intelligentsia in the 1920s and 1930s dismissed MAFS as "eating and drinking clubs," portraying them as parochial and "traditional." The self-conscious, Western-educated elite wanted to see more modern forms of social organizations that would promote social change and progress.[21]

New types of MAFS emerged in the early twentieth century, reflecting the changing Vietnamese society under French colonial rule. Alexander Woodside's seminal research on the Vietnamese search for community (đoàn thể) in the early twentieth century notes the activities of "semi-modern" mutual-aid organizations created for employees in different trade, service, and professional sectors.[22] The Association of the Industrial and Commercial Employees of the Tonkin (Bắc-kỳ Công-thương Đồng-nghiệp Hội), for example, was a large mutual-aid organization for employees in a variety of white-collar, service, and trade sectors. Another example was the Vietnamese Medical and Pharmaceutical Society (Việt Nam Y Dược Hội) founded in the early 1920s.[23]

In writing about the new MAFS of the early twentieth century, Woodside notes that they resembled groups of the past in their insular outlook, hierarchical nature, and elitist leadership. Woodside cites particularities of Vietnamese society under colonialism, such as the French policy of divide and rule and the structure of professional training, as factors contributing to the elitist nature of Vietnamese associational life. These "undemocratic" characteristics remained prominent in the voluntary associations that emerged in the postcolonial period. However, these traits are not unique to Vietnam; they are common to many voluntary associations, even in the twenty-first century. Some civil society theorists note the paradox that "voluntary associations are often exclusionary and hierarchical and yet are nevertheless an essential element of a liberal-democratic polity."[24] Even labor unions, which are usually considered progressive, have excluded minorities in favor of their members' privileges.[25] These examples are important reminders that some notions about civil society and its components are more prescriptive than descriptive.

Trade unions made their appearance in Vietnam by the late 1920s. Although trade unions are distinct from mutual-aid societies, the main purpose of both types of organizations is the protection and advancement of their members' interests. In some countries, MAFS contributed to the development of trade unions. In Mexico during the Porfiriato period (1876–1911), some occupation-specific MAFS in sectors such as the railroad and textiles "began acting like trade unions in all but name."[26] In Argentina MAFS played a role in the development of trade unions and the welfare state of the early twentieth century.[27] Trần Ngọc Angie's research on trade unions in colonial and postcolonial Vietnam shows that ethnic and other social identities were important in union formation and recruitment.[28] These examples reinforce Weller's and Luong's arguments that MAFS can create social connections, which can be channeled to support the development of civil society.

Although the French colonial government permitted the formation of voluntary associations, especially MAFS, trade unions were outlawed. Despite the ban, Vietnamese left-wing activists and communists were secretly organizing dock, factory, plantation, and mine workers in the late 1920s. The Red Trade Union Federation—an affiliate of Communist International—began operating

publicly in 1929.[29] By the late 1940s, politically moderate unions began to organize workers. Notable was the work of Gilbert Jouan, a French civil servant in
the customs office. Influenced by the Catholic trade union movement, Jouan was
convinced that taking control of the labor movement was an effective way to
counter the growing influence of radicals and communists in Indochina. The
French authorities evidently found Jouan's reasoning sound and allowed him to
organize. Jouan joined forces with Trần Quốc Bửu, and together they founded
the Vietnam Confederation of Catholic Workers (VCW).[30] As discussed later,
the VCW continued to operate after the country's division and became the largest labor confederation in South Vietnam.

The French colonial authorities' response to the VCW highlights the state's
ambivalence toward the associational life of the colonized. Although the government closely scrutinized civil society, it also recognized the potential benefits of organizations such as unions, which did not even have legal status. From
the state's point of view, voluntary organizations could help maintain social order and spread state-approved messages. In the case of the VCW, the authorities hoped it could address workers' needs without inciting class warfare, disrupting the colonial economy, or calling for social revolution.

Another compelling reason for French administrators to tolerate voluntary
associations was that these groups provided social services to their members.
Colonial administrators in Indochina were constantly struggling with fiscal
shortfalls and were happy to transfer some of the responsibility to the local population. Such attitudes were particularly pronounced during food crises, which
were frequent events in the Red River Delta region. In these economically strained
periods, colonial officials encouraged people to rely on their local communities
and associations rather than look to the government for aid. The Commission on
Famine Prevention was created in 1906 after a major famine earlier that year, and
Governor-General Paul Beau suggested that provinces consider resurrecting self-
help institutions, such as communal granaries. Ignoring the existence of many
active mutual-aid organizations, some colonial officials suggested that the Vietnamese people should be taught the value of mutual aid so that they could assist
one another during subsistence crises.[31]

It is clear that both the colonial government and the local population saw
practical and social value in voluntary associations in general and mutual-aid
organizations in particular. For the colonial state, the MAFS provided a way to
cut spending and bolster the state's claim to rule. Participants in MAFS were no
doubt motivated by a multitude of reasons, some of which were rooted in self-
interest (e.g., economic protection), while others were motivated by the desire to
forge socioeconomic connections and maintain values and customs. This latter
desire was likely shaped by the immense changes that accompanied colonialism,

capitalism, and modernization. Socioeconomic changes in the postcolonial period made the raison d'être of associational life just as compelling.


# Forging Ties in the RVN

According to a 1956 government survey, of the 400 voluntary organizations in
South Vietnam, 148 were classified as MAFS.[32] Many of groups were organized
around traditional bonds such as religion, native place, and lineage. Other groups
were established around shared experiences and identities such as employment,
alma mater, and recreational interests. During the 1960s and 1970s, MAFS continued to be established and maintained. In 1971 the Interior Ministry registered
forty-four new voluntary associations, 86 percent of which were MAFS (see
table 2.1).[33]

The mutual-aid associations of the RVN bore many similarities to those of
the French colonial period. Like the French colonial state, the new republic required voluntary groups to register with the government and pledge to stay out
of politics. The police conducted thorough background checks on founding
members. Like their counterparts in the colonial administration, RVN officials
recognized the benefits of MAFS and valued voluntary associations' potential
to inculcate loyalty to the state and create bonds among citizens. Authorities also
realized that in addition to extending state hegemony, civil society could bolster the state's modern image. In responding to the application of the Association of History and Geography Professors, an official noted in the margin that
"organizations like this should be encouraged" because of their contributions
to cultural life. Interestingly, the official pointed out that many such organizations existed in other countries, specifically the United States.[34] In other
words, if South Vietnam wanted to be like the United States and other modern
nations, it needed to demonstrate that it was an open society where voluntary
organizations operated freely.

MAFS identified group solidarity and mutual help as their main objectives,
although many groups set other goals as well. Associations typically had detailed
charters that set out club regulations regarding membership, election of the executive, and duties and rights of members. Almost all groups had membership
fees. The Friends and Family Mutual-Aid Society charged an initial fee of 200
dong, in addition to monthly dues of 50 dong (in US dollars, approximately 87
cents and 23 cents, respectively), while the Society for the Worship of National
Saints and Heroes charged 120 dong annually.[35] The Society of Engineers and
Technicians, recognizing that the cost of membership might be a barrier for new
graduates, instituted a 50 percent discount on the application fee, charging only

**TABLE 2.1** MAFS that received state permission to operate in 1971

| | |
|---|---|
| **General and place-based mutual-aid groups** | Kim Giang Mutual-Aid Society, Saigon |
| | Mỹ-Xuyên Mutual Aid, Saigon |
| | Mutual-aid and worship group of Nguyện Công Shrine |
| | Tân Thao Mutual Aid, Saigon |
| | Ninh Bình Mutual Aid, Gia Định |
| | Quất Động Mutual Aid, Saigon |
| | Bạch Sam Thường Xuyên Mutual Aid |
| | Saigon Bưu-Hoa Mutual Aid, Saigon |
| | Buddhist Mourning Society, Nha Trang |
| | Hội Thánh Chơn-lý Định-Tường (Cao Đài), Định Tường |
| | Tổng Đoàn cư-sỉ phật-tử VN, Saigon |
| | Hội Kiều-Yêu Tương-Tế, Saigon |
| | Hội Ái-Hữu Thân Thượng, Gia Định |
| | Hội Hương Lão Bác Ái Kế-Sắt, Biên Hoà |
| | Thanh Nguyen Văn Hóa Hiệp Hội, Saigon |
| | Hội Tương Tế Chàm-Lạc-Tri, Bình Thuận |
| | Hội Ái hữu Quảng [unclear word], Gia Định |
| **Lineage associations** | Five organizations for surnames Phùng, Thích, Triệu, Thọ, and Lai |
| **Professional groups** | Vietnam Nursing Mutual-Aid Society, Saigon |
| | Society for Periodical Publishers, Gia Định |
| **Alumni associations** | Apprentices of Nguyen Thanh Nhan's pharmacy, Gia Định |
| | National Post Office School, Saigon |
| | Reserve Officers Training, year 2 (sĩ quan trừ bị khóa 2), Saigon |
| | Reserve Officers Training, year 2, Thủ Đức |
| | Lái Thiêu Catholic boarding school for the hearing impaired, Saigon |
| | Nguyễn Trải School, Bình Dương |
| | Bán Công Dĩ-An High School, Biên Hòa |
| | Phú Yến High School, Chợ Lớn |
| | Vỏ Bị Military Academy, Đà Lạt |
| **Parent-student associations (Hội Phụ-Huynh Học)** | Pupils of Saigon |
| | Elementary public schools of Trà-kha "A" |
| | Elementary private school of Việt Trí, Saigon |
| | Cái Đội School in Vĩnh Long |
| | Elementary public school Ngô Tâm Thông in Vĩnh Long |
| | High school of agriculture, forestry, and animal husbandry of Định Tường |
| | Elementary public school Liên-Ấp Bình Đức |
| | Elementary public school My-An, Vĩnh Long |
| | Quảng Ngãi High School for Girls |
| | Elementary public school Mỹ-Hoà, Vĩnh Long |

*Sources*: Documents found in PTTD2 4412: Tập Nghị Định của Bộ Nội Vụ v/v cho phép thành lập hội năm 1971.

100 rather than 200 dong.[36] Though not exorbitant, association fees were still out of reach for the vast majority of the population. During the period 1956–1974, the average daily wage was 98.7 dong for a skilled worker and 68.7 dong for an unskilled worker in Saigon.[37] Thus, even the reduced entrance fee charged by the Society of Engineers and Technicians exceeded a skilled worker's daily wage. Although many groups' charters stated that membership was open to all regardless of ethnicity, religion, and gender, the cost of joining and maintaining membership made these groups accessible only to people with higher incomes. Moreover, some groups required current members to vouch for an applicant's character or sponsor an applicant's bid to join. This requirement, similar to membership rules of exclusive country clubs in the West, made some voluntary associations elitist and exclusionary.

Another commonality among many MAFS and other voluntary organizations was the practice of holding annual or biannual general membership meetings, where the main business was electing a new executive. Associations typically had an executive and/or a management committee of about half a dozen people. In 1960 the Confucian Studies Society, established in 1957, had an executive committee of seven members and an advisory committee of six. The Association of US University Graduates, founded in 1959, had an executive committee of eight.[38] Along with the business of electing a governing body, the general meeting was an opportunity to perform rituals (an important aspect of some MAFS) and socialize. Because encouraging ties and affection among members was one of the primary goals of MAFS, these social gatherings were important. Some associations also used the general meeting to enhance the status of the organization. The general meeting of the Association of Technical School Graduates was a grand event that took place at the Navy Club in 1970. This alumni group boasted 320 members, the majority of whom held professional and executive positions in state-run and private companies. Perhaps because of its members' connections, the group invited President Nguyễn Văn Thiệu to its meeting in 1970.[39]

In addition to holding general meetings, social events, and celebrations, some MAFS published newsletters or journals to keep members informed. These publications included essays, poetry, short stories, advocacy pieces, club news, and technical discussions pertinent to the group.[40] The Saigon branch of the Vietnam Veterans Legion published the annual *Veterans* magazine (*Cựu Chiến Sĩ*) during the Lunar New Year in the 1960s and early 1970s. It included traditional New Year's greetings, poetry, and essays about that year's zodiac animal and other entertaining topics. In addition, the magazine reported association news, such as past and upcoming activities of the club's Saigon branch and other chapters. The magazine also featured in-depth information about policies and laws relevant to veterans. The 1967 issue, for instance, explained the services and benefits to which veterans, wounded veterans, and widows and children of veterans were entitled.

Similarly, the General Association of Educators produced a periodical titled *Discussion (Luận Đàm)*. This association was established in 1959 for university, high school, and elementary educators, and its members included respected scholars such as Nguyễn Đình Hòa. The organization aimed to improve education and develop a national culture.[41] By 1960, the group had become a member of the World Confederation of Organizations of the Teaching Profession and had participated in many international conferences. Its periodical contained essays about philosophies of and approaches to teaching and learning. In 1960 *Discussion* carried articles examining unemployment among the educated, the mission of high school education, the benefits of humanities versus technical studies, the role of youth in the current national crisis, and views about the state of education in the RVN.[42] This periodical provided opportunities to exchange ideas not only about the profession of teaching but also about the broader role of education in society. This suggests that although MAFS publications were produced primarily to advance the objectives of a specific organization, they also provided a forum for the discussion of issues relevant to the wider society. In other words, some MAFS publications contributed to the public sphere by providing opportunities for critical engagement on matters of public interest.

To get a better sense of the workings of MAFS, the remainder of this chapter examines three popular types: native place and kinship organizations, alumni (school-based) organizations, and professional employment-based organizations.

# Native Place and Kinship Organizations

Organizations established around members' native place existed in Vietnam before the twentieth century and remained important, especially during the turmoil of the mid-twentieth century. When the country was divided at the conclusion of the First Indochina War in 1954, close to 900,000 people left their homes and moved south of the seventeenth parallel (see chapter 1). Although the RVN government considered the northern migrants settled by 1956, social and cultural integration remained challenging, and issues of displacement continued throughout the 1960s and 1970s. As the political struggle over unification between the communist north and republican south developed into a military conflict by the early 1960s, the number of internal refugees rose to a crisis level in the RVN. Many people fled because their homes had been destroyed by either communist or republican forces. In addition, US-RVN joint forces designated some contested areas free-fire zones, where anyone would be considered an enemy combatant and could be killed on sight. Displacement of civilians worsened when the United States deployed combat troops in 1965 and the DRV started to wage major offensives in the south. The war created tens of millions of refugees. According to Louis Wiesner, in South Vietnam "close to 12,000,000 civilians, over half the population, fled from one side or the other or from armed conflict, or were evacuated or relocated, some of them more than once."[43] In these circumstances, it is not surprising that people felt a need to seek solace among compatriots with a common identity.

As a result, many same-place associations were established, including the mutual-aid society for people who originated from the central province of Quảng Trị but were living in Saigon, the mutual-aid society for prominent people from Ninh Bình province in North Vietnam, and the society for retired officials from the southern province of Vĩnh Long.[44] Migrants from the northern provinces of Bắc Ninh, Bắc Giang, Bắc Kạn, Vĩnh Yên, Phúc Yên, and Thái Nguyên could join the Friendly Society for Residents of the Kinh Bắc Region (Hội ái hữu Kinh Bắc). Father Nguyễn Hòa Nhã and National Assembly representative Nguyễn Hữu Đức founded this society in 1969 to maintain solidarity among Catholic migrants from these provinces.[45] More of these groups would be established in 1971 (see table 2.1).

For similar reasons, many lineage (họ) mutual-aid associations were established in South Vietnam. Mutual-aid groups for the Hứa, Tất, Ngô, Trần, Vương, Thích, Phùng, and Triệu lineages were established. The main goal of these groups was to strengthen ties among members by conducting ancestral veneration ceremonies.[46] In addition, some lineage groups built cemeteries or ancestral halls for their rituals. The Ngô lineage was particularly ambitious; its goals were to perform ancestor worship twice a year, construct an ancestor temple, establish a scholarship fund, and build a school (presumably for children of the lineage).[47] About this last goal, the director of the General Secretariat of the Presidency, Mai Quốc Đống, stated that this was a matter for the Ministry of Education and Health to decide.[48] What troubled Đống was not that the group wanted to build a school but that they were Vietnamese citizens of Chinese ancestry. In other correspondence, Đống expressed concerns that ethnic Chinese were trying to reestablish the congregation system.

Congregations were banned in 1960 as part of the RVN's attempt to assimilate Chinese residents and win their political loyalty. Chinese communities had existed throughout Vietnam since at least the seventeenth century, and they had managed to remain semi-independent. Contributing to the Chinese community's distinction was the existence of the congregation system, which provided a range of services and support to members. In the early 1950s there were five active congregations: Canton, Fukien (Hokkien), Hakka, Hainan, and Triều-Châu (Chaozhou).[49] Powerful and wealthy, these congregations established hospitals, schools, cemeteries, and credit systems for their members.[50] Under French rule, this arrangement worked well, since it was more efficient and effective for congregation leaders to administer and control the ethnic Chinese population than for the colonial government to undertake these tasks.

The congregation system did not suit the president of the new Republic of Vietnam, however. Like many other postcolonial states in the region, the RVN was in the throes of nation building in the mid-1950s. At the heart of nation building—which involves both building a state apparatus and creating a sense of national belonging—is the need to accrue the moral authority and coercive power to reach, influence, and control the population. The people of the RVN were now citizens endowed with rights and duties, and they owed their allegiance to the central state. Vietnamese citizenship had automatically been given to all Viet ethnic residents, and ethnic Chinese were strongly encouraged to become citizens. Children of Chinese parents were automatically considered citizens of the RVN. To compel the Chinese to accept Vietnamese citizenship, the Diệm government decreed in 1956 that foreigners were barred from eleven trades, all of which were dominated by ethnic Chinese.[51] In other words, the Chinese population was coerced into adopting Vietnamese citizenship There was resistance, but eventually most ethnic Chinese submitted to the law. By 1969, there were 1.1 million ethnic Chinese with Vietnamese citizenship and 3,000 without.[52]

Other decrees followed, including the dissolution of the congregation system, the mandatory adoption of Vietnamese names, and the use of the Vietnamese language in schools. While the ethnic Chinese community complied with the government's policies, these laws did not destroy their ethnic identity or kinship ties. This lack of success was clear to the special commissioner for Chinese affairs, Nguyễn Văn Vàng. In 1959 he wrote to city mayors and provincial chiefs urging them to try harder to arouse a sense of (Vietnamese) national spirit in the ethnic Chinese population. One way to do this, Vàng advised, was to encourage people of Chinese descent to join sports clubs, mutual-aid associations, and professional societies established by Viet ethnic people.[53] Moreover, he advised officials in the Ministry of Labor that ethnic Chinese should be encouraged to join the Vietnam Confederation of Labor rather than form their own unions.[54] In 1962 Vàng alerted the minister of the interior about two ethnic Chinese sports clubs that had applied for official status. Because these clubs comprised only Chinese members, he suspected that the motive behind their establishment was to reassign and hide the assets of the now defunct Chinese congregations. Upon their dissolution, the congregations' property and assets were supposed to be transferred to the government, but the process of confiscating this property had stalled due to strong resistance. Vàng therefore asked that permission for these clubs be withheld.[55] He also wrote to the mayor of Saigon to warn him that Vietnamese of Chinese descent were trying to reestablish their own ethnic associations in the guise of sports clubs and mutual-aid societies.[56] Despite Vàng's efforts, by the mid-1960s, the congregations were once again active though not officially recognized.[57]

In the aftermath of the Tet offensive (1968), a new complication was added to the "Chinese problem." During Tet 1968, the DRV launched a surprise offensive with PAVN and PLAF troops, targeting towns and cities throughout South Vietnam. Because some of these attacks were launched from Chợ Lớn, a Chinese-dominated suburb of Saigon, RVN officials had to reconsider their approach to the Chinese community. In light of the failed assimilation policy and what they perceived as communist infiltration of the Chinese community, government officials discussed how to bring the Chinese population into the nation-state without alienating them. Officials from the Ministry of Defense suggested imposing stricter regulations on the associational and cultural lives of ethnic Chinese, including limiting the number of Chinese-language newspapers, publications, and films produced. They also recommended that the government restrict the number of Chinese-only associations and increase efforts to encourage ethnic Chinese to integrate with the majority population. Other officials, however, advocated a more pragmatic approach. These officials noted that since the government's main enemy was communism, easing restrictions on the ethnic Chinese community might be more effective in gaining its support.[58]

Although RVN officials were clearly reluctant to permit Chinese-only voluntary groups, Mai Quốc Đống rightly admitted that ethnic Chinese had the same rights as other Vietnamese citizens to form voluntary associations.[59] He and other officials, however, continued to express concerns. Therefore, when the Ngô lineage proposed to build private schools for its members, Đống was suspicious. Similarly, when some groups proposed associations based on places in China, such as the Vĩnh Long Society for natives of Triều Châu (or Chaozhou, in China's Guangdong province) or a welfare society for people from Mai-Huyện (or Meixian, a Hakkah-dominated district in Guangdong), there were strong reactions from President Thiệu's office.[60] Đống averred that it was inappropriate for Vietnamese citizens to establish a club bearing the name of a foreign place, particularly because this practice was reminiscent of the former Chinese congregations.[61] The Ministry of the Interior therefore proposed that any such applications be rejected in the future.[62]

The government's handling of ethnic Chinese voluntary associations is telling on a number of counts. First, the sociopolitical turmoil of nation building and civil war influenced associational life. Amid the dislocation, people sought others with shared identities and ethnicities to form communities. Second, the government considered MAFS and other voluntary associations as vehicles for the spread of both dissent and government influence. Even though native place and lineage organizations professed no larger sociopolitical goals, RVN officials saw their potential to challenge the status quo and effect change. Consequently, each association and its founding members had to be vetted. Voluntary associations also offered the government an opportunity to shape society. Nguyễn Văn Vàng and his colleagues therefore wanted to use MAFS to integrate ethnic Chinese into the wider society in the hope of gaining their political loyalty.

The authorities recognized the importance of civil society and saw it as a sphere over which they could assert their influence. RVN officials' thinking actually aligned with Antonio Gramsci's understanding of civil society: he saw civil society as another superstructure over which the state could exert control without the use of force.[63] South Vietnamese officials knew firsthand that coercion had only a limited effect. Their forced assimilation policies of the mid-1950s had not worked, and they were hoping that influence through associational life might be more effective. The irony was that they were still forcing ethnic Chinese to join Vietnamese organizations rather than using more subtle tactics. At the same time, ethnic Chinese were using voluntary associations to exercise their rights and protect themselves. Forming lineage organizations allowed them to maintain their ethnic identity and strengthen community ties; moreover, members could leverage the social capital gained through such associational activities for personal economic and political advantages.

# Alumni Associations

An important aspect of nation building is establishing a comprehensive national education system. With funding and advice from the United States and its agencies, the RVN reformed and expanded education. Student enrollment increased dramatically in the first five years of the RVN.[64] Both secondary and postsecondary schools became important centers for social networking, and high school and university students played important roles in the sociopolitical life of South Vietnam. In 1963 they led a mass protest against Ngô Đình Diệm's government and continued to act as a thorn in the side of subsequent governments. Later, left-leaning and communist students would take control of some university groups, most notably the Student Union of Saigon University. Chapter 5 discusses student groups in more detail, so the focus here is on alumni associations. Although they were less vocal than student unions in the public sphere, alumni groups were popular and prevalent.

Like other mutual-aid groups, alumni associations focused on building connections among members and were generally not overtly political. Alumni groups were established for well-known, prestigious schools such as the elite

Quốc Học high school of Huế, as well as for less famous schools outside the urban centers. For example, there were alumni associations for students from Phước Tuy and Sóc Trăng provinces, for graduates of the Lái Thiêu Catholic boarding school for the hearing impaired, and for graduates of a Japanese-language school.[65]

For the most part, the alumni groups' priority was to forge social connections among members. Therefore, organizing social events, particularly their annual meetings, became the centerpiece of their activities. Some alumni meetings were high-society events that included dignitaries and government officials. Some groups strove to take on commemorative or philanthropic projects in addition to their networking objectives. In 1969 the alumni association for the elite Pellerin Catholic School had several major projects under way: constructing a community center in Thủ Đức, repairing the school's roof, performing relief work in support of victims of the Tet offensive, and building a dormitory. The last project was accomplished with donations of land and money from the association's members.[66] President Thiệu was an alumnus of this school and was the group's honorary president.[67]

The National Institute of Administration also had an active alumni association. The institute was established under French tutelage in 1953, but the United States, through Michigan State University, helped expand and restructure it.[68] The institute was a training ground for civil servants, and its graduates were influential people who maintained connections with one another through the alumni association, which continues to be active outside of Vietnam. With chapters in different cities, the association published a bulletin (*Bản Tin*) to keep members informed. In 1969 members were busy raising funds for a memorial project to honor former students who had died in battle.[69]

The most elite high school in South Vietnam, Quốc Học (National Institute), counted among its famous graduates communist leaders Hồ Chí Minh, Võ Nguyên Giáp, and Phạm Văn Đồng and nationalist leader Ngô Đình Diệm. The school was founded in Huế in 1896 under the initiative of Diệm's father, Ngô Đình Khả, with the approval and support of the governor-general of Indochina. Until March 1945, when Japanese troops led a coup against French forces in Indochina, classes were taught in French and the school was directed by French administrators. Thereafter it offered classes in the Vietnamese language and was the first high school to be directed by Vietnamese educators and offering a Vietnamese curriculum.[70]

During the First Indochina War, Quốc Học was taken over by the French military, and the school had to relocate in smaller units to several different places in Hà Tĩnh and Nghệ An provinces. The school was reestablished in its original location on January 29, 1955, after ten years in exile. The alumni association was founded in 1958, but it lapsed into inactivity in the early 1960s. By 1963, it was active again, and many Quốc Học students joined other students throughout the country in the protest movement against Diệm that year. Many students were arrested. During the Tet offensive, leading to the temporary communist take-over of Huế, the school was occupied again. Afterward, it housed seven thousand refugees for several months. Perhaps not by coincidence, the alumni association reestablished itself on July 6, 1969, and scheduled a general meeting for December. The association's charter outlined three objectives: strengthen bonds of friendship among former students, support students from the central provinces in obtaining an education, and contribute to the rebuilding of the nation by bolstering morality and Vietnamese culture. The last objective perhaps reflected the trauma the city of Huế experienced during the Tet offensive. During the three weeks of communist occupation, approximately two thousand people were executed by the communist forces.

By 1971, the alumni association had seven chapters throughout South Vietnam and was in the process of opening three more.[71] The association reported in a letter to President Thiệu that it was publishing a periodical on national culture and providing scholarships to needy Huế students attending universities in other cities. It also aspired to build dormitories for Huế students in Saigon.[72] In addition, the association was planning to refurbish the school's entrance, which featured a mythical dragon (long mã)—an iconic motif in Huế architecture and a symbol of Huế culture.[73]

The Quốc Học Alumni Association, like many alumni groups in the RVN, focused on maintaining ties and friendship among its members. When alumni organizations engaged in civic activities, they tended to limit themselves to the philanthropic or cultural sphere, rather than venturing into the realm of politics. For these reasons, the government generally had no objections to the establishment of alumni associations. However, there were a couple of exceptions. The alumni association of Vạn Hạnh Buddhist University encountered problems with its application for official recognition. Vạn Hạnh University was founded in 1964 by the Buddhist leaders who were the moving force behind both the 1963 protest movement against Diệm and the 1966 Buddhist standoff against Prime Minister Nguyễn Cao Kỳ and the military. The university's connection with Buddhist leaders such as Thích Trí Quang, who commanded enough authority to mobilize mass protest movements, no doubt made the government reluctant to grant the alumni association permission to operate. An official with the Ministry of the Interior flagged this group, citing Vạn Hạnh University's close affiliation with Thích Trí Quang and the Ấn Quang Buddhist group.[74]

In this light, Nguyễn Xuân Liêm, cabinet chief of the Ministry of the Interior, suggested that the application be temporarily set aside. Mai Quốc Đông wholeheartedly agreed with Liêm's concerns. Đồng asserted that groups with "tendencies that are not beneficial to the authorities" often use people with clean political records to represent them. He also warned that after they get permission to operate, it might be difficult to control their actions or their membership.[75]

Based on the same reasoning, officials were reluctant to recognize the parent association of the Buddhist Bồ Đề school of Đà Nẵng.[76] Buddhists had established the Bồ Đề network of private secular schools in 1952 as part of the Buddhist revival movement to make Buddhism more influential and relevant in society (see chapter 3). In the end, officials decided to set aside the Bồ Đề parent association's application as well. In both the Vạn Hạnh and Bồ Đề cases, the authorities based their decisions on fear of possible infiltration and not on actual evidence. Police background checks on the founding members of both groups uncovered nothing of concern. They were denied recognition because of their schools' affiliation with a group the government deemed subversive. Although Thích Trí Quang and the Ấn Quang monks had led two major protest movements in the past, by 1969, they were more involved in the electoral process and no longer led large street demonstrations.[77] Vạn Hạnh University had embraced a more moderate political stance, even though, like many other South Vietnamese universities, it had its share of radical students. Although the government's decisions with regard to these two specific Buddhist alumni groups were unwarranted, their fear of seditious infiltration into seemingly apolitical groups was not unfounded. By 1969, a number of groups, including student unions, had been infiltrated by communist and NLF supporters. Some of these undercover agents and activists were discovered in the aftermath of the Tet offensive, making it clear that some volunteer organizations were highly politicized.

As the examples of the Buddhist alumni associations and the ethnic Chinese organizations suggest, the government perceived MAFS as a double-edged sword. On the one hand, officials recognized that voluntary associations were important for social cohesion, conviviality, and support. On the other hand, officials were worried that such associations, no matter how benign, could be used for coordinated social and political actions.

## Professional Employment-Based Associations

As the number of postsecondary institutions in South Vietnam grew, so did the number of associations for professionals and technocrats. Unlike the organizations discussed so far, professional organizations emphasized mutual benefit to individuals as well as promotion of the profession, including raising its profile and prestige in society. Associations existed for a multitude of professions, ranging from academia to business, health care, and the arts. Teachers, business managers, small business owners, pharmacists, engineers, and medical personnel established their own organizations. The Society for Agricultural Experts and Technicians is a typical example. According to the association's charter, the group received state permission to operate throughout the RVN in March 1965. Its purposes included supporting the interests of its members, encouraging cooperation and exchange among members, and elevating members' professional knowledge.[78] Another example is the Association for Health Engineers and Hygiene Specialists, whose stated purposes were to develop the profession, promote reform in society, and contribute to nation building.[79] Associations like these attracted the emerging class of technical experts, many of whom had been trained abroad. Many of these careers were not new, but they were newly professionalized.

## Library Association

Another good example is the Library Association of Vietnam, established in 1958 to promote the field of library science and libraries and archives in general. The founders were Phan Vô Ky, Nguyễn Gia Phương, and Hoàng Tuấn Anh, all of whom had leading roles at important state libraries. Ky was the director of the National Library, Phương was head librarian for the Ministry of Education, and Anh was head librarian for the Ministry of Information.[80] At the Library Association's first general assembly in 1959, which was well attended, all three men were elected to top executive positions in the organization.[81]

The founding of this group coincided with the state's interest in building and centralizing a national library system. In 1956, within nine months of becoming president, Ngô Đình Diệm called for the building of a new national library.[82] Consequently, the Ministry of Education was tasked with supervising the amalgamation of existing libraries to create a centralized national institution. Housed at 34 Gia Long Street, the old national library was cramped, and a new building was needed.[83] The symbolic cornerstones were laid in 1956, but construction was stalled for many years, and the building was not completed until 1971. In the meantime, the government continued to reorganize and streamline the national library system. In 1959 the government created the Directorate of National Libraries and Archives within the Ministry of Education to guide and supervise the development of public libraries, including managing services, personnel, and international relations.[84]

It is not surprising that a voluntary association for librarians was established during this period when libraries were receiving administrative attention. Reflecting the government's attitude about the importance of the library as an institution of a modern nation, the Library Association stressed the critical role libraries play in society and culture. In the premier issue of the association's journal *Library Review* (*Thư Viện Tập San*), association president Phan Vô Ky suggested that books and libraries are important for cultural development.[85] Another writer and staff member at the National Library, La Văn Thu, argued that just as a household's bookshelf reveals a lot about the cultural and moral development of a family, a country's libraries reflect its level of civilization.[86] Thu maintained that libraries exhibit each society's unique contribution to civilization. In other words, Vietnam's international reputation as a civilized country depended on it having a modern library system. In stressing the importance of libraries to the country's development and international status, the contributors to *Library Review* were claiming that the Library Association was much more than a voluntary professional society; it was an organization that could contribute to the nation-building process. Indeed, the group saw itself working side by side with the government to build an ideal society at a time when the "nation's revolutionary endeavor was in its most ardent phase."[87]

Because of the state's interest in building a modern library system in the late 1950s, the Library Association received a great deal of official support. The association had powerful patrons such as Ngô Đình Nhu, who became its honorary president; the minister of education, Trần Hữu Thế, acted as an adviser.[88] The Michigan State University Vietnam Advisory Group, US Information Services, and Asia Foundation played significant roles in the association's founding and provided encouragement, advice, and guidance.[89] In addition, these agencies supplied financial and infrastructural support for the association's operation. The Asia Foundation, for example, funded many of the group's activities, including the publication of library and archival reference books and library directories.[90] In 1974 alone, the Asia Foundation funded the association's library training courses (with 295,000 dong), conferences and meetings (1,050,000 dong), and publication of four issues of *Library Review* (488,000 dong) and seven newsletters (235,000 dong).[91]

US support for the Library Association was propelled by the larger geopolitical goal of maintaining a noncommunist South Vietnam. To support this agenda, the United States promoted the expansion of modern educational and intellectual institutions, which included the building and modernizing of libraries. The US nation builders viewed education, along with other cultural establishments, as the perfect channel to transmit US influence without appearing imperialistic. As such, aid money was funneled into educational and cultural organizations and activities. In 1967 the US Agency for International Development (USAID) launched a library development program as part of its education development project in South Vietnam. In 1966 a USAID report had painted a bleak picture of the state of libraries in South Vietnam and recommended that, along with training staff and reorganizing the system, all "efforts should be taken to assist the formation of an effective library association."[92] It was therefore not a coincidence that the US government and some foreign aid agencies were supportive of the Library Association.

As many historians have established, international aid agencies and nongovernmental entities were by no means neutral in their activities in Vietnam.[93] US technical experts, educators, and aid workers shared the US government's ideology and goals regarding nation building in Vietnam. These experts operated with the neocolonial belief that by spreading US-style education and other social institutions, Vietnam's "backward and traditional" society would be uplifted.[94] The Asia Foundation had a close relationship with the US government, and according to Grace Chou, it had a "parallel agenda" with the US government when it came to keeping Asia free of communism.[95] The Asia Foundation's founding members were selected by officials in Washington, with the approval of the US National Security Council. In 1967 the Asia Foundation and American Friends of Vietnam were both implicated in a scandal related to their receipt of indirect funding by the CIA.[96] These and similar groups were therefore not purely social and cultural organizations; they operated with a definite political agenda.

The extensive government and foreign support given to the Library Association raises the question of its independence. While many of the association's activities depended on foreign aid and it collaborated with the government on numerous projects, none of the activities contravened the association's stated goals and aspirations. The group's leadership seemed just as eager to pursue funded projects as the donors that supported them were. There was no indication that foreign aid agencies persuaded the association to carry out projects its members did not endorse.

Although there were close ties between the Library Association and the RVN government, the relationship was not always smooth. Even with Nhu as its honorary president, the organization still encountered red tape in its application for legal status.[97] Furthermore, the association struggled to obtain adequate office space throughout its existence. Its original office in the old national library building was insufficient, and after the new national library was built, the association failed to secure office space there. This prompted a bitter remark from the group's president that, after fifteen years of activity, the public and the government still did not recognize the organization's contribution to the country. In 1973 the association was given an office at Vạn Hạnh University.[98]

While foreign funding was certainly important, the Library Association also raised money from its membership, which consisted mainly of library employees but also included other professionals such as teachers and professors. Members had to pay 50 dong to join and then an annual fee of 200 dong. In 1960 the association collected 7,200 dong in membership fees, but unfortunately, most of the seventy-six members had not paid their dues in full.[99]

The association also raised funds through private donations and the sale of its books. In 1960 the Library Association raised 620 dong by selling its Vietnamese-English dictionary to the Asia Foundation and US Information Services. In 1968 Nguyễn Thị Cút, the treasurer and managing director of the association's journal, donated the 15,000 dong she earned in royalties for her translation of a book on library cataloging and classification.[100] Toan Ánh, an executive member and prolific author on Vietnamese culture and society, donated fifty copies of his book to raise funds.[101]

The Library Association's aim was not only to support the building of national libraries but also to promote the profession. The work of librarians had become specialized, requiring higher education and training. The president of the association in 1974, for example, held a master of library science degree from a US university and was employed at various university libraries in the RVN. Librarians needed a forum for social and professional exchange where they could share new knowledge and best practices. The Library Association also lobbied to improve the profession, such as creating more training programs and scholarships for librarians and technicians. To this end, the *Library Review* was essential.[102] It contained material aimed at specialists, such as features of a national library, the importance of school libraries, and how to organize official documents. The *Library Review* also published minutes of the association's meetings, details regarding the election of new executive members, notices of upcoming events, and membership news.

The Library Association was small and likely had little impact on the majority of the RVN's population, but it provides an interesting and useful case study for MAFS in South Vietnam. The organization and its activities reflected the changing sociopolitical environment. In essence, the Library Association was a by-product of South Vietnam's nation-building process. The association's raison d'être, activities, and goals mirrored those of the new republic. Both were propelled by aspirations to build a modern and independent country. Both were subjected to the US desire for influence, and both benefited from US aid. The Library Association was influenced by these national and international forces, but it continued to operate because of its members. The people who joined, administered, and participated in the Library Association did so voluntarily. It is safe to assume that many participated because they believed the association benefited them as practitioners of the profession. And, no doubt, many believed that libraries played an important role in the health of the nation.

# The Vietnam Confederation of Workers

Even though trade unions are not typically considered MAFS, they have in common the mandate to protect their members. The history of trade unions in Vietnam is rich and complex and has been studied by scholars Trần Ngọc Angie and Edmund Wehrle. Relying on their research, this section focuses on the Vietnam Confederation of Workers and how it negotiated the many politico-economic forces that impinged on its activities. This example illuminates the challenging state-society dynamics of wartime South Vietnam.

Although labor organizing took place during the French colonial period, trade unions became legal only in 1952, when the semiautonomous government of Bảo Đại reformed the labor laws.[103] As of 1968, there were 507 legal unions belonging to six different officially recognized confederations. The largest was the Vietnam Confederation of Workers (VCW), with 396 unions and 214,500 workers under its purview. The second largest, the Vietnam Confederation of Labor (VCL), oversaw 48 unions. It was more left leaning and was allegedly controlled by NLF cadres. In the 1960s the VCL was weakened by internal leadership rivalries.[104]

The VCW had its beginnings in the late 1940s and dominated the labor movement in the RVN until the end of the Vietnam War. Its longevity can be attributed to its moderate approach to labor organizing and to the willingness of its leader, Trần Quốc Bửu, to make strategic alliances with various RVN governments, the US government, and the anticommunist AFL-CIO (American Federation of Labor–Congress of Industrial Organizations). Bửu pursued these alliances to strengthen the labor movement against rivals, especially communist-led labor groups, and state repression.[105]

In addition to these pragmatic reasons, Bửu's alliances were based on his political convictions. He was a nationalist with strong anticommunist views. In 1940 he was sentenced to ten years in the notorious Côn Sơn (Paulo Condore) French prison for anticolonial activism. When he was released at the end of World War II, Bửu joined the Viet Minh movement to fight for Vietnam's independence. However, he soon became disillusioned with the Viet Minh because it was dominated by communists.[106] When Bửu moved into trade union work in the late 1940s, his distrust of communism deepened. He and the VCW became targets for communist repression. The VCW's activities among rural workers, plantation laborers, and tenant farmers put the organization in direct competition with the DRV-controlled labor union, the Vietnam Federation of Trade Unions, established in 1945. VCW leaders working in areas under DRV control found themselves under attack. Many were arrested and sentenced to hard labor. Therefore, when the country was divided, Bửu worked hard to evacuate VCW members to the south.[107] This experience made the VCW, and especially Bửu, willing to ally with South Vietnamese authorities and other hawkish political forces.

The VCW's alliance with various RVN governments is emblematic of the challenges voluntary groups encountered in South Vietnam. During the First Republic, Bửu supported Ngô Đình Diệm and courted the patronage of Ngô Đình Nhu. He even joined Nhu's Cần Lao Party.[108] This semisecretive political party acted as a vehicle for the Ngô brothers to extend their influence and control. Its many members, well placed within the civil service and the military, allowed the Ngôs to surveil officials and bureaucrats for signs of disloyalty.[109]

The Ngô brothers' patronage of the VCW enabled them to co-opt the labor movement and fashion themselves as progressive leaders.[110] Their decision to nurture the trade confederation also stemmed from their own ideology and nation-building goals. Inspired by personalism, which promoted a communalistic and humanist approach to nation building, both brothers supported the creation of state-guided voluntary organizations that would encourage people to work collectively to contribute to society. To this end, they established mass organizations such as the National Revolutionary Movement and the Republican Youth. These groups, however, much like the Cần Lao Party, were political tools of the Ngôs rather than voluntary organizations. In essence, they helped mobilize support for Diệm and his government's policies.[111]

With the support of Diệm's government, the VCW grew and organized a number of major strikes involving workers at the Saigon port, electric plants, a cigarette factory, and plantations in 1956.[112] To maintain state support, however, the VCW had to make compromises. The confederation had to openly and covertly support Diệm's policies. For example, the VCW had to allow undercover police agents to participate in its May Day parade in 1956.[113]

The relationship between the VCW and the state grew tense when it became clear that the Ngô brothers were keen to assert more control over the confederation. Meanwhile, government distrust increased when communists infiltrated the organization, leading to a crackdown on the VCW. To counter state repression, Bửu looked to the United States and the AFL-CIO, whose support allowed him to avoid arrest and save many of his union leaders from jail sentences.[114]

As with the Library Association, US aid and support were critical to the survival of the VCW. The US government and the AFL-CIO provided financial aid, advice, and training.[115] The AFL-CIO leadership was fiercely anticommunist and supported the US government's global fight against communism. The AFL-CIO even collaborated with and received funding from the CIA. With AFL-CIO support, the VCW was able to compete with rival unions, including those led by NLF cadres and numerous smaller noncommunist labor confederations. The VCW's alliance with the United States, like its alliance with various RVN governments, also provided rivals with fodder to accuse the VCW of being an American puppet and not representing workers' interests.

The VCW's history epitomizes the challenges that faced civil society in South Vietnam. Because of its large membership and mobilizing potential, the VCW was of interest to many rival political forces. The RVN government, along with the US government and the communists, wanted to assert influence over the organization. This complex web of political forces also acted on the activities of other voluntary groups throughout the Republican period.

Throughout the period 1954–1975, South Vietnam experienced numerous sociopolitical changes and upheavals caused by the end of colonialism, the division of the country, US intervention, and warfare. Residents of South Vietnam searched for ways to cope with these uncertainties, but they also actively sought to take advantage of opportunities that came their way. By focusing on one aspect of civil society—mutual-aid and friendly societies—this chapter has demonstrated that South Vietnam's associational life was pluralistic and dynamic. A wide array of MAFS were operating simultaneously. Some were based on older social connections, such as shared native place and lineage, and others reflected changes that came with nation building and the growing US influence. Some MAFS were protective in nature and helped members deal with the changes and dislocations that visited South Vietnam. Other groups were formed to help members increase their influence in society, extend their social network, and contribute to society.

Like the French before them, the South Vietnamese authorities had an ambivalent relationship with the MAFS. On the one hand, RVN officials saw the social good these groups could bring about. MAFS had the potential to be catalysts for social cohesion, self-help, civic responsibility, and national unity. Club activities reinforced the rule of law and democratic procedures. Associations were regulated by charters that outlined procedures for the election of executives, the admission of members, and club functions. These were useful habits to instill in citizens. On the other hand, there was great potential for subversion. The labor unions, for instance, had an enormous capacity to disrupt the economic and political status quo. Even among MAFS that had narrow and conservative goals, officials were concerned about the infiltration of antistate elements. Associational activities afforded opportunities for the propagation of antistate ideas and social mobilization. It was believed that radical elements infiltrated groups, and some did gain access. Another way to spread radical ideas was through the associations' publications, which were meant to communicate club activities but were sometimes used to discuss issues affecting the wider society.

The challenge for the state was to determine which organizations to support and which to circumscribe. The Library Association was one group whose goals aligned exceptionally well with the nation-building project of both the South Vietnamese and US governments. As such, the association received a great deal of support and aid. Other groups were more ambiguous. Although Buddhist and Chinese associations professed no antistate purposes, they represented potential challenges to state authority because their members had alternative identities that might compete with the state for their loyalty. As for labor unions, the VCW had clear economic priorities that could not always be reconciled with the state's agendas and goals.

# PERFORMING SOCIAL SERVICE IN SOUTH VIETNAM

In April 1975, as it became clear that South Vietnam would collapse, Western humanitarian organizations mounted a massive effort to evacuate orphans, particularly Amerasian children. These efforts culminated in the US government's
Operation Babylift, with a budget of US$2 million. It remains the largest mass
overseas evacuation of children to date. Some critics have questioned the wisdom
of removing these children, some of whom were not orphans, from their country.[1]
Despite these concerns, Operation Babylift has been celebrated in the popular media as heroic, and it continues to be commended decades after the war's end. On
the thirtieth anniversary of the fall of South Vietnam, ABC News remembered
one American woman's effort to "rescue" children from Saigon.[2] Betty Tisdale,
known as the "Angel of Saigon," single-handedly brought 219 children from the
An Lạc orphanage to the United States. Her feat was highlighted again on the fortieth anniversary.[3] Little was said, however, about Vũ Thị Ngãi, the woman who
founded and ran the An Lạc orphanage in Saigon, or any of the other Vietnamese
people who worked at the many orphanages in South Vietnam. Vũ Thị Ngãi's contribution to the orphanage was diminished in an essay by Tisdale, who attributed
its founding to a US naval physician, Tom Dooley.[4] The postwar narrative about
the rescue and the Americans' appropriation of credit obscure the role played by
the Vietnamese in the area of charity and social service. The reality was that orphanages in South Vietnam were, for the most part, operated by Vietnamese voluntary organizations and volunteers. The vast majority of these volunteers were
female; some belonged to religious orders, while others were middle- to upper-class
laywomen.

People in South Vietnam established and joined not only mutual-aid groups but also social service organizations. This chapter examines Vietnamese participation and leadership in the many voluntary organizations that provided support, relief, and services to their communities. Some groups were local branches of prominent international organizations such as the Lions Club, Scouts, and Red Cross, which were widely popular and highly visible. There were also many Vietnamese-initiated and -led endeavors. This chapter focuses on the latter, as they are less well known and less studied.

Like the mutual-aid and friendly societies discussed in chapter 2, the social service organizations considered here were diverse in terms of their approaches, analyses, and actions taken to achieve social improvement and nation building. These activities illustrate how the Vietnamese people were active agents trying to navigate the circumstances of their society and ameliorate conditions for themselves, both individually and collectively.

Like the mutual-aid societies, these charitable organizations did not operate in a vacuum. They were shaped by social conventions, such as dominant views about gender and social status. The economic reality also influenced participation. Generally, the working poor could not afford the time or resources to participate in philanthropy. The upper class, in contrast, had access to the necessary financial resources and time, as well as connections to the political and military establishment, which could be leveraged to an organization's advantage. In colonial and postcolonial Vietnam, the elite were defined not by wealth alone but also by their attainment of a high level of education, culture, and social status. Their participation in associational life, therefore, had the potential to increase their standing in society. As some theorists have demonstrated, social capital accrued through participation in civil society often contributes to reifying the status quo and social hierarchy, rather than creating more horizontal linkages.[5]

Domestic and foreign political forces were instrumental in facilitating or limiting the activities of these organizations. The RVN government in particular had an impactful role. By law, all voluntary organizations had to apply for permission to operate and had to refrain from participating in politics. As such, organizations that were sympathetic to communism or critical of the current government or the war found it difficult to receive official approval. Some groups, however, managed to function quietly without state sanction. They leveraged their connections with foreign governments or international nongovernmental organizations (NGOs) to obtain funding and support in a bid to bypass RVN rules and restrictions.

# Tending to the Unfortunates before 1954

Just as mutual-aid societies had strong roots in Vietnamese history, so did charity and social service. As discussed in chapter 2, the ethics of benevolence and mutual support were important in the period before French colonial rule and were often evident during subsistence crises. Within Confucian ideology, the emperor and the scholar-official class were responsible for the welfare of those they governed. The Nguyễn dynasty's multilevel system of granaries illustrated the state's responsibility to society but also emphasized the elite's role in helping society's less fortunate members. The imperial state encouraged the elite to act charitably during hard times with promises of rewards such as imperial recognition, title, rank promotion, and tax exemption. The Nguyễn monarchs also directed the building of homes (*nhà dưỡng tế*) to provide refuge for people with no familial or community support, although this practice was probably not prevalent. The expectation was that relatives and the local community would take care of the elderly, orphaned, and those in need.[6]

Confucian ideals regarding social responsibility reinforced another important belief system practiced by the majority of the population. Central to Mahayana Buddhism is the belief in compassion and benevolence. Buddhist "doctrine raises the benevolence advocated by Confucianism to a higher degree, encompassing all living creatures."[7] Buddhist saints (bodhisattvas) exemplified compassion above all in their decision to delay reaching nirvana in order to remain in the world to teach and guide others. Buddhist teachers therefore exhort believers to be compassionate and help their fellow beings. As a result of these multiple sources of moral teachings, the importance of social aid was heavily emphasized from the state down to the village level. In some places, this ideal was enshrined in village covenants, which stipulated how villagers should support their poorer members, especially in times of need.[8]

During the French colonial period, notions and practices of charity were also supported by Roman Catholicism, which, like Buddhism, emphasizes the importance of compassion and altruism. By the late nineteenth century, the Missions Etrangères de Paris had founded a host of welfare institutions, including orphanages, hospitals, dispensaries, and schools. By 1918, there were more than nine hundred Catholic institutions throughout Indochina.[9] These institutions were open to all, regardless of religious affiliation. Nevertheless, non-Catholics may have been suspicious about the motives of these charitable institutions, since religious proselytization was intrinsic to the curriculum and culture at Catholic schools and care institutions.[10]

Nuns played a notable role in Catholic charitable endeavors and typically directed orphanages and schools. The Sisters of Saint Paul of Chartres (Dòng nữ tu Thánh Phaolô) were especially active in running these welfare facilities.[11] One of the oldest orphanages, established in 1861 in Chợ Lớn, was directed by this order.[12] As the later discussion shows, this gender pattern also characterized charity institutions belonging to other religious denominations and secular organizations in both colonial and postcolonial settings.

Another characteristic of Catholic charities was their relationship with the colonial state. Charles Keith suggests the existence of an interdependency between French authorities and Catholic institutions. The colonial administrators facilitated Catholic missionary activities, and in return, Catholic welfare activities bolstered colonial rule. Catholic charitable institutions not only demonstrated the magnanimity of the French rulers but also reduced costs for the colonial government.[13] Comparable mutually beneficial partnerships between private charities and governing authorities were observed in other societies. In nineteenth-century Bordeaux, for instance, city officials looked to charities to deliver social services and provided funding to these institutions in return.[14] Because of this symbiotic relationship, private charities "were neither free agents . . . nor helpless pawns of an over-powering state."[15] In the RVN, a similar dynamic operated between the government and officially recognized charities.

In addition to establishing schools and orphanages, Catholics were involved in various lay associations that provided mutual aid as well as social relief. The Society of Saint Vincent de Paul, for example, was established in 1933 in Vietnam and carried out charitable work throughout Tonkin (one of the five regions of Indochina).[16] For children and youths there was an array of Catholic associations, including the Eucharistic Crusade, Valiant Hearts, Valiant Souls, Catholic Boy Scouts, Catholic Youth Association, and Young Catholic Workers.[17] These were chapters of international organizations that spread rapidly throughout the Catholic world in the 1930s because of a resurgence of the Catholic action movement (Công Giáo Tiến Hành). Begun in the late nineteenth century as "a way to organize lay Catholics and prevent them from being drawn too deep into mass politics," the movement paid special attention to workers, young people, and women.[18] Its ultimate goal was to increase the role and influence of the Catholic laity in spreading Catholic teachings. The Catholic action movement inspired the founding of an assortment of associations that allowed Catholic men, women, and children to participate not only in devotional and church-related activities but also in civic and community affairs. Members of the Catholic Youth Association, for example, visited hospitals, orphanages, and other care institutions and helped with relief activities and community improvement projects.[19] These Catholic associations facilitated Catholics' participation in civil society. As chapter 5 shows, these activities continued into the 1970s.

Around the same time, Buddhists were experiencing a religious movement of their own. Known as the Buddhist revival (Chấn Hưng Phật Giáo), this was a transnational phenomenon that affected many Buddhist countries in Asia at the turn of the twentieth century. The movement was propelled by the perception that the religion needed to be modernized and reformed. This led to concerted efforts to organize, institutionalize, and unify Buddhist education, training, and administration.[20] One important area targeted for reform was how Buddhism engaged with the wider society. According to Elise DeVido, Vietnamese Buddhist reformers were influenced by Chinese monk Taixu's notion of "Buddhism for this world," which emphasized "the centrality of education, modern publishing, social work, and Buddhist lay groups to Buddhism's future in the modern world."[21] In other words, Buddhists needed to participate more actively in the wider society if they hoped to make their religion relevant and central to the modern nation-state. Like the Catholic action movement, the Buddhist revival led to an increase in public activities, including the creation of lay associations and institutions directed by Buddhists. Particularly important was the founding of the Buddhist Youth Family Movement (later known as Buddhist Family, or Gia Đình Phật Tử) in 1940.[22] This organization proliferated and played a significant role in social and political activism. The Buddhist Family network facilitated the participation of Buddhist children and their families in charitable and civic activities.

The upshot of the revival movement was involvement of the clergy and laity in voluntary social service and relief activities. Buddhists, particularly women, became active in founding associations, volunteering at pagoda schools and orphanages, fundraising to repair temples, and participating in relief activities.[23] It was also common for Buddhist pagodas to offer medical care. Since the Trần dynasty (1225–1400), a strong association between Buddhist monks and medical care had developed. The famous fourteenth-century Buddhist physician Tuệ Tĩnh, considered the founding father of Vietnamese medicine, consolidated monks' and nuns' traditional role as healers with knowledge of herbal medicines and other remedies.[24] Charitable and fee-based medical dispensaries were found at many pagodas.[25] Through their religious organizations and institutions, both Buddhists and Catholics became prominent participants in civil society.

Secular philanthropic and civic organizations were also active in French Indochina. The upsurge in voluntary activities was supported not only by preexisting local beliefs but also by new Western ideas about society and the individual's role in it. By the early twentieth century, a colonial strain of French republicanism was making its mark in Vietnam, shaping the sociopolitical outlooks of educated Vietnamese.[26] Along with their beliefs in secularism, democracy, and rationality, republicans promoted the idea of civic responsibility.[27] Participating in charity and philanthropy was seen as more than a moral or religious act; it was a duty of modern citizenship, a contribution to building a rational and modern society. Consequently, urban Vietnamese society was regularly called on to contribute to and participate in charity. Common foci of philanthropy were orphans, impoverished students, and victims of natural disasters. The Great Depression created an even greater need, and I have written elsewhere about the many Vietnamese-led fundraising events and charitable endeavors of the 1920s and 1930s.[28] Vietnamese newspapers were instrumental in mobilizing support for charitable projects. Publications such as Saigon's highly popular *Women's News* (*Phụ nữ tân văn*) and the Hanoi-based newspapers *French Asia* (*Báo Đông Pháp*) and *Women's Herald* (*Phụ nữ thời đàm*) regularly carried promotional information about various charitable events and projects.

Some newspapers also initiated their own social aid projects. *Women's News*, for example, helped found the Dục Anh Society (Society for Nourishing Children) in 1931. Cao Thị Khanh, co-owner of *Women's News*, was the society's secretary, and the wife of district chief Nguyễn Trung Thu was its president.[29] Other founding members were prominent professional women in Saigon society, including a dentist, a lawyer, and an engineer.[30] With the promotional support of *Women's News*, the society collected enough donations and garnered enough support to open two charitable day-care centers for the children of working parents in Saigon. These may have been the first secular child-care institutions established by Vietnamese people.[31] The society continued to operate its orphanages after 1954 and did not close shop until the end of the war.

Another notable example of a voluntary social project of the French colonial era was the League of Light (Đoàn Ánh Sáng), which sought to improve housing and basic infrastructure in poor urban and rural neighborhoods. Begun in 1937, this was an initiative of the respected Self-Strength Literary Group (Tự Lực Văn Đoàn), whose journals and literary works were immensely influential throughout the twentieth century and into the twenty-first. According to Martina Nguyen, this was a comprehensive reform movement and arguably "the largest philanthropic grassroots organization founded by Vietnamese during the colonial period."[32] The group received support from the French authorities, who hoped to head off more radical demands and communist-led agitation for economic justice.[33] As such, the League of Light developed a collaborative relationship with the colonial state, similar to the link between the Catholic Church and the Vietnam Confederation of Workers. This civil society–state dependency was also evident in the postcolonial period, when the state relied on reformist and politically moderate groups to provide social services.

Another pattern that carried into the postcolonial period was the dominant role played by the upper class in leading philanthropic activities. Cao Thị Khanh,

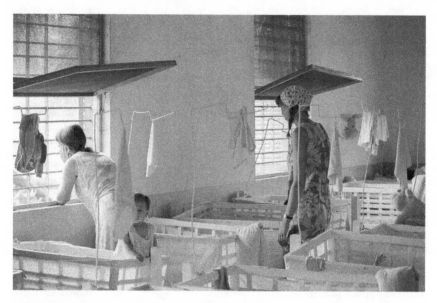

**FIGURE 3.1**   Infant room at Dục Anh orphanage, Saigon, 1969. Photograph by Harry Hallman.

founder of the Dục Anh Society, came from a wealthy family steeped in Confucian learning. She was evidently well educated, for she wrote poetry, critical essays, and social commentaries for her paper.[34] As prominent and influential writers and publishers, members of the Self-Strength Literary Group wielded significant cultural capital. This pattern was also evident in the West, where society's elite, particularly the middle class as of the nineteenth century, had the resources and time to participate in charitable work. In French colonial Vietnam, those in the upper class with access to Western education possessed the French-language skills, self-confidence, and ability to navigate official regulations and solicit state support. Philanthropy, in turn, had the potential to reinforce the elite's social standing in society.

# Social Service in the Republic of Vietnam

After 1954, the Vietnamese people continued to participate in voluntary social welfare activities. There was a great deal of continuity, as some charities and service groups moved their facilities south when the country was divided, and those already in the south continued to operate. An Lạc orphanage was an example of the former. Founded by wealthy widow Vũ Thị Ngãi in Thanh Hóa province at the beginning of the First Indochina War, An Lạc orphanage relocated multiple times because of warfare. Ngãi first moved the orphanage from her home in Thanh Hóa to Nam Định and then to Hải Phòng in 1949 to avoid the fighting.[35] By this time, the orphanage was housing a thousand children. In April 1955 she moved the orphanage again to the south. Ngãi's personal wealth helped sustain the orphanage, which also garnered significant support from her extensive social network among wealthy Vietnamese and foreigners. In addition, she had strong supporters in the French and later US navies, who proved useful in facilitating the smooth transport of Ngãi, the children, and their belongings when they relocated to the south. According to US Navy physician Tom Dooley, every piece of furniture and all the household items, including beds, bassinets, blankets, desks, barrels of chopsticks, and a Ping-Pong table, were moved.[36] The American Wives Club received the children in Saigon and helped them settle in their new abode. Dooley was an important supporter of the orphanage. He became famous for his medical humanitarian work in Southeast Asia and for the anticommunist sentiments in his book *Deliver Us from Evil*. A decade after his death, a foundation was established in his name, and it continued to support the An Lạc orphanage. It was through this foundation that Betty Tisdale became involved with the orphanage, leading to her efforts to evacuate the children in 1975 to escape the communist takeover of South Vietnam.[37]

Some organizations not only continued to operate after the 1954 division of the country but even expanded their operations. The Dục Anh Society, for example, grew to support an orphanage with 160 children and two day-care facilities for 210 children. The society also held workshops to teach women embroidery, sewing, and cooking. Like the An Lạc orphanage, the Dục Anh Society remained active until 1975.[38] Another example of continuity was the One Piaster for Students Society. Originally founded in 1930 in Bến Tre, this organization reemerged after a period of dormancy. It moved to Saigon in 1950 and began operating orphanages, discount eateries, and a charitable primary and secondary school. Members raised funds from the sale of livestock, rice, and coconuts.[39]

In addition to existing organizations, new voluntary associations were established, both religious and secular. Like earlier social endeavors, most focused on helping orphans, people with disabilities, and the poor. Many groups opened orphanages, medical clinics, free primary schools, and skills workshops. Some provided services to specific individuals, such as societies to help the blind, the mentally ill, and those with leprosy. The Society for the Blind had three hundred members in 1971, all of whom were blind, and the group helped blind people find work and learn Braille.[40] The Friends of the Mentally Ill provided support to psychiatric patients at two hospitals. One of its initiatives was to build separate living quarters for patients' children at the Biên Hòa mental institute. Similarly, the Friends of People with Leprosy established a center in Gia Định province for 130 people suffering from the disease.[41]

Other charities were larger in scope and size. With the help of international Christian organizations, Vietnamese Christians established many projects and institutions. From 1954 onward, the Catholic Relief Service (CRS), Caritas International, Mennonite Christian Service, and others worked with Vietnamese charity groups. Vietnamese nuns from many Catholic orders were involved in directing orphanages and schools sponsored by these international agencies. The most active order was the Daughters of Charity of Saint Vincent de Paul (Bác Ái Vinh Sơn). These nuns were involved with four charities associated with Caritas: a day-care center, orphanage, social hub, and nutrition center.[42] Other religious groups, such as the Sisters of Saint Paul de Chartrès, Lovers of the Holy Cross, and the Redemptorist order were also on the forefront of charitable work throughout the RVN.

Similarly, the number of Buddhist social service organizations increased. The Buddhist revival movement continued to be important and in fact experienced an upsurge during the 1950s and 1960s. In 1951 Buddhists from all three regions of Vietnam established the General Buddhist Association of Vietnam (Tổng Hội Phật Giáo Việt Nam). Although the General Buddhist Association would be superseded by the Unified Buddhist Congregation (UBC; Giáo Hội Phật Giáo Việt Nam Thống Nhất), a more inclusive and powerful organization in 1964, its creation was significant because not since the fourteenth century had there been a unified Buddhist organization in Vietnam.[43] In 1952 the first secular school—Bồ Đề—directed by Buddhists was opened in Huế. The school followed the national education curriculum but also included Buddhist teachings. Soon, more Bồ Đề schools were built in other cities and towns, and by 1970, there were 170 Bồ Đề schools throughout South Vietnam.[44]

Starting in 1951, various Buddhist associations established medical clinics, many of which were located in Thừa Thiện and Ninh Thuận provinces.[45] The Vietnam Buddhist Charitable Association (Hội Từ Thiện Phật Giáo Việt Nam) was established in Chợ Lớn in 1959 by Mrs. Trần Văn Kim and a group of Buddhists.[46] They ran a free primary school, four sewing classes, and a clinic that dispensed both Western and Eastern medicine at prearranged times.[47] In 1965 the Vĩnh Nghiêm Buddhist pagoda in Saigon received permission to operate a charity clinic where patients paid a token fee for medical care. The clinic consisted of twelve rooms, including a laboratory and an x-ray facility.[48] In 1972 alone, the clinic provided medical care for 24,000 people, dental care for 10,000, and x-ray services for 650.[49]

The number of Buddhist orphanages increased as well. By 1973, there were sixteen registered Buddhist orphanages, many of which were associated with the

**FIGURE 3.2** Catholic nun and orphans, no date. VA044338, James M. Kraft Collection, Vietnam Center and Sam Johnson Vietnam Archive, Texas Tech University.

UBC. The UBC leadership included those who had participated in the 1963 protest movement to denounce anti-Buddhist discrimination and Ngô Đình Diệm's autocratic and nepotistic behavior. Edward Miller argues, however, that the Buddhist revival movement was the larger context for this protest.[50] The movement's goals were to make Buddhism more relevant in society and to assert Buddhism's centrality in national affairs and identity. Fueling Buddhists' sense of urgency was the perception that Diệm, who was Catholic and had strong connections to the Catholic Church, was prejudiced against Buddhists. Some Buddhists also feared that Diệm was attempting to turn South Vietnam into a Catholic nation.[51]

Creating the UBC was an important step toward achieving the goals of the revival movement. At its inaugural congress, UBC founders emphasized the need to develop projects linking religion and society. A leading monk, Thích Thiên Minh, outlined steps to realize this goal: build more charitable institutions such as orphanages and day-care centers, increase and systematize the Bồ Đề Buddhist schools, establish Buddhist student dormitories, and encourage students to participate in social work.[52] As a result, the UBC had many orphanages, old-age centers, and dispensaries throughout Vietnam. The Buddhist Social Welfare Organization, under the leadership of Thích Nhật Thiện, loosely coordinated these endeavors but did not have the capacity to fund them. Consequently, the affiliated institutions had a great deal of autonomy and relied on local communities for funding.[53]

One of the social projects initiated by the UBC was the Quách Thị Trang orphanage, located at the Quốc Tự pagoda. The orphanage was established in August 1965 to care for children orphaned or displaced during the previous year's typhoon season, one of the worst in Vietnamese history up to that point. Consecutive tropical storms in the fall of 1964 had devastated the central provinces in South Vietnam. Ninety percent of homes in Quảng Tín province were destroyed by Typhoon Violet; Typhoon Joan killed seven thousand people and flooded five million acres in the central provinces.[54]

To coordinate and encourage relief efforts, the RVN government established a committee chaired by Vice Prime Minister Nguyễn Xuân Oanh.[55] To mobilize people's support, the government framed participation in relief activities as an act of patriotism and part of the struggle against communism. This message was clearly enunciated in published communications, pamphlets, and posters produced to promote participation. One poster exhorted people to set aside their religious and political differences and focus on helping their compatriots in need. Another poster depicted communists shooting down helicopters loaded with flood victims.[56]

The NLF's actions in this relief campaign provided fodder for the RVN's propaganda machine. US and Vietnamese news outlets reported that communists had sabotaged aid efforts. Independent and respected newspapers such as *Dân Chủ* (*Democracy*) and *Chính Luận* (*Political Discussion*) reported that communists had ambushed relief workers. A *Dân Chủ* article published November 13, 1964, alleged that communists had killed six aid workers and wounded six others. It also alleged that 50 percent of the helicopter flights transporting flood victims had been shot at, and some had been shot down.[57] The *New York Times* reported that communist fighters had shot at low-flying US aid planes and helicopters. There were allegations that communists were seizing aid material, either for themselves or to give to flood victims for propaganda purposes.[58] The flood relief effort of 1964 became highly politicized, providing opportunities for the republican, communist, and American sides to shape the narrative for propaganda purposes.

The Quách Thị Trang orphanage was built in the context of this concerted and politicized relief endeavor.[59] It is relevant that the orphanage was named after a fifteen-year-old girl who was killed by the police during the 1963 Buddhist protest movement. The UBC's decision to memorialize a victim of state violence is another example of the how disaster relief was politicized. The orphanage symbolized not only the Buddhists' charitable work but also their struggle against state oppression and discrimination. It was the embodiment of what Buddhist revivalists were advocating: Buddhists playing a more prominent role in society to influence the direction of the country. The Quách Thị Trang orphanage represented the impact Buddhists could have on both the social and the political stage. On the practical side, the orphanage provided care to children in need. In 1971 the orphanage was still operational and had 389 children in its care.[60]

As the war intensified through the 1960s, voluntary groups directed their attention toward refugees and families of wounded and fallen soldiers. In 1964 wives of high-ranking military officers founded the Association for the Protection of Servicemen's Families (Hội Bảo Trợ Gia Đình Binh Sĩ).[61] This organization had significant support from the government; no doubt their husbands' military positions paved the way for access to state resources. For example, the group was allowed to use government office space in Chợ Lớn. The government also collaborated directly with the organization in operating its hospital in Phú Thọ. The Trùng Vương hospital, which had three hundred beds, was free for military families and fee based for nonmilitary patients. The Ministries of Defense and Health paid the salaries of the hospital's medical staff, while the association paid for other staff, who were mainly military wives, widows, or orphans.

The group also managed a sewing workshop with two hundred sewing machines. This enterprise created jobs for military wives while providing income for the association. Other sources of funding came from donations, sale of the organization's weekly publication (*Hoa Tình Thương, Compassionate Flowers*),

**FIGURE 3.3** Buddhist nuns and children at an orphanage in Phan Rang, no date. VA063238, Carter Taylor Collection, Vietnam Center and Sam Johnson Vietnam Archive, Texas Tech University.

and charity fairs. Since the 1920s, Vietnamese voluntary groups had been holding fairs to raise money, and as in the past, they were organized predominantly by prominent women and featured handicrafts made by women.

Another organization that focused its attention on the impact of the war was the Friends of Children and Female War Victims Society (Hội Bạn Trẻ Em Và Nữ Nạn Nhân Chiến Cuộc), which was founded in the summer of 1970 in Gia Định province and had branches in Vũng Tầu, Đà Lạt, and Quí Nhơn. Composed mostly of public civil servants and professionals, this society opened the Chung Thủy children's village in Vũng Tầu to provide care and education to street children, with special attention to the children of wounded soldiers. Because of the group's limited funding, the village was small, but by early 1972, it was able to care for forty-two children and had established a school for them.[62]

**FIGURE 3.4**  Boy at Dục Anh orphanage, 1969. Photograph by Harry Hallman.

The Friends of Children and Female War Victims Society also created a micro-credit program that allowed poor women to borrow small amounts to start or grow small businesses. Named Flowering Vines (Giây Hoa), this project started with 900,000 dong for issuing loans. Later, when the project proved successful, the Ministry of Social Welfare gave it 500,000 dong to extend the program. In addition, the group established a temporary care center in Saigon for children displaced by the Easter offensive in 1972. The center housed the children while the society looked for foster families to care for them. The society also helped disadvantaged widows by providing free child care.[63]

Some organizations attended to the welfare of political prisoners and enemy combatants. For example, the Unified Social Relief Association, established in 1965, helped refugees and victims of natural disasters, but its members also vis-ited inmates at the all-female Thủ Đức prison, which held both political and nonpolitical prisoners.[64] One organization even visited North Vietnamese sol-diers at an Australian base hospital in Vũng Tầu. Members brought gifts such as books and comics, which were very popular among the young soldiers; mem-bers also helped the soldiers write letters.[65]

# Women and Social Service

As the preceding discussion shows, women featured prominently in the realm of charity and social welfare. On the one hand, women were often the recipients of charity in South Vietnam. Many associations were established specifically to support women, particularly working-class women, military widows, and mili-tary wives. On the other hand, women were the agents of charitable initiatives; they founded, led, and provided the labor for numerous voluntary organizations. Female participation was particularly high in endeavors that provide care to or-phans, widows, and mothers.[66] As historians of Europe and the United States have observed, in the late nineteenth and early twentieth centuries, maternal and child welfare was perceived as a feminine realm where women could participate without disrupting gender norms.[67] Women capitalized on this perception to gain entry into public life. This was also the case for Vietnamese women. In both religious and lay organizations, women participated in philanthropy, most no-tably by caring for orphans, widows, and the sick, areas that did not transgress gender expectations.

Even though women's participation in social welfare did not challenge gen-der conventions, their work was not without political or national significance. For example, Seth Koven and Sonya Michel have shown that women's charita-ble work contributed to and shaped the welfare states of Germany, France, Great

Britain, and the United States.[68] As discussed later, women in the RVN played an important role not only in providing care for those in need but also in developing the social work profession.

On a theoretical level, women's leadership in public welfare activities challenges the conceptualization of the public sphere as generally masculine and devoid of women.[69] Many theorists perceive the public sphere as a domain where free and critical engagement about issues of public concern transpires.[70] Because civil society provides the institutions and networks supporting the public sphere, it is reasonable to postulate that most social interactions enacted through voluntary activities and associations have the potential to facilitate this critical engagement. However, in much of the literature, the arenas considered for such interactions tend to be narrowly focused on print media and debates in male-dominated spaces such as coffeehouses, political clubs, and academies.[71] By not including places such as orphanages and day-care centers, where women dominate, the public sphere has had "masculinist gender constructs" built into its conceptualization.[72] When these female spaces are considered, it becomes clear that women were engaged with social issues. In performing voluntary social work—which entailed working in welfare facilities, soliciting donations, organizing charity fairs, and attending meetings—women were active in public and were engaging with a large cross section of society. Their participation and activities were the articulation of their concerns about social problems and how to solve them.

In Vietnam, during both the French colonial and Republican periods, orphanages and day-care centers were the domains of female volunteers. This trend reflected the dominant perception in Vietnamese society that child rearing is the natural responsibility of women. Therefore, Buddhist and Catholic nuns, who might not have had any child-rearing experience, ran the orphanages. The executive committee of the Dục Anh Society, founded in 1931, was composed entirely of women and continued to be so until 1975.[73] By the 1920s, attitudes in colonial Vietnam toward women's education and their role in society were changing, and women were becoming involved in organized public activities. Nevertheless, there was still significant prejudice against women who were active outside their homes, especially in the company of men who were not their relatives.[74] In light of societal views, and considering the colonial restrictions against radical social and political activities, supporting child and maternal welfare appeared to be a safe venture for upper-class women who wanted to engage in and contribute to society.

From the 1950s onward, more women's philanthropic organizations emerged, including the Social and Cultural Women's Group, Women's Goodwill Society, Society to Protect Women, Buddhist Women's Society, Military Widow Society, and Vietnamese branch of the International Women's Association.[75] In fact, from the point of view of an Interior Ministry official, there were too many women's groups in South Vietnam. Thus, when the Progressive Women's Association applied for permission to operate in 1968, he recommended that the application be rejected.[76] The official also voiced his suspicion that some women's groups were fronts for political activism. In other words, he feared these clubs might provide opportunities for political discussion, such as the type of discussion that might take place in the idealized public sphere.

As this ministry official's suspicion indicates, women's organizations did not escape government scrutiny. The experience of the Vietnam Women's Association (Hội Phụ Nữ Việt Nam) bears this out. It was founded in 1952 by newspaper publisher Tô Thị Thân, who was widely known by her husband's pen name, Bút Trà. The couple owned and published a series of popular Saigon-based newspapers.[77] It was Tô Thị Thân, rather than her poet husband, who managed the business and made editorial decisions. Unlike Cao Thị Khanh, the co-owner of *Women's News* and one of the founders of the Dục Anh Society, Thân was not a member of the social elite. Although she was wealthy, she did not have the requisite cultural capital. Thân had made her money from a string of pawnshops she owned with her first husband, who was ethnic Chinese. For marrying outside her Viet ethnic group, she was subjected to slights and derogatory nicknames. Perhaps because of her nonelite background, she was vocal about making her newspaper accessible to the masses rather than just a small group of educated readers.[78] Similarly, her association focused on helping working women, and its membership comprised nonelite women.

The stated purposes of the Vietnam Women's Association were to unify women in the fight for their rights, improve their livelihood, and defend the rights of working women. The organization's main activity was in the realm of education, specifically, the promotion of literacy. To this end, the Vietnam Women's Association offered literacy classes to the poor through its Literacy Society (Bình Dân Học Hội). The group also organized celebrations for children during the Mid-Autumn Festival and Lunar New Year, and its members visited and distributed gifts to hospital patients, prisoners, and orphans.[79] Thân used her newspaper to promote the activities of the Vietnam Women's Association, hoping to increase membership, donations, and attendance at events. With the newspaper's promotional help, the association had established many branch clubs throughout South Vietnam by 1960.[80]

The Vietnam Women's Association, however, was soon infiltrated by left-wing and communist members. Member and writer Lê Thị Bạch Vân (known as Mrs. Tùng Long) suggested that political activists were attracted to the group because of its large working-class membership.[81] After the secretary of the association, Ái Lan, was arrested for alleged communist affiliation in 1955, Tô Thị

Thân was compelled to invite more politically conservative elite women, such as the wives of high-ranking officials, to act as advisers or to hold executive positions. These women not only gave the association more prestige but also lessened the government's suspicion that the group was a hotbed of radicals and communists.[82]

According to Lê Thị Bạch Vân, however, the new elite members were merely window dressing; they were there to appease the authorities. In practice, Thân remained in charge, and the association's activities did not change. The new vice president was Mrs. Lê Quang Kim, a pharmacist who was involved with many other voluntary groups, including presiding over Vietnam's chapter of the International Women's Association.[83] She reportedly did not attend many meetings of the Vietnam Women's Association. Another new member was Ana Lê Văn Cang, who had little time to devote to the association because she was busy helping to run her father's newspaper Tin Điển (Express News). Moreover, when she did attend meetings, she dressed formally in the Vietnamese long dress (áo dài) and often spoke in French.[84] Her deportment did not sit well with the non-elite members. Nevertheless, the inclusion of these upper-class women kept the association from being shut down.

By 1963, however, the Vietnam Women's Association encountered a formidable obstacle when it was pressured to join the Women's Solidarity Movement (WSM; Phong Trào Phụ Nữ Liên Đới), which essentially destroyed the association's independence and therefore the association itself. The founder of the WSM was President Ngô Đình Diệm's sister-in-law Trần Lệ Xuân (better known as Madame Ngô Đình Nhu). Because Diệm did not have a wife, Xuân became the de facto First Lady during the First Republic. In 1961 she established the WSM by reorganizing the women's section of the civil servants' league, an affiliate of her husband's clandestine Cần Lao Party.[85] Composed mostly of female civil servants and wives of officials, the WSM's purported goal was to participate in social work. In reality, it was a vehicle for Xuân to promote and enact her political ideas. The movement focused on propagating her notion of modern Vietnamese womanhood, which entailed building a monument for national heroines Trưng Trắc and Trưng Nhị, organizing festivals in their honor, and establishing a female paramilitary organization.[86] These activities were intended to aggrandize Xuân and the Diệm government rather than to improve the lives of women. To increase the WSM's influence, Xuân co-opted groups such as Thân's Vietnam Women's Association.

In addition to her relationship to Diệm, Xuân was an elected member of the National Assembly, where she sponsored legislation to ban divorce, arranged marriage, prostitution, and polygamy. These laws were framed as actions to protect women and the traditional family structure.[87] Because of Xuân's powerful connections and position, Tô Thị Thân was in no position to refuse the invitation to join the WSM. Lê Thị Bạch Vân found herself in a similar situation. She noted in her memoir that Xuân offered her the position of general secretary for one of the WSM's chapters. As the mother of nine children, a full-time writer, and an active member of many voluntary groups, Vân had little time to spare, but she was advised by friends that there would be political consequences if she refused the "First Lady."[88]

Trần Lệ Xuân's use of coercive tactics to expand her movement's membership demonstrates that this was not a voluntary organization but a political tool for the ruling elite. Moreover, while voluntary organizations were required by law to remain apolitical, the WSM did not adhere to this rule. During the Buddhist protest movement in 1963, Xuân used her group for political purposes. At a sensitive juncture in negotiations between Diệm and the Buddhist leadership, the WSM issued a public statement criticizing the activist monks and questioning their legitimacy as religious leaders.[89] This intervention exacerbated tensions and damaged any gains made up to that point.

The WSM was comparable to the aforementioned Republican Youth and National Revolutionary Movement, which were created to bolster Diệm's popularity and carry out his policies (see chapter 2). The WSM essentially destroyed the Vietnam Women's Association when it was forced to amalgamate, revealing the contested landscape in which civil society operated during the First Republic (1954–1963). Although there was generally more openness and freedom in the Second Republic (1967–1975), civil society was still fraught with multiple political forces vying for influence.

As expected, the WSM was disbanded when Diệm and Nhu were assassinated on November 2, 1963. In the Second Republic, another First Lady established her own women's organization. In May 1968 Nguyễn Thị Mai Anh, the wife of President Nguyễn Văn Thiệu, founded the Women's Association for Social Service (WASS; Hội Phụ Nữ Việt Nam Phụng Sự Xã Hội). The group's logo, featuring a laborer, an elderly man, and a physically disabled boy, indicated the group's focus on helping the disadvantaged. Another stated goal was the improvement of women's material and spiritual lives. The WASS's major projects included establishing the Mê Linh Center for children who were victims of war and a charitable hospital called Vì Dân (Because of the People). The hospital was opened in September 1971 with three hundred beds.[90]

Like Xuân's WSM, the WASS was led by a group of elite women. In addition to Nguyễn Thị Mai Anh, who was president of the group, other executive members were highly educated women with political and economic power. For instance, Nguyễn Thị Hai was a pharmacist by training; she and her husband owned a successful pharmaceutical company in South Vietnam. Hai was also an elected people's representative and deputy chair of the Lower House.[91] Another distinguished officer was Phan Nguyệt Minh.[92] Educated in France and the United States, Minh taught at the National Institute of Administration and Saigon University and was an elected member of the National Assembly (1959–1963) and the Senate (1967–1973). She had been a member of the WSM and the International Women's Association and president of the Girl Scouts.[93]

As Phan Nguyệt Minh's involvement shows, it was common for people of the upper class to hold leadership positions in multiple organizations. George McT. Kahin's unpublished "Biographies of Prominent Vietnamese" confirms this observation. For example, businesswoman and House of Representatives deputy Trần Kim Thoa was a member of the Chamber of Commerce, president of the Vĩnh Hòa Mutual-Aid Society, and comptroller of the Dục Anh Society. Professor Trần Văn Quế was a member of the Biên Hòa Mutual-Aid Association and the Society for the Development of the Body and Mind and chair of the Committee for the Propagation of Caodism.[94] However, as the example of Thân's Vietnam Women's Association suggests, some of these positions were only for show, as these groups needed people with good political backgrounds to shield them from government scrutiny.

Clearly, President Thiệu's wife did not have to worry about government scrutiny, but her involvement made it easier for the group to raise funds and shepherd its major projects to completion. Indeed, the WASS received donations and aid from both domestic and foreign supporters. For instance, the Mê Linh Center was built with support from World Vision; the RMK-BRJ construction company, with links to the US Navy; and a major South Korean engineering firm.[95] No doubt some donors were keen to support this politically well-connected group in the hope of obtaining political favors and influence. Using charity to gain political influence is not unique to South Vietnam. In the West, high-society charity events are often seen as opportunities to make connections that will further one's social mobility and personal ambitions.

In addition to receiving direct donations, the WASS organized annual charity fairs to raise money and draw attention to its work. The US government gave the group US$6,000 to purchase foreign goods to sell at its 1971 charity fair. Vietnamese ambassadors were asked to send gifts from their host countries, and companies in Vietnam were approached for donations. Fourteen other charities participated in the fair to raise funds for their respective groups, many of which were women's organizations or female-led organizations.[96]

Fundraising for the hospital emphasized its benefit to society, particularly the poor. Patients who could not afford to pay could request either a fee waiver or a fee reduction, provided they presented documentation showing that they were eligible for assistance. However, according to hospital procedure, patients who received fee reductions or waivers were told that their fees were being paid by "the President's wife and the Women's Association for Social Service."[97] Obviously, this protocol was implemented to bolster the prestige of the First Lady and, by extension, President Thiệu. This practice also emphasized the charitable nature of the hospital, which raises questions about the role of the state in social welfare provision.

## The RVN State and Welfare

Well into the 1960s, the South Vietnamese government remained aloof from social welfare responsibilities. Even though the government provided health care and education and, with the help of foreign governments and NGOs, was expanding services in these areas, it played a minor role in other social welfare sectors. This was particularly true when it came to orphanages. Orphanages and day-care centers were mostly private institutions. By 1972, about 880,000 children had lost one or both parents. Many lived with their extended families, but approximately 19,000 lived in registered orphanages and 5,000 lived in unofficial orphanages. About 4 percent of the children in institutions were the result of couplings between American GIs and Vietnamese women. These biracial children often experienced discrimination, especially those whose fathers were African American.[98] By the early 1970s, the state had only three orphanages, while private organizations ran 120 registered and 40 unregistered care institutions for children.[99] The first state orphanage was the Thủ Đức national orphanage, which was built in 1956 mainly for the children of fallen and wounded soldiers. To establish this new institution, the government had taken over the Thủ Đức Catholic orphanage, which had been administered by the Sisters of Saint Vincent de Paul since the late nineteenth century. The order agreed to relocate elsewhere in Saigon (at the time, Thủ Đức was part of Gia Định province). To manage the state's new orphanage, officials asked the nuns of the Lovers of the Holy Cross order (Dòng Mến Thánh Gía) to take the lead.[100]

From 1954 to the mid-1960s, the RVN government provided aid to private institutions, but only on an ad hoc, case-by-case basis. In the summer of 1966 the government attempted to regulate orphanages and other charitable activities more rigorously. It became mandatory for all welfare institutions with more than ten people to register with the government and submit to state inspection. Private care institutions also had to conform to state health and education regulations. In return for their compliance, the state provided funding to these institutions. Orphanages were given 300 dong per child per month (68 cents in US dollars).[101] Government funding provided some incentive to register, but because state funding was meager, some private organizations preferred to remain unofficial and independent.[102]

Given the inadequacy of state funding, organizations had to find ways to raise money to survive. Some were fortunate enough to receive aid from foreign governments and NGOs. Others relied on local donations, fundraising events, and entrepreneurial activities to supplement their budgets. For example, the Women's Goodwill Society supported its orphanage with a *phở* stand, tailoring business, and hair salon. The Quách Thị Trang orphanage raised pigs and chickens, grew vegetables, and ran a bread bakery. Similarly, funding for the Dục Anh Society came from its bakery, hairdressing salon, and lottery ticket sales.[103] In 1954 an overwhelming portion of this group's budget came from its business activities; only 16 percent of the Dục Anh Society's budget came from government sources and 3.5 percent from membership dues. The Buddhist Phước Thiện orphanage, under the directorship of Mrs. Võ Duy Nhật and the pagoda's head nun, also relied heavily on raffles for its revenue. The Gò Vấp orphanage depended on a variety of economic activities, including making and selling crafts and candles. In addition, it had some success selling blossom branches made by teenage residents, who averaged ten thousand branches a month.[104]

As the government got more involved in regulating welfare institutions, it became concerned about misconduct and corruption associated with care facilities and their finances. In 1966 a Ministry of Social Welfare official admonished the Dục Anh Society for management shortcomings, particularly its lack of control over older children in its facilities. The official asked the group to make changes in its organization and operation.[105] The authorities were also concerned about corruption and fraud connected with fundraising. In 1966 an official from the Ministry of Social Welfare warned other departments about fraudsters who were running charity fairs for private gain. He suggested that applications for charity fairs be sent to his ministry so that it could confirm the status of these groups.[106] Officials also suspected that some charity fairs were being used more for gambling and less for fundraising purposes.[107] In addition, there were reports of embezzlement associated with fundraising. The governor of Ba Xuyên province, for instance, received complaints that some charity organizers in the Mỹ Xuyên district were skimming funds from the charity fairs.[108] These official reports and claims of fraud were neither surprising nor unique to Vietnam, as charity-related chicanery is common in many societies. In the case of South Vietnam, however, the problem was exacerbated because of the large influx of foreign aid (discussed later).

The state's involvement in the social welfare sector extended to establishing training facilities for social workers. Before 1970, there were few professionally trained social workers in Vietnam because there were few specialized schools.

The Caritas School of Social Work was founded in 1947 with the collaboration of the French Red Cross, and it was directed by the Sisters of Charity of Saint Vincent de Paul. The school offered a three-year training program exclusively for female students.[109] In 1957 a number of Caritas graduates established the Vietnam Army School of Social Work. Both these programs were small. By 1969, the Caritas School had produced only 106 social workers, and not all of them worked in the field.[110] It was only in 1968 that the government of South Vietnam began to make plans for a public school of social work. The United Nations Development Program (UNDP) and UNICEF, along with other UN agencies, provided funding and support for this endeavor. The National School of Social Work enrolled its first students in 1970. By 1975, the school had produced about three hundred graduates with two-year diplomas.[111] But according to a USAID report, many social work graduates worked for well-paying foreign agencies rather than Vietnamese welfare organizations. As a result, many voluntary welfare organizations in South Vietnam remained staffed by people who lacked formal training, many of whom were volunteers.[112] For example, the Dục Anh Society had twenty volunteers and thirty paid employees at its centers in 1973.[113]

Even with the professionalization of social work, the field remained gendered and dominated by women. As in the United States, where social work "was marked as a nurturing occupation appropriate for women," this profession was feminized in South Vietnam.[114] Overwhelmingly, the early pioneers of social work were women, and they included Nguyễn Thị Oanh, Phan Thị Quới, and Cẩm Hồng. Many had received their training abroad and returned to help build the profession in South Vietnam. The first director of the National School of Social Work was Phạm Thị Tự, who was a professor of sociology with a doctorate in political science.[115] Women also dominated the first professional society for social workers, officially recognized in 1970. All seven founding members were women, many of whom were unmarried.[116] Even before the group received permission to operate, it had convened three seminars and published three issues of its newsletter.

Some early social workers, such as Nguyễn Thị Oanh, continued to play an important role throughout the war years, and in the late 1980s they were instrumental in the field's revitalization. After 1975, the socialist government of a unified Vietnam banned social work because the profession was thought to be rooted in a Western bourgeois analysis of social problems. Moreover, the government believed that any social issues would be resolved with the implementation of socialism.[117] However, during the reform (đổi mới) period of the late 1980s, when a market economy was reintroduced in Vietnam, professional social work was also resurrected. To rebuild the profession, the government called on Republican-era social workers to train a new generation of experts. Women's voluntary work in the colonial and postcolonial periods led them to play an important role in the development of social work as a profession and in the state's provision of welfare in both the Republican and post–*đổi mới* periods.

Although pioneering social workers such as Nguyễn Thị Oanh played important roles in social welfare and relief, they were not oblivious to the limitations and contradictions of their efforts. By the end of the war, many social activists realized that their work was not addressing systemic problems of inequality, corruption, and oppression.[118] The war was another obstacle that prevented substantive and enduring changes from taking root. US involvement was a major issue in the provision of social services. The United States was underwriting substantial amounts of aid for welfare endeavors occurring both directly and indirectly through the RVN government and foreign aid agencies. According to Nguyễn Thị Oanh, the massive US aid for social work and development helped "smooth the negative effects of the war," thereby allowing the war effort to continue more easily. US aid also created opportunities for corruption and abuse.[119] According to a former official with the Ministry of Welfare, the abundance of aid was a temptation for both government workers and charity staff members.[120] An attitude developed among some aid workers that no one would miss the funds and no one would be hurt if some of the aid was pilfered. In some cases, donations were misused or diverted not for personal benefit but to support another cause. The leader of the Student Summer Program, for example, funneled some of that program's unused funds to help the District 8 Development Project get started (discussed in chapter 4). It is unclear whether donors were consulted before the funds were diverted or whether the funds were later returned to the summer program.[121] The abundance of aid also encouraged waste, since volunteers and officials felt no need to conserve their resources.[122] Many undoubtedly felt compelled to help others in light of the profound hardships created by the war, but one could also surmise that some people were drawn to relief activities in the hope of obtaining material aid for themselves.

This chapter examines the long history of the Vietnamese people's voluntary involvement in organizing and delivering social services. Until 1975 the realm of social welfare allowed many people in South Vietnam to participate in public life. Motivated by their religious beliefs, social responsibilities, and dreams of personal advancement, the people of South Vietnam had many options: they could join specific philanthropic groups, participate in mass relief efforts, or support charities by donating time, labor, cash, or goods.

While many Vietnamese participated in charity and welfare activities, their involvement was shaped by gender, class, and politics. Social welfare was deemed a feminine realm, affording women a prominent role in this area of public life. This was particularly true when it came to caregiving facilities such as day-care centers and orphanages. The dominant assumption was that all women are natural caregivers, and although this perception is flawed, it allowed many women to participate in associational life. As social work became professionalized, women continued to dominate the field as professors, supervisors, and students. The new cohort of social workers was mostly women, some of whom helped resurrect the profession in the 1990s.

Class and politics also circumscribed people's access to and roles in charity work. Registered organizations were typically led by the political and cultural elite in society—those with education, connections to the West, or sociocultural capital. Because these organizations needed state permission to operate, overt political dissidents were often denied. Association executives therefore tended to be politically moderate, anticommunist, and supporters of the current government. This pattern, which mirrors findings in other societies where elites tended to found and direct philanthropic endeavors, underscores the point that associational life and civil society are not always democratic and sometimes tend to reify rather than challenge the social hierarchy.[123]

This trend notwithstanding, participants in social welfare did not lack agency or independence. Though restrictive, the RVN could not regulate every aspect of civil society. Many groups resisted registration, despite funding incentives provided by the state. Well into the mid-1970s, several dozen active organizations lacked permission to operate or had only temporary permission.[124] Moreover, given the existence of diverse social groups, competing interests, and changing political situations, there were opportunities for different groups to vie for roles in the area of social aid. After all, as theorists of civil society have argued, constant competition in public life provides opportunities for counterhegemonic challenges.[125]

# VOLUNTARY EFFORTS IN SOCIAL AND COMMUNITY DEVELOPMENT

In 1964, at a summer youth work camp organized by leaders of the Unified Buddhist Congregation (UBC), a young Buddhist politician and scholar, Trần Quang Thuận, spoke to the volunteers about the meaning of social service. The young people were spending the week carrying out community work, such as building roads and bridges, in villages outside Đà Lạt city. In the evenings, they attended lectures and workshops. Thuận told the youths that social service is more than charitable giving or building roads and bridges. To him, social service should aim to change the social structure and bring about a social revolution. To that end, social activists must go deeper to achieve sustained and meaningful change.[1] Thuận was not alone in his critique of the voluntary efforts of many philanthropists and social workers in South Vietnam. Some social activists had become disillusioned with the relief work being carried out in the RVN. They realized that although these activities temporarily assuaged people's miseries, they also made it easier for the government and its US allies to wage war.[2]

This chapter examines three development projects that sought to bring about deep social change and improvement: the Popular Culture Association's Popular Polytechnic Institute (PPI), the School of Youth for Social Service (SYSS), and the New Life Development Project. These projects represented three distinct perspectives and analyses of the pressing issues facing South Vietnam. All three endeavors, however, were driven by participants' desire to stimulate change and improve society. These projects also act as case studies to contemplate the nature of South Vietnam's civil society.

# Popular Polytechnic Institute and Popular Culture Association

The Popular Polytechnic Institute (Trường Bách Khoa Bình Dân) was founded in October 1954, a few months after the Geneva Accords were signed. Amid the sociopolitical uncertainties of the time, and especially given the division of the country, PPI's founders were searching for ways to provide better access to education. Conceived as a nonprofit and voluntary organization, the institute offered free night classes to adults on a variety of academic subjects, along with literacy, language, and skills courses. The institute's founders subsequently established the Popular Culture Association (Hội Văn Hóa Bình Dân) to help coordinate PPI's expansion, as well as undertake a number of educational and cultural projects.[3]

At the time of its founding, the Popular Culture Association had forty-three members, most of them young, idealistic, well-educated men. Many had graduate degrees from abroad and were embarking on promising careers in South Vietnam.[4] According to founder Huỳnh Văn Lang, he and his colleagues were conscious of their privileges and opportunities and therefore felt the need to contribute to society. Lang was inspired by Vietnam's many modernizers and educators, including Nguyễn Trường Tộ (1830–1871), Trương Vĩnh Ký (1837–1898), and Phan Chu Trinh (1872–1926).[5] All three are important nationalist figures in Vietnamese history, but Phan Chu Trinh is particularly relevant, as he helped found the Eastern Capital Free School (Đông Kinh Nghĩa Thục) in 1907 to spread knowledge and modernize Vietnamese society. Although the school offered its four hundred students politically safe subjects such as mathematics, languages, and science, the French authorities detected its nationalistic undertones and revoked the school's operating permit.[6] In associating PPI with the Eastern Capital Free School, Lang was suggesting that it too was contributing to the modernization and strengthening of Vietnamese society.

After securing government permission to operate, Lang and his colleagues set out to find teaching space, volunteer instructors, and funding for PPI—all challenging tasks. However, the founders of the Popular Culture Association were well connected to South Vietnam's political and economic elite, and they used those relationships to get the support they needed. Lang, for example, had a position in the Ministry of Finance and later became director of the Foreign Exchange. He was also close to President Diệm's brother, Ngô Đình Nhu, and was a high-ranking member of Nhu's Cần Lao Party. Lang used his business connections and know-how to help finance the party.[7] During the First Republic, membership in the shadowy Cần Lao Party was virtually mandatory for ambitious civil servants, military officers, and professionals. Similarly, Đỗ Trọng Chu, another founding member, served in the Office of the General Commissioner for Refugees and then joined the Foreign Service in 1960. Chu's wife, Trần Thị Mậu, was the PPI director in Gia Định and had important political connections. In 1956 she was elected to a seat in the National Assembly, becoming one of the few female representatives. She became friends with another female representative, Trần Lệ Xuân (Madame Nhu), founder of the Women's Solidarity Movement (WSM).[8] In other words, the founders of the Popular Culture Association were closely linked to the president's family. Unlike the WSM and other organizations the Ngôs initiated, however, the Popular Culture Association apparently did not use coercion or unethical means to grow their organization, although the founders' political connections undoubtedly made it easier for them to get official permission to operate. The registration process was extraordinarily fast: Lang and his colleagues met on October 5, 1954, to discuss the creation of PPI, and by October 21, they had received official recognition.

The association's connections were also tremendously useful in getting funding from both government and foreign sources. In 1954 PPI received approximately 43,000 dong from the Department of Education Services and another 30,000 dong from the International Rescue Committee (IRC).[9] As PPI continued to grow, government and foreign aid agencies provided more financial help. In 1955 the Ministry of Education gave the institute 300,000 dong, and it received an additional 130,000 dong from the IRC.[10] Starting in 1956, the Asia Foundation also provided funding to the association and its activities.[11]

Despite the benefits that came from the founders' close relationship with the Ngôs, political connections can be a double-edged sword, especially when there is a regime change or a political shift. By 1958, Huỳnh Văn Lang found himself sidelined by Nhu, and Lang's role in the Cần Lao Party was substantially reduced. By 1963, Lang was secretly working with other disillusioned Cần Lao members to decrease Nhu's influence on the president.[12] After the Ngôs were removed from power, Lang was imprisoned for his role in supporting Diệm and the Cần Lao Party. The Popular Culture Association, however, outlasted the Ngôs and continued to flourish. The leadership of the organization changed hands. Lawyer Cung Đình Thanh became general director of PPI in 1967 and chair of the Popular Culture Association in 1968.[13] He held these positions until 1975. That the institute and the association survived the political turmoil of the First Republic, the interim military rule, and the Second Republic suggests that there was deep support for their work and a genuine need for the services they provided.

In addition to receiving foreign and state funding, the Popular Culture Association financed its activities through fundraising. Here again, the organizers' social status and connections were helpful. In 1957, when opera singer Marian Anderson visited Vietnam as part of a US government–sponsored cultural exchange program, Huỳnh Văn Lang met with her and convinced her to give a benefit concert for the school. Within a matter of days, Lang had managed to get permission to hold a fundraising concert, and the owner of the Đại Nam theater in Saigon agreed to allow the Popular Culture Association to use his venue free of charge.[14] These accomplishments underscored Lang's connections and his ability to use them effectively.[15]

A great deal of fundraising was required because PPI proved to be in high demand, and the Popular Culture Association wanted to open more schools and expand their activities. All the instructors were volunteers, so the funding covered administrative costs, office supplies and equipment, and the printing of student cards and test papers. In the beginning, Lang and his colleagues expected several hundred students to enroll. To their surprise, eight thousand applied, illustrating the strong desire among Vietnamese adults to improve their skills and education. However, PPI could accept only fifteen hundred students for its first session.[16] The Popular Culture Association subsequently opened more teaching centers in the Saigon–Chợ Lớn area. It eventually established sixteen chapters and associated PPIs in other cities and towns throughout South Vietnam.

PPI offered classes in a variety of major subjects such as literature and grammar, economics and business, politics and society, science and technology, and physical education. It also offered courses on many languages, including Vietnamese, English, French, Japanese, German, Mandarin, and Cantonese. Reflecting the growing importance of the United States in Vietnam, the most popular class was English, and several sections were offered. Courses on the Vietnamese language had high enrollment among Vietnamese of Chinese ancestry. They had a strong incentive to improve their Vietnamese language skills because of Diệm's Vietnamization policies, which made Vietnamese the main language of instruction in Chinese-run schools.[17]

In PPI's second session, which started in May 1955, it offered fifty-eight different classes and had fifty instructors and thirty assistant instructors. For the second session, PPI enrolled 1,869 students. Three-quarters of the students were male, and the majority were office workers in public and private sectors (33 percent), while manual and skilled workers accounted for 27 percent. The others were unemployed (12 percent), traders (8 percent), students (8 percent), and homemakers (5 percent); nurses, teachers, and military personnel made up 7 percent of the student body.[18]

In 1955 the Popular Culture Association initiated an adult literacy program with forty-seven classes and 1,889 students. The program ran six nights a week for three months, and students paid a token fee of 60 dong to attend the program. High school students were hired as instructors, and they were paid 600 dong per month.[19] This program slowly expanded, offering more sessions and levels. In 1961 it started to offer Ministry of Education–approved primary and secondary school equivalency courses and preparatory courses for the national grades ten and eleven graduating exams.[20] This adult education program was extremely popular and boasted high numbers of graduates.

Because of high student demand, the Popular Culture Association's programs and offerings grew significantly. By 1967, the Saigon–Chợ Lớn branch had six different centers and one hundred volunteer instructors during each academic session. These volunteers were teachers, professionals, and technicians who conducted classes in their areas of specialization. From 1954 to 1967, the Saigon PPI taught more than forty thousand students and graduated close to eighty-five thousand students from the adult -education program (for the period 1955–1967).[21] These figures do not include those who graduated from programs operated by the other sixteen regional chapters.[22] These statistics verify the association's impressive achievements.

Additionally, the Popular Culture Association founded public libraries and cultural centers and published one of the most respected and longest-running journals in South Vietnam, *Bách Khoa* (Polytechnic). However, the association and *Bách Khoa* parted ways in 1964 because of political differences. According to the association's 1967 report, it wanted to maintain an emphasis on education and cultural matters, but *Bách Khoa*'s editors believed the journal's "attitude of political objectivity" was no longer suitable.[23] Their assessment proved to be correct. In fact, under the leadership of Lê Ngộ Châu, *Bách Khoa* became more politically balanced as it welcomed a wide spectrum of political views from both the Left and the Right.[24] Subsequently, the Popular Culture Association began to publish its own journal called *Cultural Development* (Phát Triển Văn Hóa), which celebrated traditional Vietnamese culture. After only five issues, *Cultural Development* encountered financial difficulties and stopped publication.[25] The journal's failure suggests that the Popular Culture Association had misread its audience, who evidently wanted greater engagement with current political and philosophical issues. In contrast to the failed *Cultural Development*, *Bách Khoa* survived until 1975 and played an important role in shaping the intellectual and cultural history of South Vietnam.

As mentioned earlier, the Popular Culture Association received support and funding from the South Vietnamese government and from US charitable organizations, particularly the IRC and the Asia Foundation. The Asia Foundation was by no means a neutral cultural organization; it shared the US government's goal of keeping South Vietnam free of communism and within the US sphere of influence (see chapter 2). The IRC also had close ties to the US government and supported US war efforts. A refugee relief organization founded in 1933, the IRC played an active role in shoring up the Diệm regime in the latter half of the 1950s. The IRC leadership, including founding member Joseph Buttinger, helped create the American Friends of Vietnam, which, together with the IRC, lobbied and campaigned for US support of Diệm.[26]

The work of the Popular Culture Association fit perfectly within the mandate and ideology of the IRC and the Asia Foundation. The IRC believed the Popular Culture Association and PPI would act as an antidote to the communists who had "been allowed to initiate and control popular education movements directed toward serving their own diabolical ends."[27] In its attempt to get the Foreign Office and US Operations Mission (USOM) in Saigon to support expansion of the Popular Culture Associations' activities, the IRC noted that most of the association's founders were graduates of US universities. These men had benefited from an exchange program that aimed to cultivate young Vietnamese leaders who could "contribute to the democratic development of their country." Therefore, supporting the Popular Culture Association would be an appropriate "follow up" to "the investment already made in the Exchange Program."[28] Moreover, the type of education PPI offered was in line with what US officials considered useful for nation building: practical, applied knowledge for the masses. PPI's curriculum contrasted with the abstract philosophical material that, according to US officials, characterized French colonial education. Last, the IRC pointed out that because it was a private group, the IRC was "in a position to administer a sound program of assistance without having the PPI appearing to be too closely tied up with the American Government."[29]

From the IRC's perspective, PPI was one of its crowning achievements in Asia. The IRC's reports and retrospective publications highlighted PPI and its activities as a concrete example of the IRC's success. Its report on thirty years of global achievements (1933–1963) devoted two paragraphs to PPI. This was a significant amount of coverage, as only two of thirty-nine pages were reserved for the IRC's activities in Asia. The report mentioned PPI as one of several projects to "encourage education at various levels and to develop the kinds of talent needed by the economy and the government." The report claimed that many of the teachers and students attending school in 1963 "were the products of the Popular Culture Association."[30]

Although the Popular Culture Association received a great deal of foreign aid and its raison d'être appeared to dovetail with US objectives, it must be remembered that the group was a Vietnamese-initiated and -operated organization. Its founders were undoubtedly influenced by ideas they encountered while abroad, but they also had many other sources of inspiration, such as the nationalist Eastern Capital Free School and Vietnamese scholar-reformers who endeavored to modernize Vietnamese society.

Furthermore, considering the popularity of the programs and their longevity, it is clear that the Popular Culture Association's vision and aspirations resonated with the Vietnamese people. For two decades, thousands of volunteers offered their time and energy to teach classes six nights a week, and tens of thousands of students participated in the Popular Culture Association's programs. Countless more students benefited from the regional chapters' programs. Therefore, although the IRC claimed PPI as its achievement, its Vietnamese founders and participants also claimed it as theirs. What is not disputed is that the initiative catered to a genuine need in society.

# Buddhist School of Youth for Social Service

In 1965, a little more than a decade after the founding of PPI, Zen Buddhist monk Thích Nhất Hạnh established the School of Youth for Social Service (Trường Thanh Niên Phụng Sự Xã Hội). Although, both PPI and SYSS were voluntary social development endeavors, there were many points of contrast. In broad terms, the school's goal was to train young people for rural development. However, it aspired not only to improve people's material well-being but also to ignite a social revolution based on Buddhist beliefs and ideals.

The school was founded during a critical period for Vietnamese Buddhism. After the overthrow of Diệm, revivalist goals continued to guide the Buddhist hierarchy. In 1964 Buddhist groups throughout Vietnam formed the UBC to unify Buddhists and strengthen their position in the nation. In addition to building the Quách Thị Trang orphanage (see chapter 3), the UBC established Vạn Hạnh University, Vietnam's first Buddhist university, in 1964. Thích Nhất Hạnh was a strong advocate of the revival movement. As editor of *Vietnamese Buddhism* (Phật Giáo Việt Nam) since the 1950s, he had a forum to express his views, call for reform to the practice of Buddhism, and encourage Buddhists to engage meaningfully with society.[31] SYSS emerged in this historical context.

The school's curriculum integrated Buddhist studies with pragmatic lessons about rural development. It focused on four main areas: education, economics, public health, and organization. Students also learned about the importance of community self-reliance, empowerment, and social justice. In addition to improving people's living conditions, students were tasked with raising people's consciousness and stimulating a social and spiritual revolution based on "love, wisdom, cooperation, and communication."[32]

Central to the success of their mission was local voluntary participation. The students were instructed to refrain from carrying out development work on behalf of the villagers. Their role was to encourage villagers to articulate their needs, help them create a plan to meet those needs, and then facilitate the realization of that plan. The villagers, not the students, were to be the agents of change. To have any hope of success, the students needed to spend a significant amount of time in the area to gain the villagers' trust.[33]

It was critical that development initiatives came from the people themselves and that they voluntarily participated in the development projects.[34] The same level of volunteerism was required of SYSS students. They were not paid wages and were expected to subsist with support from the local community. In fact, like PPI, the school was operated by volunteers. Except for four full-time employees, volunteers performed many tasks, including teaching, administration, and fundraising. The school itself was built without support from the government or even the UBC. At first, the UBC hierarchy did not approve of Thích Nhất Hạnh's idea, but after seeing the success in the pilot villages, the leaders incorporated SYSS into Vạn Hạnh University in 1965. However, one year later, the university distanced itself from Thích Nhất Hạnh and SYSS because of his peace activism.

In 1966, while visiting Cornell University, Thích Nhất Hạnh issued a five-point plan for peace. Essentially, he was calling for a cease-fire and the withdrawal of US troops. From the RVN government's perspective, any call for peace was tantamount to a call for capitulation to North Vietnam. Thích Nhất Hạnh's pronouncement was therefore controversial, and it resulted in his exile. To maintain its funding and secure its own existence, Vạn Hạnh University was compelled to cut ties with Thích Nhất Hạnh and to deny his role in the founding of the university.[35]

In emphasizing local initiatives, volunteerism, and self-help, SYSS workers were employing the community development approach. Their choice of this approach was not surprising, since the philosophy of community development was widely popular throughout the developed and developing world in the 1950s and 1960s. Rivaling modernization theorists, community development proponents called for small-scale projects that emphasized social solidarity "to encourage democratic deliberation and civic action on a local level, and the embedded politics and economics within the life of the community."[36]

This approach to development had already had an impact during the First Republic and was embraced by Diệm's CIA adviser Edward Lansdale.[37] Diệm's civic action program (1955) and strategic hamlets initiative (1962), though flawed and ultimately unsuccessful, reflected the important influence of community development in the republic's early period.[38] For Diệm and the CIA, however, village development was pursued to fight the communist insurgency and to establish an anticommunist South Vietnam. SYSS had a different objective. Though concerned about improving people's lives, SYSS was also informed by the Buddhist revival movement. As such, SYSS leaders sought to establish a Buddhist social revolution based on Buddhist "principles of love, non-violence, and a willing spirit."[39]

Furthermore, as Thích Nhất Hạnh stated in the SYSS handbook, it was to be a revolution led by Buddhists.[40] This community development approach was also central to the New Life Development Project, discussed in the next section.

From 1966 onward, SYSS was directed and managed by Thích Nhất Hạnh's students, particularly Thích Thanh Văn, who was the director until 1970, and Cao Ngọc Phương, later known by her ordained name, Sister Chân Không. Having lost its affiliation with Vạn Hạnh University, SYSS existed without official status and without any chance of state funding. It had to rely on donations to finish building the school and dormitories. The school's policy regarding foreign funding also made it difficult to raise money. Unlike the Popular Culture Association, SYSS would not accept funds from agencies with political agendas. The Asia Foundation reportedly retracted its offer of funding for the school when Thích Thanh Văn refused to renounce Thích Nhất Hạnh.[41] Because of its funding policy and its founder's peace activism, SYSS's financial situation remained precarious throughout its existence. Cao Ngọc Phương and other staff had to be resourceful and persistent in their efforts to raise enough money to keep the school running and to provide scholarships for needy students. SYSS received support from wealthy Vietnamese donors as well as from the less well-off, including market women and street vendors who donated small amounts of cash, food, and other material goods. Students from Vạn Hạnh University also donated their time at the school.[42]

Although SYSS lost the approval of the Buddhist hierarchy, it found support among the students who enrolled. In its first year, SYSS received five hundred applications but could accept only two hundred students.[43] Given the lack of funding, the school and its dormitories were spartan. The rural worksites offered even less material comfort for SYSS volunteers. Nevertheless, hundreds of individuals in their late teens and early twenties signed up. Some even left other universities to attend SYSS; others were recruited from participating villages based on their commitment to the school's philosophy and approach.[44]

In addition to harsh living conditions, SYSS students faced physical danger. Some of the SYSS villages were caught in firefights between nationalist and communist forces. The school also had to contend with political assassinations and acts of terrorism. According to Cao Ngọc Phương, the school was attacked on May 16, 1966, when assassins threw three grenades into the dormitories, wounding two students, one of whom was paralyzed for life. It appeared that Thích Nhất Hạnh, who had left for the US a few days before, was the target of the attack, as the grenades were thrown into his sleeping quarters. In April 1967 the school was attacked again; this time, about a dozen grenades were lobbed into the female students' dormitories. Two women were killed and sixteen female students were wounded.[45] In two other instances, SYSS volunteers were targeted for kidnapping and execution while working in the villages.

It is unclear who ordered the assassinations and kidnappings. Thích Nhất Hạnh's peace stance earned him criticism from both the RVN government and the communists. His exile is evidence that the RVN government did not approve of his peace message. The DRV did not appreciate Thích Nhất Hạnh's peace advocacy either. According to Cao Ngọc Phương, after Thích Nhất Hạnh's collection of peace poetry came out in 1965, Radio Hanoi and Beijing's Voice of Vietnam denounced him as reactionary.[46] Clearly, neither side approved of Thích Nhất Hạnh or his school. The government could have shut down SYSS, and it is unclear why it did not, especially since the school did not have a permit. Moreover, Cao Ngọc Phương had been arrested several times for peace activism and was falsely suspected of being a communist.[47]

Perhaps the RVN government did not perceive the school as a threat. This was less likely the case for the NLF. By the mid-1960s, the NLF was active in providing social services and raising the living standards in rural areas under its control.[48] As such, SYSS's community development activities and its goal of establishing a Buddhist social revolution worked against the NLF's agenda. In other words, the NLF might have considered SYSS a challenge to its moral authority.[49] Moreover, around the same time, communist organizations in South Vietnam had started a campaign of terrorism to intimidate and destabilize South Vietnamese society. Bombing attacks were carried out against US and South Vietnamese government buildings and personnel in the cities; in the countryside, communists targeted village leaders, teachers, priests, and humanitarian workers.[50]

In any case, the violence against SYSS made some young people reluctant to participate in the program. In addition, the government's general military mobilization and the end of the draft exemption for students in 1968 made it hard to keep male students enrolled.[51] The war and the actions of both warring sides impeded SYSS's work, limiting the functioning of civil society. Despite these challenges, the school continued to operate until 1975.

# New Life Development Project

Like PPI and SYSS, the New Life Development Project (Kế Hoạch Xây Đời Mới) was another long-running social development effort that relied on volunteers. The New Life Project offers many points of comparison with the other two endeavors.

Active for six years (1965–1971), this was a community development effort originally focused on District 8, a poor section of Saigon. First known as the District 8 Development Program, its name was later changed when the project extended into Districts 6 and 7. Like SYSS, the project's commitment to grassroots development was pathbreaking. Even though community development was influential in development discourse, modernization theory, with its emphasis on large state-led projects, still dominated.[52] The New Life Project was committed to empowering the local community by encouraging residents to identify problems, come up with solutions, and execute their plans. Like SYSS, the project emphasized the importance of voluntary participation in building community spirit and cohesion.

Like PPI, the idea for this project came from a group of highly educated, well-connected young men. The core group of fifteen leaders worked in law, medicine, civil service, education, and the military. They were friends and had previously worked together on other civic projects, such as the flood relief campaign of 1964 and the summer youth camp of 1965.[53] These young, idealistic activists wanted to contribute to the building of a noncommunist country. They were mostly Catholic and were inspired by Catholic social activism.[54] Unlike SYSS, however, the New Life Project was framed not as a religious endeavor but as a secular attempt to solve the problems facing South Vietnam.

Moreover, these leaders were seeking new methods of governing, as some had become dissatisfied with the top-down approach. As Đoàn Thanh Liêm, a twenty-seven-year-old lawyer, explained, young people's cynicism and "disillusionment with the present leadership and indeed, with most of their elders have caused the youth of Vietnam to act largely on their own to attempt to rehabilitate their country from the bottom up."[55] Đoàn Thanh Liêm attributed the failure of leadership not only to the legacy of French colonialism but also to the current US military presence, both of which had eroded community values and consensus. Võ Long Triều, the group's main leader, believed that for noncommunist South Vietnam to survive, South Vietnamese leaders must provide the people with an alternative "social revolution," one not predicated on class warfare and hatred.[56]

Võ Long Triều was also inspired by the Jewish kibbutz movement in Israel. The kibbutz movement's emphasis on collective cooperation, mutual help, and social justice resonated with him, and its principles were congruent with those that guided the work of the New Life Project. Like SYSS, its leaders were advocating a grassroots community development approach. However, Triều was also attracted to how kibbutz members were committed to defending their communities. In other words, the New Life Project was not just about development; it was also about security. More specifically, the project was conceived as a way to shore up local support for the RVN and protect the population from communist infiltration.[57]

Security was indeed an issue when it came to District 8. Located in the southernmost part of Saigon, bordering on Chợ Lớn, this was a poor area lacking in basic services and infrastructure. In the mid-1960s it had a population of approximately 146,000, of which 30,000 were newly arrived refugees.[58] Because of the many canals and rivers that crisscrossed the district, it was prone to floods. The district lacked running water, indoor plumbing, and a reliable electricity supply; people had to pay for clean water, which was trucked into the area.[59] District 8 was also the location of the city's garbage dump. A deputy of the National Assembly noted that "it was not uncommon for people to build make-shift houses in between 8–10 foot high piles of refuse."[60] Not surprisingly, this area was vulnerable to outbreaks of cholera and bubonic plague. To make matters worse, District 8 was the former home of the crime syndicate Bình Xuyên, and by the 1960s, it had been infiltrated by communist operatives who established forty-five cells and used the local canals to transport supplies.[61]

In terms of infrastructure, the New Life Project focused on building roads, homes, schools, and sanitation facilities. One of its first tasks was building a new public elementary school. The one elementary school in the district had become inadequate for the population. To serve the student population, the school day was divided into three shifts: morning, noon, and afternoon. The noon shift (11 a.m.–2 p.m.) was challenging for both teachers and students because this was a stifling hot part of the day. With the new five-room elementary school, the noon shift could be eliminated.[62]

After the elementary school, two public high schools were built, one in District 8 and one in District 6. These districts had previously lacked high schools, so students living there had to travel quite a distance if they wanted to continue their education. Although the Ministry of Education agreed to pay the salaries of the teachers at these new high schools, it did not have the budget to help with construction costs. This was not surprising, since on average, 60 percent of the national budget was allocated to defense while only 6 percent went to education.[63] The New Life Project therefore had to mobilize local and foreign donations to establish these schools. Community members and New Life Project participants contributed a tremendous amount of labor to construct these schools.[64] To build the high school in District 8, for example, project workers and volunteers had to move a dilapidated cemetery because this was the only land available. With the city's agreement, project leaders began contacting families and getting them to move the graves. Unclaimed bodies were buried in a mass grave with proper rituals. The area was then filled and leveled, an enormously labor-intensive undertaking. Project leaders were able to borrow a dredger from the Ministry of Public Works, which made the job more manageable. After the war ended, the District 6 high school became a commercial space, but the high school in District 8 still stands and is now called the Lương Văn Can High School.[65] The Lương Văn Can Alumni Association still celebrates the school's humble beginnings, particularly the fact that it was built with the participation of local residents.[66]

The New Life Development Project also built houses for the local population. Meant to be a community-building process, the houses were built collectively by residents of the area. Afterward, the houses were distributed to participants by a lottery system.[67] The work was hard and time-consuming because the swampy land needed to be filled before construction could begin. The program built 748 new houses in District 8 and 198 in District 6.[68] Unfortunately, the fighting during the Tet offensive destroyed many of the homes, and the New Life Project had to repair and rebuild them in 1968. In its six years, the project built and repaired eight thousand homes in three districts.[69]

Because this was an experiment in grassroots community development, the New Life Project wanted to encourage community participation, initiatives, and leadership. It recruited about two hundred youths from inside and outside the districts (in-district volunteers were preferable) to carry out the laborious work. These recruits were paid a monthly stipend of 2,500 dong (US$25), which was comparable to the monthly wage of a skilled worker.[70] New Life Project workers were trained to interact respectfully with the local community to build trust and to empower the people to take the initiative. Like SYSS students, New Life Project participants were required to live in the community and were expected to practice the "three together" principle: live together, eat together, work together.[71]

At any one time, there might be thirty to forty young volunteers, both male and female, participating in the New Life Project for a limited period. Many were either high school or university students, and the majority became involved through their participation in other voluntary organizations such as the Scouts, religious clubs, school organizations, and Young Christian Workers.[72] Some SYSS participants occasionally joined the New Life Project to show their support.[73] Others were recruits from among current and former students of the New Life leaders, many of whom were teachers. Many volunteers came on the weekends or whenever they had time to spare.[74]

To challenge the traditional social hierarchy and conventional approach to governance, New Life Project leaders made a conscious effort to build relationships with the community and be attentive to its needs. The leaders made sure to be present in the community and to participate in the physical labor. According to Võ Long Triều's memoir, even after he became the minister of youth, he still participated actively in the project, helping to make road repairs and perform other work in the evenings and on weekends. Hồ Ngọc Nhuận, the new district chief, also took part in the physical labor.[75]

The New Life Project and its radical approach encountered some skepticism and criticism from local officials. Its leaders, however, were fortunate to have important political support at the national level. Prime Minister Nguyễn Cao Kỳ considered Triều a protégé and wanted him to participate in the government in some capacity. In fact, according to Triều, the prime minister encouraged him to come up with ideas for a community-building project that the government would help fund.[76] Without the state's support, this ambitious project would have never seen the light of day. Moreover, when Triều became the minister of youth in 1966, this lent the project even more protection and support. To overcome local bureaucratic opposition and to facilitate work in the districts, project leaders lobbied for a change in district leadership. They wanted dynamic administrators who were committed to the project's ideas and approach. With Kỳ's backing, some project leaders took administrative control. Hồ Ngọc Nhuận, who had no administrative or political experience, replaced the incumbent district chief. Triều argued that Nhuận's commitment to the project and his rapport with the people were more important than bureaucratic experience.[77] Mai Như Mạnh, a recent graduate of the National Institute of Administration, was appointed vice chief of District 8.[78]

As one might expect, with the prime minister's support, the project received significant funding from the RVN government, USAID, and other NGOs. In the first phase of its work (1965–1969), the project received 30 million dong from the national budget. In the last phase, it received 10 million dong through foreign aid. In addition, USAID provided a great deal of building material, such as cement, roofing, and iron rods. Donations also came from a variety of private aid agencies. International donors included the Cooperative for American Remittances to Europe (CARE), CRS, Asian Christian Service, Vietnam Christian Service, Oxfam, and the Adenauer Foundation.

These organizations provided machinery and equipment for training classes, including sewing machines, typewriters, and medical supplies. Meanwhile, wealthy individuals and church groups in Saigon donated furnishings for the schools and training centers.[79] The need for funds was ongoing, and project leaders continued to lobby for aid, whether foreign or domestic. Appeals were made for both general support and specific needs. For example, when project leaders were setting up embroidery and knitting classes at the Huê Lâm pagoda in District 6, they assisted the head instructor, Nun Như Châu, to procure donations from CARE. After inspecting the school, CARE representatives approved the donation of embroidery and knitting machines.[80]

Although project leaders actively sought financial and material support from foreign sources, they were aware of the problems associated with accepting too much help. US interest and support were both a blessing and a curse. The project received significant aid, advice, and support from USOM and later USAID. In addition, the project's radical approach and success drew foreign media attention. The project garnered even more interest after US Vice President Hubert Humphrey visited the site in February 1966. Accompanied by American and

Vietnamese dignitaries, including US Ambassador Henry Cabot Lodge and Edward Lansdale, Humphrey toured District 8 and met some of the participants and leaders. Humphrey praised the New Life Project for pursuing a social revolution.[81]

This international attention was encouraging for project participants, but it was fodder for communist agents who tried to discredit the project as a US initiative. From the start, New Life Project leaders were wary of being too closely linked with the US. Distrust of US motives had grown by the mid-1960s, fueled not only by communist propaganda but also by the recent deployment of US combat troops in the spring of 1965. Both Radio Hanoi and the NLF radio station called New Life Project leaders US lackeys, and pamphlets slandering their characters were distributed in the area.[82] Therefore, New Life Project leaders and cadres had to work hard to counter suspicion. For example, when the project first began, there were rumors that the area was being gentrified and houses were being built for foreigners.[83] Even when the rumors were proved false and locals were given the houses they had helped build, suspicion lingered. Hồ Ngọc Nhuận remembered hearing a satirical version of a popular children's song around the neighborhood. Rather than instructing children to be grateful to their forefathers for building the Vietnamese nation, as in the original song, the satirical version opened with the line: "This is our house that USAID, USOM have built."[84]

More serious attacks came in the form of assassination attempts. In one incident, a young volunteer was almost killed when his bulldozer was rigged with a grenade. Fortunately, he noticed the wire before he started the bulldozer.[85] Shortly after Humphrey's visit, project leaders learned that the communists had issued death warrants for two project leaders, Hồ Văn Minh and Hồ Ngọc Nhuận.[86]

While Humphrey's visit made things more dangerous for New Life Project cadres, it was an important boost to the career of Charles Sweet, one of the main contacts between the New Life Project and US aid agencies. Sweet came to Vietnam in 1964 as an International Voluntary Service (IVS) volunteer and was assigned to work with Vietnamese youth. Sweet participated in the 1964 flood relief campaign and played an instrumental role in the youth summer work camp (see chapter 5). Through these activities, Sweet met and worked with some New Life Project leaders. At the same time, however, he was working for the CIA.[87] His CIA affiliation probably became clearer in 1967, when he was recruited for Lansdale's counterinsurgency team.[88] According to Sweet, he got involved with the New Life Project by mobilizing funds and providing advice and encouragement to project leaders.[89] During Humphrey's visit, Lansdale introduced Sweet to Humphrey and credited Sweet for his work with the project.[90]

Known for his psychological warfare activities and his advisory role to Ngô Đình Diệm in 1956–1957, Lansdale returned to Vietnam in 1965 for his second tour and was assigned to be Ambassador Henry Cabot Lodge's special adviser and to focus on pacification.[91] The New Life Project's approach to community development corresponded with Lansdale's beliefs regarding the efficacy of and approach to counterinsurgency. During his time with Diệm, he had emphasized civic action, grassroots participation, and giving people a stake to defend.[92] Vice President Humphrey was a strong supporter of Lansdale and his ideas about counterinsurgency, and he had been one of the few in Washington who lobbied for Lansdale's return to Vietnam.[93] It was not surprising, then, that Humphrey visited the New Life Project site.

Although the New Life Project started before Lansdale returned to Vietnam, its approach and goals were certainly in line with his vision of an effective counterinsurgency strategy.[94] It was fitting, therefore, that Lansdale recruited Sweet for his team; Sweet was supporting a project that exemplified the effectiveness of community development in building loyalty to the state and in fighting communism. In a 1968 speech at Harvard's Kennedy School of Government, Sweet claimed that the New Life Project was successful in blocking communist infiltration into the districts. Youth and community leaders provided intelligence about irregular activities, and this resulted in the arrests of "hard-core enemy" cadres and the elimination of "enemy activities."[95]

Although there was a clear convergence in the approaches of certain Americans and the New Life Project leaders, and although there was significant US funding for the project, it would be erroneous to dismiss this as an American endeavor. The project was initiated and carried out by the project's leaders and participants and, more importantly, by the local communities. In his reports, speeches, and personal letters, Sweet was consistent in describing this project as a Vietnamese initiative. He first described the project to his family as follows: "Another project that I am involved in is the District 8 Development Project in which the students [have] actually taken control of one of the eight districts. . . . They have done a fairly good job to date but need alot of support for their effort."[96] In an economics paper written in 1970 when he was a graduate student at Harvard, Sweet wrote, "even though a substantial amount of funding and commodity aid was given, the New Life Project was a Vietnamese-initiated program and maintained this identity" until its end.[97] In another report, Sweet described his role as adviser, supporter, and friend. There is no doubt that his most important contribution was to mobilize "the resources of the US Mission to support but not to overwhelm local initiatives."[98] While both Sweet and New Life Project leaders were keen to keep US involvement quiet in order to gain the locals' trust, Sweet's explanations of his role on these occasions—when he might have been inclined to exaggerate his responsibility—ring true.

The New Life Project was brought to a close in 1971. According to Võ Long Triều, the project's success drew suspicion from President Nguyễn Văn Thiệu, who took control and essentially dismantled the project.[99] By this time, Thiệu and Kỳ had become open rivals, as both vied for the presidency in the October 1971 election. From Sweet's perspective, however, the New Life Project had lost its mandate in May 1968 when the US bombed the district in pursuit of PAVN-PLAF fighters during the second wave of the Tet offensive. The use of indiscriminate force in a dense urban setting resulted in more damage than the main phase of the offensive in February. This event created resentment and deepened the distrust of Americans, not only among residents but also among the New Life Project leaders themselves. Moreover, because these leaders worked with and accepted US aid, the bombing damaged the people's trust in them too. The erosion of credibility and trust destroyed the project's foundation.[100]

The three development projects examined in this chapter are examples of how groups of private individuals attempted to contribute to nation building. Each project was unique in its vision, approach, and experience. The Popular Culture Association and PPI endeavored to make adult education available throughout South Vietnam. The founders believed that educational attainment was fundamental to the process of nation building. As such, the mandate of the Popular Culture Association did not go beyond expanding adult education and promoting cultural activities. In its socially and politically conservative approach and aims, the association received substantial aid and support from the government and foreign aid agencies. In contrast, SYSS and the New Life Project aspired to bring about deeper and more comprehensive changes. Leaders of both projects alluded to "social revolutions" that empowered people to take charge of their lives. Influenced by the Buddhist revival movement, SYSS leaders framed their work within Buddhist ideals and principles. Although many New Life Project leaders were Christian, that project was framed not in a religious context but as a secular nation-building effort. The aim of the New Life Project was not only to improve people's lives but also to give people a stake in the nation and give them something to defend. The ultimate goal, in effect, was to generate support for a noncommunist South Vietnam.

Like the examples discussed in previous chapters, these three cases illuminate the contours of South Vietnam's civil society and highlight its limitations. It was useful for organizations to have connections to the political and social elite. These links facilitated more funding and support while reducing state scrutiny. It was no wonder that the Popular Culture Association and PPI lasted as long as South Vietnam itself did. Considering the New Life Project's goal of ridding the districts of communist infiltration and winning people's loyalty, it was not surprising that the project received strong support from USAID and from

Prime Minister Kỳ. The project's demise was partly caused by the United States' indiscriminate use of force and by the dysfunctional political leadership of South Vietnam, where political rivalry trumped nation building. It is ironic that the New Life Project was damaged by the very approach to war that counterinsurgency advocates like Edward Lansdale disavowed.

Another irony is that SYSS outlasted the New Life Project, even though the former took a more radical stance on the war. Thích Nhất Hạnh's vocal antiwar activism caused SYSS to lose support from the Buddhist hierarchy and engendered suspicion from both the RVN government and the communists. SYSS's rule against accepting aid from political entities also meant that it was often strapped for cash. In addition, the school was the target of numerous terroristic attacks. Despite these obstacles, SYSS lasted until 1975. Its survival suggests that even in South Vietnam's heavily guarded and contested civil society, some groups managed to carry out their agendas and voice their concerns.

Even more ironic than the two points noted above is the political trajectory of Hồ Ngọc Nhuận, one of the most promising leaders of the New Life Project. Because of his commitment to the principles of community development, this affable and impressionable young Roman Catholic teacher was selected to head the local government of District 8. His popularity in the district and the success of the project propelled him to electoral victory twice as the people's representative in the National Assembly. His successful leadership of the project also earned him death threats from the communists. By the 1970s, however, Hồ Ngọc Nhuận had begun to identify politically with the Third Force, an informal group of activists calling for negotiations and an end to the war. He went further than some of the others in the Third Force and worked directly with members of the NLF.[101] In a bid to win over the hearts and minds of the Vietnamese people, US-AID had poured millions of dollars into development aid and tens of thousands of dollars into the New Life Project. Nhuận's case shows that US efforts to influence civil society were sometimes unsuccessful. Rather than winning his favor, US actions pushed him to the other side.

5

# SOCIAL AND POLITICAL ACTIVISM OF STUDENTS IN SOUTH VIETNAM

Pharmacy student Nhuận Cận penned a poem that was featured in *Ý Hướng* (Intention), a periodical published by pharmacy students at the University of Saigon:

> *The Black River* (Dòng Sông Đen)
> Sunlight streams over black mud
> The stilt house totters
> Trash piles up beside the bridge
> Tips of water spinach in the water
> Matters of life rear up morning and night
> A woman silently rummages in the garbage
> Traffic dust and din flow by
> Life is fleeting
> on the Black River[1]

Following these introductory lines, the poem contemplates the bleak, transient existence of those living on the city's outskirts, in contrast to the comfortable lives of the wealthy. What is remarkable about this poem is that it was included in the 1971 Tet (Lunar New Year) issue. Instead of the typically joyful and light-hearted content surrounding celebrations of Tet, the pharmacy students published an editorial calling for students to get out of their ivory tower, an article about youth's loss of faith, and a traditional yearend roundup from the Kitchen God filled with gritty details of war and suffering. Clearly, *Ý Hướng*'s editors wanted students to remember their social responsibilities even during an important holiday.

Like their peers across the developed and developing worlds, Vietnamese students in the 1960s and 1970s were deeply involved with politics and social issues. From campuses in North America and Europe to cities in Asia and Africa, students' protest and activism affected societies in dramatic and profound ways. There is a significant body of scholarly literature on the student movements of the 1960s and on the global connection linking them.[2] Young activists fought for social justice, peace, and racial and gender rights. For many, particularly those in the United States, the Vietnam War was a catalyst. In the RVN, the war loomed powerfully over students' public activities and their lives.

Although street protests and school strikes caught national and international attention, many South Vietnamese youths were engaged in social and community activities that were less dramatic but just as significant. Like the adult participants in civil society, youthful activists had to navigate state control, competing influences, and the demands of warfare. Regardless of their political ideologies, motivations, or choice of public engagement, their involvement in society revealed their agency, aspirations, and hopes.

# The War's Impact on Youth

It is debatable the extent to which youth activism changed the course of the war (if at all), but it is certain that the war had a deep impact on Vietnamese youths. For young men, warfare carried the dread of conscription. Women also served in the ARVN, but they were not drafted. After the Tet offensive in 1968, legislators debated a bill to conscript women, but it did not pass. Nevertheless, by the end of 1969, there were four thousand women in the Women's Armed Forces Corps and approximately one million in the People's Self-Defense Forces.[3]

In the early years of the republic, the ARVN relied on volunteers, but it did not take long for it to become a predominantly conscripted army. From 1955 to 1959, a one-year period of military service was mandatory for men between twenty and twenty-two years old.[4] In 1959 the length of service climbed to eighteen months and then to twenty months in 1961. Three years later, the period of service was extended to thirty-six months, and the age range was widened to include men from twenty to twenty-five. After the Tet offensive, the general mobilization law was promulgated on June 19, 1968, further expanding the draft-eligible population to all males aged eighteen to thirty-three. The new law also suspended military discharge, except for health reasons.[5] University and high school students were exempt from the draft, but those sixteen years and older were required to serve in the reserves or in the People's Self-Defense Force.[6] In addition, starting in 1968, high school students older than seventeen were expected to participate in a new military training program created for them.[7] If a student refused to complete his military training, he would lose his exemption and be drafted. This military training was initially incorporated into the regular school term, but in 1971, after much lobbying from students and teachers, the program was moved to the summer.

Life for Vietnamese youths in the 1960s and 1970s was marked by uncertainty and stress. This assessment corresponds with findings published in the June 1966 issue of Đối Thoại (Dialogue), a student journal of the Faculty of Letters at Saigon University. The journal's editors interviewed five hundred students and published excerpts focusing on their opinions of the war and the war's impact on their lives.[8] Several students did not want to talk about the war or did not think they had much to say, but many related diverse personal experiences and views. Some interviewees mentioned traumatic events they had experienced, including losing family members to the First and Second Indochina Wars.[9] One interviewee, an officer in the air force, expressed remorse for the many people he had killed while carrying out his duty. According to him, each "war medal he received was paid for by countless deaths."[10]

Interviewees also offered their perspectives on the war. A student of Vietnamese literature, Phan Anh, stated his objections to both communism and US intervention. Unfortunately, as in a number of other published interviews, more than half of Phan Anh's response was censored. An equally strong opinion was voiced by Phạm Vân Phải, who was bitter because the war was caused by the Vietnamese themselves. Much of Phải's answer was also redacted by the censors.[11] In contrast to Phải's depiction of the war as a Vietnamese civil conflict, one respondent, Eastern philosophy student Bách Ái Tâm, opined that the RVN was being invaded by a foreign force (the DRV) that worshipped a foreign ideology, and he expressed concerns about South Vietnam's readiness in the face of this communist invasion.[12] It is notable that his long answer, which was in line with the government's prowar view, was published in full.

Although these interviews are anecdotal and impressionistic, they illustrate the wide range of outlooks and experiences among youths. It appears that although the war affected individuals to different extents and in diverse ways, few escaped its impact completely. The Đối Thoại survey underscores the fact that in the late 1960s and early 1970s, the vast majority of Vietnamese youths had grown up with war and had no knowledge of life without war.

The US Information Agency (USIA) also conducted a survey in May 1966 with more than five hundred Saigon postsecondary students, questioning them about politics, education, and war.[13] Like Đối Thoại's survey, the USIA's study revealed a general war weariness among students. USIA director Leonard Marks found it significant that a third of the students surveyed wanted a postsecondary education for their own personal advancement, and only 5 percent were pursuing an education for the benefit of society.[14] Also significant for US officials was that only 10 percent of the respondents belonged to any student organization—a low level of engagement compared with other Asian countries such as India and Japan.[15]

Although the USIA's report emphasized Saigon students' lack of social engagement, it also noted that the survey was conducted during the Buddhist struggle movement, which led to several months of violent confrontations between Buddhists and the government. The report cautioned that this event might have influenced students' answers, but it did not comment on the discrepancy between the findings of low social engagement and high levels of student involvement in the movement. During this period, Buddhist youths throughout the RVN participated in street demonstrations and other protest activities. Their activism was so prevalent that the government threatened protesters with an end to the student draft exemption.[16] Their participation suggests that young people were socially concerned, contrary to the findings of the USIA survey. High levels of engagement were also observed by David Marr, who was researching urban Vietnamese youth in the mid-1960s. According to Marr, while some older intellectuals showed signs of resignation and alienation, high school and university students remained engaged and passionate about their country's fate.[17] The vibrancy of the student associations examined in this chapter certainly confirms Marr's findings.

# Youths and Social Work

Archival records show that many youths were involved in voluntary associations and youth movements of all types. There is no indication that the war or political instability hindered their enthusiasm for associational life. In fact, in the mid-1960s, as the war became more intense, the number of youths joining associations increased dramatically. In 1965 approximately 69,000 young people were members of various organizations. This number jumped to 200,000 in 1966 and then to 260,000 in 1967, a nearly fourfold increase in three years.[18]

Although this growth was remarkable, the number was low relative to the total population. The population of South Vietnam in 1966 was approximately sixteen million, of which 24 percent were between the ages of fifteen and twenty-nine.[19] As such, the 260,000 participants represented only 7 percent of this age group (assuming that most of the youthful participants fell in this age bracket). However, because the majority of youth groups were located in towns and cities, the level of participation should be calculated based on the urban population. According to the US Department of Labor, the population for South

Vietnam's nine largest urban centers in 1965 was a little over 3.2 million. As-suming that, like the general population, 24 percent of urban residents were be-tween the ages of fifteen and twenty-nine, the participation rate jumps to 34 percent.[20] This rough estimate indicates that the majority of youths did not participate in voluntary organizations, but a substantial number did get involved. Moreover, the 260,000 did not include individuals who joined unofficial groups, such as various Buddhist and Catholic youth groups that operated throughout South Vietnam.[21] Nor did this figure include those who participated in ad hoc public activities such as rallies, protests, and relief projects.

There are several possible explanations for the significant increase in youth involvement in the mid-1960s. As I discuss later, students' involvement in the protest movement against Ngô Đình Diệm in 1963 probably empowered youth activists. Another reason might have been related to the intensification of the war itself. Research has shown that in periods of socioeconomic and political uncertainty, people tend to join voluntary groups to form networks for protec-tion and mutual help.[22] It seems highly plausible that, in the face of a seemingly endless war and an increasing number of young men being drafted into the mil-itary, getting involved in a social cause offered a needed distraction and helped combat feelings of helplessness. Last, the spike in the number of association members occurred shortly after a major flood relief campaign in 1964 and a popular summer youth program in 1965. Both events involved thousands of young volunteers. Exposure to these voluntary public activities likely encour-aged many youths to join other clubs and to participate in civic work.

The most active and vocal student groups were the university student unions. Universities in major cities such as Saigon, Huế, and Đà Lạt had dynamic stu-dent associations. Perhaps the most powerful was the Saigon Student Union (SSU; Tổng Hội Sinh Viên Sài Gòn), which was composed of students from twelve different faculties and colleges at the University of Saigon. The SSU was preceded by the National Student Union (Tổng Hội Sinh Viên Quốc Gia), which received official permission to operate in 1955. The National Student Union was active until at least 1960, at which time it was reorganized and became the SSU.[23] By 1972, there were three public universities—Saigon, Huế, and Cần Thơ—and three private ones—Vạn Hạnh Buddhist University and two Catholic universi-ties, Đà Lạt and Minh Đức. In addition, the National Institute of Administra-tion provided a two-year training program for civil servants. Saigon University was the largest, with thirty thousand students in 1970.[24]

In addition to school and university associations, youths had many other ways to participate in public life. Typically, they got involved through personal con-nections made in their schools, churches, pagodas, or neighborhoods. Like adult voluntary associations, youth groups were usually organized around a common interest, pursuit, or faith. For children, groups that inculcated good civic or re-ligious behavior were popular. The Boy Scouts and Girl Scouts, for example, at-tracted many members and had nearly six thousand participants in the mid-1960s.[25] The Scout Association of Vietnam first appeared in 1916 but did not receive official recognition from the Scouts' international organization until 1957.[26] Older Scouts were often recruited for social work. The Red Cross and other aid agencies, for instance, asked Scouts to help distribute aid and take part in other disaster relief activities. This was the experience of a former Boy Scout I interviewed.[27] He joined the organization when he was in university and still has fond memories of the social events and camping trips it sponsored. He also found civic work rewarding. His group participated in a vaccination program in highland villages, in addition to providing disaster and war relief.

Both Catholics and Buddhists had youth associations that aimed to make the religion more relevant to the younger generation and encourage adherents to play more prominent and positive roles in society. Buddhist children could join the Buddhist Family Association (Gia Đình Phật Tử), sometimes referred to as the

**FIGURE 5.1**   Saigon Girl Scouts collecting donations for victims of the Tet offensive, 1968. VA000463, Douglas Pike Photograph Collection, Vietnam Center and Sam Johnson Vietnam Archive, Texas Tech University.

Buddhist Scouts. This organization was founded in 1940 and was one of the many manifestations of the Buddhist revival movement.[28] It endeavored to make Buddhist values and teachings more meaningful to children and youths and to persuade Buddhists to be more engaged with society. With both male and female members, this organization was modeled on the Boy and Girl Scouts. It employed similar techniques for organizing and activities, and members' uniforms and hats even resembled those of the Scouts. Like the Scouts, Buddhist Family members also participated in civic and charity work. In 1964 the Buddhist Family Association was reorganized and expanded, and it came under the national control of the UBC's Viện Hóa Đạo (Institute for the Propagation of the Faith). At that time, the Buddhist Family Association had ninety-six thousand members, the majority of whom were located in the central provinces.[29]

Buddhist university students had their own associations at their respective schools. The Huế University Buddhist Student Association was particularly popular, attracting five hundred members out of a student population of three thousand in 1964. This group was involved in social projects such as road building and well drilling, literacy programs, and hygiene promotion.[30] The Buddhist university student associations played an important role in both the 1963 and 1966 Buddhist protest movements, as well as in the fight for peace and social justice.

Like their Buddhist counterparts, Catholic children and youths had many religion-based organizations, including the Eucharistic Crusade, Valiant Hearts, Valiant Souls, and Catholic Scouts. Those aged sixteen and older could join organizations such as the Catholic Youth Association and Young Christian Workers (YCW; Thanh Lao Công).[31] Like the Buddhist youth organizations, the Catholic groups aspired to promote religious values and teachings, along with civic and social responsibility.

The YCW was particularly active in the 1960s and 1970s. Founded in Belgium in 1925, it focused on the needs of workers. It made its appearance in Vietnam in the early 1930s and had subgroups for women, men, pupils, rural youths, and working families. At the helm of YCW were left-leaning Roman Catholic priests, including Fathers Phan Khắc Từ and Trương Bá Cần.[32] Prominent female social activists, such as Nguyễn Thị Oanh, Vũ Thị Kim Liên, Đặng Thị Thân, and Trần Thị Trinh, also provided leadership for the organization.[33] With the support of the archbishop of Saigon, YCW spearheaded the establishment of a center for working-class youths. The youth center was built in the Vườn Xoài parish (now in District 3 of Ho Chi Minh City), where there was a large, poor Catholic refugee population. The district lacked even the most basic infrastructure; a former resident of the neighborhood, Trần Thị Nền, recalled that there were no private toilets until after 1975.[34] The center encouraged youths to get involved in community work and develop a sense of social responsibility. Trần Thị Nền credited her participation in the YCW community center for her decision to pursue a career in social work.[35]

According to Nguyễn Văn Nghị, a former priest involved with the group, YCW focused on systemic problems that created poverty. As such, members linked up with other organizations and movements, including various Buddhists groups, student organizations, labor unions, progressive newspapers, and politicians, to bring about change.[36] YCW activists also played an important role in labor organizing in the 1960s and 1970s. Despite some members' leftist sympathies or communist connections, YCW was not an NLF organization.[37]

In addition to religious groups, there were many secular social service organizations that youths could join. One of the oldest was the Voluntary Youth Association (Thanh Niên Thiện Chí), which was founded in 1956 and received official approval in 1960.[38] The founders were inspired by their experience with youth camps organized by the Asia Foundation, Mennonite Central Committee, and American Friends Service Committee. Though based in Saigon, the Voluntary Youth Association had chapters in Huế, Đà Lạt, and Cần Thơ.[39] Throughout the 1960s this association organized youth work camps that allowed participants to carry out village development projects, work in refugee camps, build and renovate schools, and organize public talks and musical events.[40]

The Đà Lạt branch was particularly dynamic. Established by Nguyễn Tường Cẩm in 1964, this group was involved in projects in villages outside of Đà Lạt.[41] Like the Buddhist School of Youth for Social Service and the New Life Development Project, the Đà Lat branch of the Voluntary Youth Association followed the principles of community development and emphasized self-help and grassroots participation. Local communities were asked to identify the projects they wished to pursue, and residents were expected to participate with association members in carrying them out.

The trips to project sites were no doubt memorable, and probably physically challenging, for many members of the Voluntary Youth Association. A university education was not affordable for most of the population, so these university students came from middle- and upper-middle-class urban families. The majority of them had little experience with manual labor. One member recalled that, during her involvement in the mid-1960s, the Đà Lạt chapter made approximately a dozen weekend work trips annually; each excursion included twenty to thirty students.[42] These trips were typically rough. The students had to bring their own food, and they slept on floors in community halls or schools. One member recalled cooking a pot of stew to take along for their meals.[43] The group received help with logistics and transportation from the government as well as the ARVN.

In Vietnam, two important events boosted young people's participation in public life: the 1964 flood relief campaign and the summer youth program of

1965.[44] As mentioned in chapter 3, the typhoon season in the fall of 1964 was the worst in sixty years, killing about seven thousand people and destroying countless homes.[45] With the government's help, a committee was established to coordinate relief activities. A host of civic, religious, school, and social groups joined forces to raise funds, deliver aid, rebuild, and care for the dislocated population.

Students established their own flood relief committee, with representatives from many high school and university student unions and other voluntary youth groups, including the Voluntary Youth Association, Scouts, and Buddhist and Catholic youth groups. One student group brought together fifty different organizations to raise funds and collect material donations. The campaign lasted a little over three months, during which time about eight hundred students traveled to the affected areas and hundreds of others participated in fundraising events in their communities.[46] Those who went to the central region distributed food and aid, addressed health and sanitation issues, rebuilt roads and other infrastructure, filled in swamps, and even provided entertainment.[47] The volunteers also helped bury the bodies of those killed in the flood. As discussed in chapter 6, tending to the dead has important implications in Vietnamese society. It is widely believed that unless proper funeral rites were carried out, spirits cannot rest peacefully and would haunt their families and the locality where the deaths took place. Accordingly, the work of these young volunteers had a deep spiritual, emotional, and psychological impact on the local society.

Despite encountering some problems because of the scale of the project and the difficulty of coordinating so many organizations and levels of government, the students gained experience in relief work and confidence in their ability to contribute to society.[48] After the flood relief campaign was over, some youth leaders discussed how to encourage more students to participate in social service.[49] Years later, many still recalled their experience with fondness and described this collective action as the beginning of youth volunteerism in South Vietnam.[50] Their enthusiasm about their involvement in the flood relief effort prepared them for later calls to action, including the aftermath of the Tet offensive (1968) and the Easter offensive (1972), both of which created hundreds of thousands of refugees and massive numbers of casualties.

The 1964 flood relief experience also led to the founding of the Vietnam National Youth Voluntary Service (NYVS; Đoàn Thanh Niên Chí Nguyệt Việt Nam). During the flood relief campaign, Vietnamese youths worked closely with the International Voluntary Service (IVS), which in turn helped them establish this new service organization. Not surprisingly, the NYVS modeled itself on the IVS, and like its international counterpart, the NYVS trained youths to carry out development work in rural areas, sending them out in the field for a period of one year. The goals were to raise villagers' standard of living and to help young

**FIGURE 5.2**   Student volunteers making concrete blocks to build a dormitory for war orphans at the Buddhist Institute of Social Affairs in Saigon, no date. VA000026, Douglas Pike Photograph Collection, Vietnam Center and Sam Johnson Vietnam Archive, Texas Tech University.

people understand village life, which was considered the basis of national culture. Participants were paid a stipend of US$25 a month (equal to the amount received by New Life Development Project volunteers). In its early years, the NYVS received more applicants than it could accept. In 1965, for example, three hundred people applied but only sixty-five were accepted.[51] Like other youth programs, however, the NYVS saw its pool of applicants shrink after the 1968 general mobilization law took effect.

The second important event that bolstered youth participation was the summer youth program in 1965. The impetus for this project came from officials working for US government agencies and their affiliates. Edward Britton, a RAND consultant, and Charles Sweet, an IVS volunteer and undercover CIA operative, approached prominent Vietnamese youth leaders and offered to support any community projects they wished to pursue. Subsequently, thirty students developed the idea for the summer youth program.[52] One of its leaders was Đỗ Ngọc Yến, a twenty-three-year-old student with extensive involvement with the Scouts.[53] The project was supported by USAID, RAND, and IVS, and it attracted a cross section of participants, including Buddhist and Catholic students. To recruit participants, the program tapped into preexisting organizations, such as the Girl and Boy Scouts, religious groups, and university unions. In total, close to eight thousand young people from twenty-six provinces participated in the summer program, which consisted of short-term work projects of about two weeks' duration or longer term-projects lasting one to two months. These projects ranged from building roads, schools, and refugee housing to providing musical entertainment and medical care throughout the countryside.[54]

Instrumental to the success of the summer youth program was Charles Sweet, who secured 30 million dong from USAID for this program (equivalent to US$2 million at 2020 rates).[55] Sweet's assignment when he came to Vietnam in 1964 was to work with students as both an IVS volunteer and a CIA operative.[56] He participated in the 1964 flood relief and the New Life Development Project. In a letter to his family, Sweet wrote that USOM officials believed students were "key to the war effort" and that the US could "win the war in the next five months if 'those students' are under control."[57] Consequently, when he arrived in Saigon, Sweet made contact with SSU student leaders and provided them with equipment and furniture for their headquarters. He also enrolled in Vạn Hạnh University to learn about Buddhism and to befriend Buddhist students. Sweet's main project, however, was the summer youth program, on which US officials placed a great deal of hope. Sweet wrote to his family about the "tremendous pressure from Washington to produce" results, noting that he had to "send a cable every week giving a progress analysis."[58]

Did Vietnamese students question how Sweet—a young volunteer fresh out of college himself—could have made such important connections and could have mobilized such a large sum of money? According to Karen Paget's 2006 interview with Sweet, many "Vietnamese students eagerly accepted these funds, said Sweet; they knew their source but rarely discussed it."[59] As previous chapters have shown, the United States funneled substantial aid into the RVN. In addition to the US government, American and international NGOs provided a significant amount of financial, material, and personnel support to the RVN. The American Council of Voluntary Agencies estimated that the total budget of thirty-one organizations surveyed was approximately US$12.6 million in 1970, not including material aid.[60] Not surprisingly, some of this aid went to youth organizations. The Asia Foundation provided financial support to the Voluntary Youth Association's main chapter in Saigon. The Saigon group, in turn, supported the creation of affiliates in other cities. The Đà Lạt chapter received funding from the association, as well as support from the IVS. According to the chapter's founder, the IVS offered to fly him to and from Saigon to take care of club business and attend meetings.[61]

For the United States, funding youth activities (as well as other voluntary and charitable organizations) was essential to the larger objective of winning over the South Vietnamese population. From the US perspective, development and relief work provided a way to influence South Vietnamese youths for the purpose of neutralizing their opposition to and mobilizing support for the war. As the US embassy in Saigon reported in 1966, USAID and IVS had established important personal links with youth and student leaders in Saigon and had been successful in promoting youth participation in civic action programs. Both agencies were providing "extensive commodity support" to these "constructive activities" to make youth less distrustful of the United States and less easily influenced by radicals.[62] In this context, the IVS was critical to the US nation-building endeavor in the RVN, for it forged ties with Vietnamese youth through a supposed NGO. Sweet's double role was useful because it allowed the US government to extend its influence without provoking distrust. However, by 1967, the IVS's image as an independent, nonpartisan organization was effectively destroyed when several of its leaders publicly alleged that the IVS was carrying out the US government's war agenda. Don Luce, head of the IVS in Vietnam, along with three other program and regional leaders, resigned in protest. Their resignation letter caused waves when it was published in the *New York Times*.[63]

For many Vietnamese youth leaders, dependence on foreign support and affiliation with the United States were difficult issues.[64] This explains why some student leaders criticized the summer youth program and refused to participate.[65] The Vietnamese press was also critical of the program, disparaging participants for allowing the United States "to buy them off."[66] Fear of this type of criticism led many organizations to secure funds from local communities rather than foreign donors. One member of the Voluntary Youth Association in Đà Lạt stated that she and other members worked hard to make the association financially independent so it did not have to rely on US aid.[67] Their reluctance to be affiliated with the United States reflected the position of their mentor and rector of Đà Lạt University, Father Nguyễn Văn Lập. He was reportedly wary of US intervention and had once refused US aid for expansion of the university.[68] Beyond ideology or national pride, there were real dangers with being linked to the US government. Communists sometimes threatened or even assassinated people they perceived as collaborators or supporters of US-led organizations and projects. Unfortunately, this was the case for volunteers with the New Life Development Project and probably the Buddhist School of Youth for Social Service as well (see chapter 4).

Distrust of the United States and anti-American sentiments were prevalent among Vietnamese youths. Even among noncommunist youths, this attitude was widespread. An article in *Vietnamese Bell* (*Chuông Việt*) exemplifies this attitude.[69] The author blamed the US presence in Vietnam for all the negative changes that had occurred in Saigon during her years away while studying abroad. She held the Americans responsible for inflation, traffic jams, and electrical outages; she even blamed the Americans for how difficult it was to flag down a taxi, because the drivers preferred the high-tipping American customers. Author Nguyễn Ngọc Ngạn notes in his memoir that anti-American attitudes were rampant and ubiquitous among Vietnamese university students.[70]

In addition to their reluctance to be associated with the United States, young people shied away from participating in social service because of the high level of mismanagement and corruption. An article in the Huế University Student Union's newspaper discussed these problems in detail, claiming the 1964 flood relief campaign in central Vietnam had been marred by incompetence and malfeasance.[71] The author raised questions about missing material aid and funds and criticized the officious attitudes of civil servants sent to organize the relief effort.

Despite issues related to corruption and US influence, relief work remained a popular form of voluntary activity and associational life. Like adults, Vietnamese youths participated in community and relief work for a variety of reasons. In many cases, altruism was probably a motivation, but other, more selfish reasons no doubt played a role as well. The altruistic and the selfish are not mutually exclusive; they can and do coexist. Undoubtedly, many Vietnamese youths recognized that social capital could be accrued through participation in voluntary associations and volunteer work. Voluntary associations in the RVN were often founded and led by prominent members of society, so joining such an organization could provide a young person with the right connections to secure entrance to a prestigious school, win a scholarship, or gain employment. Not everyone was motivated by self-interest, but associational life provided the opportunity to gain social capital, which could lead to tangible economic benefits. This aspect of associational life underscores Pierre Bourdieu's and other scholars' suggestion that civil society and its associated social capital can reproduce socioeconomic inequality rather than challenge it.[72]

Another reason for participating—one mentioned by several people I interviewed—was the distraction and fun offered by associational life. Community work projects provided young people a chance to socialize, escape strict parental supervision, enjoy some entertainment, and experience adventure.[73] When work projects took place outside of the city, recreational activities and excursions were often part of the agenda. It is no wonder that decades later, participants still remembered their voluntary work with fondness. Interviewees recalled the fun they had organizing charitable events, such as musical and theatrical performances. One woman recalled with affection her role as master of ceremonies for many benefit shows. Even when the work was difficult, participants found it bearable because they shared the experience with others. Years later, many participants still kept in touch with one another. For example, former members of the Đà Lạt branch of the Voluntary Youth Association still maintained close ties, even though many were living abroad.[74]

Finally, relief and civic activities attracted many youths because this was a safer arena of public engagement than involvement in politics. As discussed in the next section, participating in political activism could land young people in jail or make them targets of communist violence. As a USIA report commented, being an activist in South Vietnam's polarized and divisive society required "considerable courage."[75]

# Students' Political Activism

The history of Vietnamese students' political activism extends back to the French colonial period. High school and university students had their first encounter with nationalist politics in 1926, when they defied the colonial state and skipped school to attend the funeral of nationalist leader Phan Chu Trinh.[76] During World War II, many youths joined the Viet Minh or other nationalist organizations, and during the First Indochina War, they joined the war effort.

In the RVN, students made their debut on the political stage in the spring of 1963 during the Buddhist protest movement (see chapter 1). Buddhist students, particularly members of the Association of Buddhist University Students in Huế and Saigon, played a critical role in the protest.[77] Similarly, the Buddhist Family Association and its extensive network of members provided mobilization, logistical, and intelligence support.[78] Non-Buddhists also joined because, by 1963, anti-Diệm sentiment had reached a critical mass. Many South Vietnamese were unhappy with the regime's repression, nepotism, and autocracy. Student groups had been infiltrated by police informers, and students' elections were "supervised." Young People were pressured to join the government's Republican Youth, controlled by the president's brother and adviser Ngô Đình Nhu.[79]

As the anti-Diệm movement expanded, prominent politicians and public figures added their voices to the protest. On August 21, 1963, foreign minister Vũ Văn Mẫu resigned from his post and shaved his head to show his solidarity with the Buddhist clergy.[80] His resignation and symbolic gesture, coupled with his founding of the group Intellectuals against Dictatorship (Trí Thức Chống Độc Tài), inspired students to organize their own protests. Students at the Phú Thọ

Institute of Technology staged a strike on the afternoon of August 21. At Saigon University, the dean of medicine was arrested when he resigned to protest the mistreatment of Buddhist demonstrators. Responding to this arrest, students from the Faculty of Medicine formed the Inter-Faculty Student Steering Committee on August 23.[81] The committee called on the government to respect and protect religious freedom, release activists from jail, end the repression of Buddhists, and allow freedom of speech.[82]

In the months following its founding, the Inter-Faculty Steering Committee, in conjunction with Buddhist activists, organized strikes and protests. On August 25 the committee led a protest near Bến Thành market in Saigon, where approximately three hundred students participated. The city was under martial law, but this did not deter them. The police reacted brutally, shooting into the crowd of protesters. Some students were injured, and about two hundred were arrested.[83] By late August, fourteen hundred students had been arrested, and another twenty-four hundred were imprisoned in early September.[84] Not surprisingly, shortly after this event, Diệm was overthrown in a coup on November 1. It was clear that the joint student and Buddhist opposition played a significant part in the erosion of Diệm's reputation and credibility.

After the November 1963 coup, political control was in the hands of General Dương Văn Minh, chairman of the Military Revolutionary Council, and the other eleven generals who had taken part in the coup. In the aftermath, there was youthful enthusiasm among the student activists who had played a role in displacing Diệm; no doubt, their confidence was bolstered by their ability to instigate political change. In the writings from this period, there was a tone of excitement and hope. Student groups continued their political agitation, and some focused on rooting out Diệm's supporters or former members of Ngô Đình Nhu's Cần Lao Party. Students from the Science Faculty of Saigon University boycotted their classes to protest against the administrators they accused of being sycophants of Diệm.[85] Similarly, twenty-five hundred students at Nguyễn Văn Khuê high school staged a demonstration to demand that the school director resign because of his alleged close ties with Diệm's government. The director and another despised administrator resigned the same day.[86]

Although the new military leaders found the students' denunciation of former Diệm supporters helpful during their initial period of consolidation, they soon became the target of student protests themselves. The new prime minister, General Nguyễn Khánh, was the first of many leaders to feel the full force of the students' opposition. In August 1964, in the wake of the Tonkin Gulf incident and the subsequent retaliatory air strikes by the US, Khánh provoked mass demonstrations with his declaration of martial law on August 8 and the introduction of a new constitution on August 17. Referred to as the Vũng Tàu Charter, the new constitution would have given Khánh more power. Leading the protests against Khánh were student and Buddhist activists who believed Khánh was laying the groundwork for a dictatorship.[87] The intense protests caused him to back away from the charter. According to a CIA report, the "violent student demonstrations... were instrumental in forcing Prime Minister Khánh out of office in August 1964."[88]

Shortly thereafter, students faced more troubling developments. In March 1965 the US deployed combat troops to South Vietnam and began a sustained bombing campaign against the DRV. Many student groups called for an end to the bombing and voiced concerns about the growing US presence in the RVN. Among the most vocal antiwar groups was the SSU. From 1966 onward, the presidency of the SSU was held by a succession of youths who were secretly working with the NLF, the People's Revolutionary Party (PRP), or both.[89] Prior to this time, SSU leaders such as Lê Hữu Bội and Nguyễn Trọng Nho had not been affiliated with communists or the Left. Both of them had played leading roles in the anti-Diệm protest movement and had advocated for a liberal democratic political system. Lê Hữu Bội would later be assassinated by the communists during the 1968 Tet offensive, while Nguyễn Trọng Nho would continue his political activism as an elected representative in the Lower House for two terms (1967–1975).

The new slate of SSU leaders with communist connections included Hồ Hữu Nhựt (president of SSU in 1966–1967), Nguyễn Đăng Trừng (1967–1968), Nguyễn Văn Quỳ (1968–1969), and Huỳnh Tấn Mẫm (1969–1970).[90] The president of the Saigon High School Student Union, Lê Văn Nuôi (1970–1971), was also a secret member of the Revolutionary Youth Union, the youth wing of the PRP.[91] Similarly, student leaders with ties to various communist-controlled organizations took over the student unions at Huế and Vạn Hạnh Universities.[92]

Considering their political engagement and radical tendency, it is remarkable that so many major university student unions were not officially registered with the government. The SSU was operating under the 1955 registration of the National Student Union, so technically, it was operating illegally. The SSU finally became official in May 1970.[93] According to RAND research consultant John Donnell, before the Tet offensive, RVN authorities appeared to be lenient when it came to student groups' registration.[94] They might have been reluctant to act against youth groups and risk appearing repressive. More importantly, the authorities likely wanted to avoid provoking massive student protests. They also apparently lacked the capacity to monitor public and associated activities, whether conducted by youths or adults.

Even though student unions did not adhere to the registration requirement of Decree 10 of 1950, they operated openly, and some even received government funding. In 1964 the SSU received 200,000 dong for its activities, and in 1966 it received 100,000 dong for its annual general meeting. In 1967 SSU president Hồ

Hữu Nhựt requested 500,000 dong to organize the upcoming executive elections and to reestablish a national student association.[95]

Despite being lenient about registration, RVN officials were not oblivious to the political potency of student unions. Officials were certainly worried about the many political forces competing to influence youth groups. These included not only the communist NLF but also other oppositional political parties. In the summer of 1964 interior minister Tôn Thất Đính suspected that Faculty of Letters students were being influenced by the Vietnamese Nationalist Party and the Buddhist hierarchy. Students of the Science Faculty, in contrast, were supposedly close to the communists and were being manipulated by them.[96] Because of their suspicions, RVN authorities kept a close eye on student activities and politics. Government officials routinely watched and reported on student elections, communiqués, and protests, as well as academic and social events.[97] Student publications were also monitored. The SSU's *Sinh Viên* (University Students) was read regularly by US and RVN officials to stay informed of student views and activities.[98]

By the mid-1960s, as some student unions came under the leadership of individuals with communist affiliations, student groups became more vocal and adopted antiwar and anti-American positions. University student unions allied with other communist and noncommunist organizations that were fighting for social justice and peace, such as the NLF-affiliated Committee for the People's Right to Live, an antipoverty group. They also participated in Father Chân Tín's Committee for Prison Reform (see chapter 7).[99] Student union representatives were often present at demonstrations for a variety of social justice causes. They also organized their own protest activities, including school strikes, all-night rallies (*đêm không ngủ*), "sing for the people" concerts (*hát cho đồng bào*), and street demonstrations.

In addition to these public activities, students used their publications to voice their concerns. Faculty-specific publications, such as the pharmacy students' *Ý Hướng*, existed alongside student union periodicals. The student unions of Saigon, Huế, and Vạn Hạnh each had its own publication—all of them entitled *Sinh Viên*—that contained articles on current political and social issues, along with poetry and fiction.[100] David Marr correctly assessed that *Sinh Viên Huế* was the most vocal and direct, publishing criticisms of the government and the war.[101] The periodical's editors did not mince words when it came to criticizing national leaders. In an article appearing on December 17, 1964, the writer condemned the Trần Văn Hương government's use of force against students who were protesting the expansion of the draft. The article derided the government's depiction of the protest as instigated by communists. The author called the prime minister immature, dictatorial, and unfit to lead a democratic country. The January 5 issue reported that the Huế Student Association had issued a resolution calling for the National Assembly to be dismissed and for Hương to step down, since the National Assembly had become merely a tool for him.[102]

Politically moderate student publications also carried critical discussions of the war and politics. The student population at Catholic Đà Lạt University, known for its moderate politics, also offered critiques of the government's conduct of the war, US involvement, and official corruption in the journal *University Student Forum* (*Diễn Đàn Sinh Viên*). For example, an article published in 1966 suggested that the war was a political as well as a military conflict and that the government must work to gain the trust and support of all the people.[103] Another article criticized the government's ineffective policies and economic mismanagement.[104] An article in a politically moderate journal published by Catholic students studying in the United States called on the South Vietnamese government to take charge of the war and limit US intervention. The author stated that the war could not be won with the use of US military force and that US bombing of the DRV would only alienate the South Vietnamese population.[105]

In addition to politically moderate groups, anticommunist groups also participated in the public. One example was the Student Confederation for Freedom and Democracy (Tổng Liên Đoàn Sinh Viên Học Sinh Tự Do Dân Chủ,) a small group of militant anticommunist students. Many of these students were from Catholic families that had left North Vietnam in 1954. This group, with support from prominent anticommunist Catholic priests, was the backbone of the May 1965 agitation against Prime Minister Phan Huy Quát. The protesters were incensed at Quát's suggestion to open talks with the NLF. They were also unhappy with what they saw as his pro-Buddhist bias.[106] Their demonstrations and lobbying efforts no doubt played a role in Quát's resignation.[107] Another group, the National Anti-Communism Student Corps (Ngũ Sinh Viên Quốc Gia Chống Cộng), was active in the mid-1960s, providing students with an alternative to left-leaning associations. Similarly, the National Organization of University Students Who Love Freedom (Tập Thể Sinh Viên Quốc Gia Yêu Tự Do) was created mostly by law students who aimed to expose and denounce the communist infiltration of student groups.[108] This goal also motivated an ad hoc committee to form in 1968, composed mainly of students in the architecture and electrical studies programs. These students lobbied the government to remove Trần Thị Ngọc Hảo from the SSU leadership. The former SSU president, who had just been outed as a communist agent, had picked Trần Thị Ngọc Hảo as his successor, so these students did not recognize the legitimacy of her appointment.[109]

There was deep tension between the student groups holding these two extreme views, and violence sometimes erupted. The communist-affiliated students accused their opponents of being stooges for the government and the US and of accepting bribes from the authorities.[110] Although I have found no evidence of students accepting bribes, there are indications that the US and South Vietnamese authorities interfered with student affairs and elections. In March 1965 Charles Sweet hinted in a letter to his family that he had done just that: "One of the people who was runnin[g] for office was a leader of the peace movement and we were hoping he would be defeated—for some reason he was."[111] In May, Sweet confided to his family that communist student leaders had taken control of the summer youth program in Nha Trang. However, with "strong American guidance, these leaders were ousted." Sweet explained that US interference in this case had damaged the relationship with the provincial government, and he was working to repair it.[112] The Left accused the government of infiltrating demonstrations with undercover agents who instigated violence, giving the police reason to arrest the protesters.[113] The Left could also point to the illegal detention and torture of students; this escalated after the Tet offensive, when RVN officials discovered the identities of many NLF and communist student agents.

Those on the right accused procommunist students of intimidating and terrorizing students who opposed them. Lê Văn Nuôi, a communist member and president of the High School Student Union, related two examples of communist intimidation.[114] In April 1970 a group of procommunist students armed with weapons disrupted the meeting of a progovernment student organization. Sufficiently frightened, the progovernment students broke up their meeting and fled. In July of the same year, student Nguyễn Tiến Thành wrote several newspaper articles condemning the dominance of communist leaders in the High School Student Union. Lê Văn Nuôi reported this student to his superior, and a directive was issued that the student should be shot in the foot to cripple him. Before this order was carried out, Nguyễn Tiến Thành's father apologized and made his son retract his criticisms.

More alarming was the shooting of two students at a student-organized concert featuring Trịnh Công Sơn and Khánh Ly on December 20, 1967. A special armed task force of the Youth Revolutionary Union broke into the concert venue, and two members took over the stage to announce the seventh anniversary of the founding of the NLF. When Ngô Vương Toại, one of the student organizers and a member of the National Anti-Communism Student Corps, tried to regain control of the stage, he and another student were shot; they both survived.[115] Exactly a year later, the former leader of the National Anti-Communism Student Corps, Bùi Hồng Sỹ, was wounded when two assailants on motorcycles shot him in the neck.[116] Finally, Lê Khác Sinh Nhật was shot to death on June 28, 1971. The assassination occurred eight days after Nhật and Lý Bửu Lâm, both political moderates, had defeated the communist-affiliated candidates for the SSU leadership.[117]

Clearly, by the late 1960s, student politics was characterized by polarization, violence, and extremism. Students supporting the NLF-communists were willing to resort to violence, while those on the right were willing to work with the state and its US ally to dislodge their opponents from leadership roles, sometimes through coercive methods. However, student support of the government was prevalent beyond the militant anticommunist student groups and leaders. Despite the many street protests and scathing editorials, there was general support for the government. The student response to the 1968 Tet offensive supports this proposition. For many urban students, the offensive—which took US and RVN forces by surprise and displaced more than half a million people—was probably their first direct encounter with the violence of war. In this national crisis, student leaders called off protests and cooperated with authorities to restore order and help with relief efforts.[118] In the immediate aftermath, male students underwent basic military training and carried out guard duty in the city, while female students learned basic first aid and worked as support staff in hospitals and clinics.[119] Many helped build refugee shelters, coordinate the distribution of aid, and teach literacy classes. Antiwar activist and manager of the Buddhist School of Youth for Social Service, Cao Ngọc Phương, participated in a Red Cross–led project to collect corpses from the streets of Saigon and Chợ Lớn.[120] John Donnell notes that the offensive "brought . . . vigorous cooperation between the GVN [government of South Vietnam] and private associations."[121] Communist-affiliated students organized their own relief efforts in the aftermath of the Tet offensive. However, according to these participants, their main goal was to provide a safe haven and cover for communist cadres operating in the towns and cities.[122]

Contrary to the hopes of the Lao Động Party, youths and students (along with the adult population) cooperated with the government and did not take advantage of the chaos to organize a mass insurrection to overthrow the South Vietnamese government.[123] The main architect of the Tet offensive, Lê Duẩn, believed that, if given the opportunity, the people of South Vietnam would overthrow the government.[124] Despite some student groups' strong and vocal opposition to certain government policies, students rallied behind the government rather than against it. This suggests that although some student leaders were affiliated with the communists, the majority of the students were not. And as much as they found the authorities deficient, they were not willing to overthrow the government.

Some writers have suggested that many students joined the communist side during the Tet offensive. For example, Gareth Porter reported that Hồ Hữu Nhựt and six other students joined the communists in the aftermath of the offensive.[125] However, Nhựt had already been working with communist-affiliated organizations since at least 1966, when he became SSU president. During the offensive, many undercover students and cadres joined in the operation, and in doing so, they lost their cover. Consequently, they had to take refuge at one of the communist bases. SSU president and law student Nguyễn Đang Trừng was one of those students who had to leave Saigon. Trừng had been affiliated with communists groups before 1968, but during the offensive he openly joined the communist-sponsored Alliance of National, Democratic, and Peace Forces, revealing his affiliation.[126] Similarly, Lê Quang Lộc, a communist undercover operative assigned to work with students in the Faculty of Letters in 1966, had to flee. Having discovered their communist connections, the South Vietnamese government issued arrest warrants for both Trừng and Lộc.

The general student population's cooperation with the government is significant because it underscores the fact that Vietnamese youths harbored myriad political opinions and political identities. Their political diversity defied the narrow confines imposed by Cold War politics, which equated opposition to the war, US intervention, and other government policies with support for communism. This prevalent Cold War attitude, and the intense polarization of politics, made it easy for the authorities and US officials to dismiss antiwar protesters as agents or pawns of the communists. However, as intelligence reports and contemporaneous political analyses suggest, although the majority of students were tired of the war, and many were against the war, they did not see communism as a viable alternative.[127] Similarly, John Graham, adviser to the US Civil Operations Revolutionary Development Support (CORDS), observed that antiwar, anti-American sentiments pervaded the general student population not because students supported communism but because they were tired of war.[128]

Communist student leaders confirmed that communist-affiliated students were few, even during the period of intense antiwar protest.[129] According to Huỳnh Tấn Mẫm, SSU president in 1969–1970, a large number of communist members in these organizations was not necessary, as their main functions were to provide support for the students' activities and to forge connections with other groups, rather than direct activities themselves. This point was reiterated by other student leaders, such as Lê Văn Nuôi, president of the High School Student Union.[130] One US government report estimated that there were about five hundred student agents in the Saigon–Chợ Lớn area before the Tet offensive.[131] If this figure is correct, this accounted for only about 1.4 percent of university students in Saigon.[132] The percentage would be even lower if secondary students were factored into the calculation, since communist recruitment was just as vigorous, if not more so, at the high school level. After 1968, owing to a combination of casualties, arrests, and compromised covers, the number of agents decreased to 150 in 1971 and 50 in 1972.[133]

After the crisis of the Tet offensive was over, the students' truce with the government ended. Politicized student groups quickly returned to their oppositional stance, protesting the war's escalation, the lack of freedom, and government corruption.[134] Over the next two years, students' political activism continued to increase and reached a peak in 1970 in terms of intensity and organization. Not surprisingly, students were especially troubled by the government's general mobilization law, which extended the draft age and made the duration of military service indefinite. They were also unhappy about the new law mandating military training for male high school students. Students throughout the country took to the streets to protest. In Saigon, Huế, Đà Lạt, and Cần Thơ, they stormed military training offices and burned documents and files. In Huế, students broke into the military training office and destroyed equipment, harassed office staff, and incinerated 60 percent of the documents.[135]

Parents and educators were also concerned about the military training requirement. They complained that the training, which was supposed to take place during the academic year, would be too disruptive and could affect students' performance on exams. With complaints from adults and street protests by students, the government was forced to modify the military training program in 1971. It was moved to the summer, when male students were required to participate in five weeks of training.[136]

The South Vietnamese students' antiwar movement received support from their international peers. On July 11, 1970, Vietnamese student protesters in Saigon were joined by an international group of peace activists who were on a study mission in Vietnam. Included in this group were US student leaders Charles Palmer, Sam Brown, and Timothy Butz. As the Americans marched with several hundred students carrying a three-foot coffin to symbolize the war's deathly impact, the police stopped them near the US embassy and fired tear gas into the crowd. About thirty Vietnamese students and three Americans were arrested.[137]

In this case, the student protesters were released later the same day, owing to the US peace delegation's pressure. Others were not released so quickly. Student leader Huỳnh Tấn Mẫm was in and out of jail eleven times. He was recruited into a secret revolutionary cell at age fifteen and was inducted into the PRP in 1966 at age twenty-three.[138] Despite his connection with the party, Mẫm also had supporters among RVN leaders, such as Vice President Kỳ and Buddhist politician General Dương Văn Minh.[139] In the 1971 presidential election, both Kỳ and Minh had been barred from running (see chapter 7), so they were keen to support radical students who were protesting Nguyễn Văn Thiệu's one-man election. In fact, Kỳ provided Mẫm and the SSU with office space in the vice president's official residence because SSU headquarters had been confiscated after the Tet offensive. Kỳ also gave student protesters thousands of MK3 grenades, which they used to blow up mock ballot boxes during the presidential election campaign.[140] Such was the politics of South Vietnam: one of the most prominent and effective undercover communist student leaders had the support of top politicians and government leaders. With their help, Mắm was able to elude arrest or, when he was arrested, win his release. As chapter 7 shows, members of civil society fought hard to publicize his detention without trial. Eventually, however, his activities landed him back in jail, where he was tortured brutally. Mắm remained in prison from 1973 until the war ended in 1975.

This chapter shows that the RVN government, foreign powers, and political groups saw young people as an important constituency that they vied to influence. Youth organizations were subjected to intervention, infiltration, and intimidation from these powerful groups. Despite the risks in both arenas of public life, students participated in politics and social service. Thousands took part in demonstrations and school strikes, and thousands more cooperated in relief activities and joined social service organizations. Youths participated in civil society for a variety of reasons— for self-interest, for the collective good, and for some combination of both. Whatever the reason, students had choices because of the competitive nature of South Vietnam's civil society. Students could join antiwar or progovernment groups. Though the highly contested public sphere could be challenging to navigate, it also afforded some leeway for students, particularly those with counterhegemonic stances. The state could not easily silence or imprison students, who could mobilize domestic and foreign political groups for support. Youths were keenly aware of the competing forces at work, and some, such as Huỳnh Tấn Mắm, managed to leverage the competing forces to their benefit.

# SÓNG THẦN NEWSPAPER AND THE "HIGHWAY OF HORROR" PROJECT

On July 1, 1972, during the Easter offensive, Vietnamese journalists Ngy Thanh and Đoàn Kế Tường used a heavily damaged railway bridge to cross the Bến Đá River, which bisects Highway 1 between the cities of Quảng Trị and Huế. What met them on the other side was a scene of carnage: hundreds of bodies of civilian and military personnel littered the highway, the result of an attack two months earlier. Their article and Ngy Thanh's photographs were published in the daily newspaper *Sóng Thần* (Tsunami), and this ten-kilometer stretch of road was christened the "Highway of Horror" (Đại Lộ Kinh Hoàng).[1]

Based on a variety of sources—newspapers, published personal accounts, and interviews—this chapter examines the attack along Highway 1 in late April and early May 1972 and its aftermath. I focus on *Sóng Thần*'s humanitarian endeavor to recover and bury the victims. When the newspaper's staff learned about the large number of bodies along the highway, they mobilized readers to provide proper burials for the victims. As a grassroots undertaking relying on volunteers, this project provides useful insights into South Vietnam's civil society. Like the voluntary work of many organizations already examined in this book, *Sóng Thần*'s activities suggest that residents of South Vietnam were engaged in social and civic life. Moreover, despite the many years of war, the South Vietnamese people did not resign themselves to victimhood. Instead, they led, organized, and participated in humanitarian activities such as *Sóng Thần*'s burial project.

In addition to considering people's public activities, this chapter explores an often overlooked spiritual and psychological impact of the war on Vietnamese society. *Sóng Thần*'s burial project was important to the community on many levels. Giving the massacred victims a proper burial not only dignified the dead but also provided emotional, psychological, and spiritual comfort to the families and the local community. In Vietnam, it is widely believed that customary funeral rites ensure the spiritual well-being of those who have passed away.

Works by anthropologists have highlighted the profound trauma caused by the Vietnam War's violence and the massive number of deaths.[2] As in many other societies, the Vietnamese people attach great significance to proper funeral and commemorative rituals. One predominant belief is that the souls of the departed are condemned to wander without rest if proper mortuary and commemorative rites are not conducted. These restless souls become angry ghosts that haunt their families and the communities where they died. This is an especially troubling prospect for those killed in brutal and violent ways, because they are forced to relive their painful deaths and endure the injustice of their fates in perpetuity.[3] Writing about the villages of Mỹ Lai and Hà Mỹ, where civilians were massacred by US and Republic of Korea troops, respectively, Heonik Kwon demonstrates that long after these massacres, the communities continued to suffer because of their inability to provide the proper burial rituals.[4] Similarly, Mai Lan Gustafsson suggests that the war continues to haunt Vietnamese society in a literal sense. Because of the war's violent nature and the tropical environment, many corpses could not be recovered, making it difficult if not impossible to carry out the prescribed mortuary rituals.[5] *Sóng Thần*'s endeavor to collect, identify, and bury those who died along the highway was profoundly important for both the victims' families and the surrounding communities.

## The Quảng Trị Killing

In the spring of 1972 the DRV mounted a major campaign commonly referred to as the Easter offensive. Even though there were clear signs that the DRV was planning a major operation, the RVN and its US ally were surprised by the magnitude of the offensive and by the DRV's decision to attack across the demilitarized zone.[6] The first of three assaults took place along the northern border of Quảng Trị province. On March 30 three infantry divisions of the PAVN (North Vietnam's army) crossed into Quảng Trị and, in just two days of fighting, took over twelve military bases.[7] In subsequent days, PAVN troops attacked Kon Tum province in the Central Highlands and the provinces of Bình Long and Kiến Tường.

The Easter offensive resulted in many casualties for both sides. The PAVN suffered roughly 100,000 casualties, while the ARVN reported approximately 30,000 killed, 78,000 wounded, and 14,000 missing in action.[8] Journalist Arnold Isaacs captured the magnitude of this violence when he reported that the United States and RVN fired 25,000 artillery rounds and carried out as many as forty B-52 raids daily in an effort to retake Quảng Trị city.[9] Because of these US-RVN attacks and earlier PAVN shelling, nearly every building in Quảng Trị city was leveled.

Despite the massive destruction, there have been no studies of the Easter offensive's impact on civilians. Only a handful of authors have mentioned the killing along the highway.[10] Based on disparate contemporary and postwar reports, publications, and personal accounts, it is clear that at various times from April 28 to May 1, the PAVN shot into columns of civilians and soldiers moving southward from Quảng Trị city.

Vietnam's state-sanctioned historical narrative acknowledges the incident but contends that PAVN troops were shooting only at retreating ARVN soldiers. According to Vietnam's Military History Institute, the event unfolded as follows:

> The [PAVN] 324th Infantry Division attacked strong points in the rear of the enemy's defensive network, cutting Route 1 south of Quang Tri city. Surrounded and isolated, the enemy troops in La Vang-Quang Tri broke and ran. Our troops clung to and pursued them. Accurate fire from our long-range artillery positions created added terror among the enemy troops. . . . Route 1 from Quang Tri to northern Thua Thien province became a "highway of death" for the enemy.[11]

The event is described in a similar manner in a *People's Army* newspaper article commemorating the fortieth anniversary of the offensive. The author, Major General Lê Mã Lương (former director of Vietnam's Museum of Military History), states that on May 1, as the PAVN was poised to take Quảng Trị city, the PAVN's 66th Infantry Regiment of the 304th Division "blockaded and attacked the puppet [RVN] troops at La Vang, while at the same time the field artillery fired furiously into the column of retreating puppet troops, causing them to abandon their vehicles and artilleries and flee in a chaotic manner."[12]

Currently, the government of Vietnam still maintains that the war was predominantly one of resistance against US imperialism, waged for the reunification of Vietnam and the liberation of the RVN. As such, in the official historiography, the RVN is portrayed as illegitimate and without agency. Publications on the Easter offensive therefore focus on the military success and heroism of the communist forces and on the destructive and relentless US air strikes. Accordingly, Quảng Trị was considered "liberated" on May 2, 1972, the day the PAVN took control of the province.[13] It follows that the attack along Highway 1 has been framed as a legitimate assault on retreating enemy troops, without any reference to the presence of civilians.

In contrast, the RVN government (before it was defeated in 1975) claimed that the PAVN intentionally targeted civilians in the attack on Highway 1.[14] Bolstering the RVN's assertion was the confession of Private Lê Xuân Thủy, who was serving as a radio operator for the PAVN's 4th Battalion, 324th Division, when he defected on July 31, 1972.[15] At an RVN government-organized press conference on September 8, Thủy revealed that his unit had been ordered to "maintain an ambush position along Route 1" for six days to allow other PAVN troops to capture Quảng Trị city.[16] His commander had instructed the unit to shoot into the column of people fleeing Quảng Trị, even though it was clear that many civilians were present. The troops were told that the refugees were the enemy because they were opting to leave. The soldiers were commanded to shoot at all vehicles, including civilian cars, buses, and bicycles. According to Thủy, this event shook his faith in the DRV and led to his defection. The testimony of one defector in state custody does not, by itself, provide sufficient proof. His assertion that the PAVN fired on civilians, however, corresponds with other contemporary reports and eyewitness accounts. Many observers reported that the civilian presence on the road was clearly discernible during the attack.

The event in question unfolded throughout the last days of April as the PAVN closed in on Quảng Trị city, causing many ARVN troops to flee south on Highway 1. In addition to the southbound troops, other ARVN troops were moving north on a mission to clear the road for retreat and to supply posts still under ARVN control.[17] Many eyewitnesses maintained that a considerable number of civilians were mixed in with this military traffic. Taking into account that the population of Quảng Trị city—around twenty thousand—was panicked by the impending loss of their city and the "rampant" rumors that the PAVN "was about to unleash a massive artillery attack," it is not surprising that a large number of civilians were on the highway.[18] Colonel Gerald Turley, senior adviser for the 3rd ARVN Division in charge of defense of the demilitarized zone, estimated that by April 30, only eight thousand to ten thousand people remained in the city, and more would leave over the next two days.[19]

Both American and Vietnamese newspapers consistently reported that the PAVN fired on the column of civilians and ARVN soldiers on the highway. Fox Butterfield of the New York Times, for example, reported that "South Vietnamese troops and refugees fleeing south toward Hue came under small-arms fire from Communist troops on both sides of Route 1 just south of Quang Tri."[20] Sydney Schanberg of the New York Times stated that the PAVN "dug in only 50 feet from the road on both sides" and was shooting at military trucks, some of which carried refugees.[21] Schanberg's article was accompanied by two photographs, one of them an aerial view of the highway congested with people, many of them wearing conical hats and burdened with their belongings—clearly civilians. Peter Braestrup of the Washington Post wrote: "on April 26, the enemy began shelling Quang Tri and refugees streamed south 40 miles to Hue. Hundreds of them were slain by North Vietnamese ambushers firing rockets at close range on Highway 1."[22] More graphic is Holger Jensen's account in the *Boston Globe* and *Chicago Tribune*: "On Highway 1, South Vietnam—bodies and parts of bodies litter this unhappy highway southeast of besieged Quang Tri city. A baby's torso. The head of a woman. A leg."[23] Two photographs accompanied the article: one of a toddler crying along the side of the road, and the other of a bus packed with soldiers and civilians, some hanging over the sides and others on top. Reporting from the highway for a respected Vietnamese daily, Nguyễn Tú described the road as "a corridor of blood" (*hành lang máu*).[24]

In the confusion of the attack and the retreat, it is not surprising that there is a lack of data regarding the number of civilians and military personnel among those fleeing Quảng Trị; most reports simply emphasize the significant presence of both. In a classified incident report for the US Air Force, Captain David Mann estimated that although most of the vehicles were military, most of the people were civilians:

> As the combat activity surged towards Quang Tri City, refugee foot and vehicular traffic congested the highways leading to Hue. The first and largest group of refugees assembled in Quang Tri City early on 29 April and then moved approximately six miles south on Route 1, to the vicinity of Hai Lang District Town. . . . At this point, the convoy came under attack by NVA [North Vietnamese Army] direct and indirect fire. Lead vehicles were stopped immediately, and mass confusion ensued. *Although three quarters of the people in the convoy were civilians, 95 percent of the vehicles in the column were military*; the majority were two and one-half ton trucks plus a considerable number of flatbeds, tankers, small trucks, jeeps, and 15 ambulances.[25]

In addition to journalistic and military reports, eyewitnesses confirmed that many civilians were on Highway 1. These eyewitnesses included US Marine Corps senior advisers Robert Sheridan and Donald Price, who were positioned along the south bank of the Mỹ Chánh River; this gave them an "unobstructed view" of Highway 1 for at least eight miles north toward Quảng Trị.[26] On April 29 Price was also tasked with accompanying the 5th Battalion to open up the highway, which the PAVN had blocked at several places. Majors Sheridan and Price reported seeing "civilians brought under fire by 130-mm artillery shells fired over their heads with delayed action fuses." The bursts "literally shredded the refugee column."[27]

Stories from survivors provide another dimension to this tragic episode. Lê Trong Lộc, who is now a physician in the US, was just a boy when his family of twelve fled Quảng Trị. The family's motorcycle blew a tire, and they ended up pushing the vehicle down Highway 1, which was choked with civilian and military vehicles. He recalled: "It became increasingly more difficult for my father and us two brothers to push the motorcycle along because there was no more room on the pavement. Blood ran all over the road. Corpses were no longer intact, their arms and legs were scattered here and there."[28] In the congestion and confusion, Lê Trong Lộc noticed a monk riding a bicycle. At that moment, he envied the monk because his bicycle allowed him to maneuver through the mass of people. A little later, he saw the monk again—lying beside the coveted bicycle with his severed head a few feet away.[29] Fortunately for Lê Trong Lộc's family, they all managed to make it to Huế unscathed. Some of his siblings avoided the highway altogether by using village roads.

Similarly, Phan Văn Châu relates a harrowing story of leaving Quảng Trị on April 29 with his family.[30] In the chaos of the attack, he lost track of everyone except for his nephew. After the barrage of fire stopped, Châu and his nephew started to look for the rest of their family; in desperation, they even turned over corpses. They ended up spending the night on the highway, huddled among the bodies. The next day they left the highway and used the back roads to get to Mỹ Chánh, where they reunited with the rest of the family.[31]

The full extent of the attack was unknown until July, when the ARVN regained the southern parts of Quảng Trị province. *Sóng Thần* reporters Ngy Thanh and Đoàn Kế Tường were among the first to return to that section of the highway, arriving with ARVN troops in the southern part of Quảng Trị province on July 1.[32] At the Bến Đá bridge, which had been destroyed in late April, the reporters made their way across the river using a damaged railway bridge. They therefore arrived at the "Highway of Horror" before the rest of the troops and witnessed the macabre scene.

According to Ngy Thanh and Đoàn Kế Tường's article, published on July 3, the ten-kilometer stretch of highway southeast of Quảng Trị city was a scene of mass destruction. The road was obstructed by damaged tanks, buses, cars, and Red Cross vehicles with stretchers still inside. Motorcycles were abandoned with keys in the ignition. Strewn in and around these wrecks were hundreds of bodies; some were soldiers, but most were civilians, including women and children.[33] Many more bodies lay in the sand along both sides of the highway. The reporters noted that because the corpses had been there since the end of April, they had begun to decompose.

In an essay written shortly after breaking the news, Đoàn Kế Tường described his reaction to seeing the "terrible hell" along the highway, "burst[ing] into a loud sob, full of indignation and resentment."[34] Encountering the aftermath of the attack was particularly difficult for him because he had been among the thousands fleeing southward on the highway in late April. Wrestling with survivor's guilt,

**FIGURE 6.1**   "Highway of Horror," July 1, 1972. Copyright by Ngy Thanh.

Đoàn Kế Tường, a Quảng Trị native, confessed: "In fleeing, I trampled upon the bodies of my brothers, sisters, and relatives without daring to look back."[35]

Other Vietnamese journalists reported equally horrifying sights when they returned to the highway in July.[36] In their joint memoir, war correspondents Vũ Thanh Thủy and Dương Phục recorded the eerie and surreal sight they encountered along this stretch of highway.[37] There were so many bodies that it was difficult for journalists to walk along the shoulders of the highway, and they had to use walking sticks to avoid stepping on the corpses.[38] Isaacs, who arrived in Quảng Trị a couple of days after the ARVN, described the highway as "one of the most appalling scenes of the entire war."[39]

Like many other wartime mass killings, there is some dispute about the number of people who died.[40] On the low side, Jensen placed the number between two hundred and six hundred. On the high side, correspondents Dương Phục and Vũ Thanh Thủy estimated five thousand dead.[41] According to Dale Andradé, former senior researcher and writer for the US Army Center of Military History, the Red Cross estimated two thousand deaths, including many who had been evacuated from the Quảng Trị hospital.[42] Majors Sheridan and Price believed approximately two thousand people had been killed. They revealed that there were actually two assaults on refugees, one taking place on April 24 and another on April 29–30.[43] According to Sóng Thần's record, 1,841 bodies were recovered.[44]

It is also unclear what percentage of those killed along Highway 1 were civilian as opposed to military. Based on the aforementioned reports and accounts, the civilian presence was significant. As already noted, Captain Mann estimated that three-quarters of the people in the convoy were civilians. Nguyễn Kinh Châu recalled that most of the bodies recovered by *Sóng Thần* were civilians, some were ARVN troops, and about one hundred were PAVN soldiers.[45] Based on data published in *Sóng Thần* at the time, it appears that most of the bodies recovered were civilians. Until late September, *Sóng Thần* regularly printed descriptions of each corpse recovered, providing names (when available) and any distinguishing characteristics to help families with identification. According to the lists published from July 20 to August 9, out of 129 bodies recovered, only 35 were military; the rest were women and children (42), men (35), and unidentifiable (17); of the last category, 11 were evidently civilian because of the clothing found on the remains.[46] In other words, 68 percent of the bodies were civilians, and 27 percent were soldiers. Although this is only a small sampling of the data, it suggests that a significant number—if not the majority—of those killed along the highway were civilians.

Even though the civilian death toll was high, some scholars do not consider this a "massacre" because of the considerable and obvious presence of military personnel and vehicles. Within the conventions of modern warfare, attacking a retreating army is acceptable.[47] The civilian victims in these cases would typically be considered "collateral damage," an unfortunate but common consequence of modern warfare. Others differ. According to some scholars of mass killings and atrocities, one defining characteristic of a massacre is the asymmetry of power at the time of the event.[48] Consequently, Mark Levene writes that it is possible to have a military massacre "when remnants of a defeated army are cut down in flight."[49] Many may not agree with Levene's definition of a military massacre, but the act of mowing down a group of retreating soldiers and civilians raises moral and ethical issues. Although some contemporary observers used the term "massacre" when writing about it, other did not.[50] But regardless of the term used, all were united in expressing shock and horror. Even Jensen, who rejected the notion that the PAVN had deliberately targeted civilians, described the event as "carnage" and "slaughter" and wrote that the PAVN showed a "callous disregard for civilian targets."[51] Unfortunately, the DRV was not the only side guilty of indiscriminate violence against civilians. It is well documented that the US and RVN were just as culpable.[52]

## *Sóng Thần* and Its Activities

Reports of many hundreds of unburied corpses strewn along the highway prompted *Sóng Thần*'s staff to take action. They named their endeavor 'Thắc Một

Nấm Mộ' [one dies in a grave], alluding to the Vietnamese proverb that underscores the importance of basic accommodations for the living and the dead: one lives in a house and dies in a grave.[53]

*Sóng Thần* was not unique in its civic activism. As discussed in chapter 3, Vietnamese newspapers and Vietnamese people in general have a long tradition of engaging in philanthropic work. During the Easter offensive of 1972, the need for relief intensified. The attacks in all four military regions produced hundreds of thousands of refugees. According to a US embassy report, as of mid-June there were 800,000 refugees, and 500,000 of them were from Military Region I.[54] Because of the ongoing fighting, much of the relief work had to be undertaken by local officials and volunteer groups, such as the Vietnam Confederation of Labor and the Ấn Quang Buddhist Welfare Organization.[55] Vietnamese newspaper reports confirmed the high level of voluntarism. The teaching faculty at Saigon University, for example, spearheaded a campaign in which members donated one day's pay to a refugee fund.[56] The students of Saigon University put on a benefit show, and Vạn Hạnh University raised 500,000 dong in addition to providing material aid. Likewise, *Sóng Thần* staff were ready to help the victims and survivors of this tragedy. Their relief efforts took the form of recovering and burying the corpses along Highway 1.

*Sóng Thần's* voluntarism was not unique, but the newspaper's origin was singular. It was founded for the purpose of exposing official corruption.[57] Corruption had been an ongoing issue in the RVN, but by the 1970s, it had become more flagrant and pervasive, especially among the political and economic elite. Characterizing the situation as "endemic and brazen," Dương Vân Mai Elliott recounts in her memoir that someone she knew had to pay 6 million dong in bribes just to get a passport and an exit visa to go to France.[58] Some writers and intellectuals considered corruption an important issue with negative implications for the war and for the country's survival. Consequently, many popular newspapers investigated scandals and corruption, but *Sóng Thần* made this its priority.

The newspaper's founders were inspired by the work of anticorruption activist Dr. Hà Thúc Nhơn, who was waging a battle against corruption when he was killed. The events surrounding his death on August 31, 1970, were highly controversial, and the details remain murky today. According to his supporters, Hà Thúc Nhơn was a highly principled physician who exposed corruption at the Nguyễn Huệ military hospital in Nha Trang city. As tension escalated between Nhơn and hospital administrators, he was accused of murdering one of the administrators. This eventually led Nhơn, along with some wounded soldiers who were patients at the hospital, to take it over by force. The standoff lasted several days and ended with the death of Nhơn and a number of bystanders. The government claimed he committed suicide, but others believed he was shot by the police or someone connected to the corrupt officials. Nhơn's supporters did not condone his radical action, but they believed the severe and endemic corruption at the hospital had driven the doctor over the edge.[59]

His death moved many people in the city of Nha Trang and throughout the country. It was estimated that five thousand people came to his funeral.[60] Newspapers reported various theories about his demise. His death inspired a group of intellectuals, writers, and professionals to form the Hà Thúc Nhơn group, an organization dedicated to continuing the doctor's fight against corruption. Officially established on November 9, 1970, the Hà Thúc Nhơn group coalesced around the weekly journal Đời (Life); its publisher, Chu Tử, joined the group and was well known for his staunch anticommunist stance.[61] After Nhơn's death, Đời reported extensively about his life and provided details about his anticorruption endeavors and his death. Readers of Đời wrote letters of support and expressed a desire to join the group; some requested that Đời reserve a section in the journal to provide updates about the group's activities.[62] Shortly after its formation, the group launched a cooperative publishing company, and its first job was to produce Sóng Thần, a daily newspaper devoted to exposing corruption and injustice.

Sóng Thần would become a collaborative effort that involved numerous people throughout Vietnam. Chu Tử became the editor in chief, and Trùng Dương was named publisher. As publisher, she was the person who had to go to court whenever an issue of Sóng Thần was confiscated for allegedly violating the censorship law, something that happened frequently.[63]

Another important person involved in Sóng Thần was Uyên Thao, the newspaper's general manager and considered the soul of Sóng Thần by his colleagues.[64] An idealist and ardent nationalist in his youth, Uyên Thao, like many Vietnamese, had wanted independence from France. However, he refused to join the communist-dominated Viet Minh. As a teenager, Uyên Thao had witnessed the execution of a teacher at the hands of communists for teaching classes in French to refugee youths (including Uyên Thao) at a makeshift school during the First Indochina War. The injustice and brutality of this act made him wary of communism. In 1953 Uyên Thao went south to join the Cao Đài Alliance (Cao Đài Liên Minh), a militia faction that had splintered from the main Cao Đài politico-religious organization.[65] Led by Trình Minh Thế, this group opposed collaboration with the French as well as with the Viet Minh. Considered an ultranationalist and "an unflappable patriot," Thế represented himself as "a champion of the people and a fighter against corruption."[66] In 1955, shortly after he agreed to join Ngô Đình Diệm's efforts to consolidate power in the Republic of Vietnam, Thế was assassinated. His death was officially attributed to the Bình Xuyên crime syndicate, which Diệm was fighting, but others believed Diệm had ordered Thế's assassination because of his growing popularity.[67]

After Thế's death, Uyên Thao left the Cao Đài and went into broadcasting and journalism.[68] It appears, however, that Thế's commitment to fighting corruption and representing the common people continued to resonate strongly with Uyên Thao. These views greatly influenced how he managed Sóng Thần and the direction the paper took. According to its founders, "Sóng Thần is the people's paper: it is the voice of protest for the entire country."[69]

Accordingly, the paper covered important issues affecting not only the major cities but also outlying regions and small towns. In fact, every issue devoted a couple of pages to regional news. Moreover, Sóng Thần had a distribution system that allowed the paper to reach readers in these outlying areas as well. There were regional offices in Huế, Quảng Ngãi, Đà Lạt, Nha Trang, Pleiku, Đà Nẵng, Qui Nhơn, and Phan Rang. In September 1971, before the first issue had even been published, three thousand of its five thousand subscriptions came from regions outside of the Saigon-Cholon area.[70]

Another interesting aspect of Sóng Thần was that it was a cooperative newspaper—possibly the only one in South Vietnam. People were encouraged to contribute by buying shares and thereby become collective owners of the paper. The Hà Thúc Nhơn group estimated that it would need 10 million dong (approximately US$25,000) to begin publishing.[71] The group wanted to raise half this amount by selling shares and the other half through loans. To allow people of all economic circumstances to participate, shares were available for as little as 500 dong (approximately US$1.30). Dividends would be assessed every six months, and 60 percent of the profits would go back to the shareholders; the other 40 percent would go toward paying employees' salaries (20 percent), reinvesting in the paper (10 percent), and supporting the work of the Hà Thúc Nhơn group (10 percent). The cooperative management committee would be elected at an annual general meeting to which all the shareholders would be invited.[72]

What is fascinating is that many ordinary people from all walks of life and from different parts of South Vietnam enthusiastically contributed to the paper's creation. Published lists of shareholders and the amounts of their contributions demonstrate the geographic and economic diversity of Sóng Thần's supporters. Many contributed, on average, between 5,000 and 20,000 dong (US$13 and US$51); others contributed as little as 500 dong, and a few wealthy readers bought 50,000 dong worth of shares.

Some contributors wrote letters of support that were published in Đời. Huỳnh Trung, a supporter from the rural district of Xuyên Mộc in southeastern Vietnam, explained that he bought shares not for financial gain but to participate in the fight against corruption.[73] Similarly, Kiều Xuân Tuất of Quảng Nam province in central Vietnam was not interested in financial returns; Hải Triều, who was writing from the front, asked that the beneficiary of his shares be a poor student.[74] A contributor from Bạc Liêu in the Mekong Delta wrote that he was contributing because, given the current dire situation, doing nothing was not an option. To afford his 10,000 dong contribution, he was cutting back on cigarettes. Many other supporters revealed that, despite their poverty, they were willing to skimp on their regular spending to contribute to the paper. Vĩnh Linh of Qui Nhơn city in central Vietnam explained that he intended to skip breakfast and smoke less in order to buy more shares in the near future. Lê Kim Hiền, a low-ranking officer's wife with six children, had debated whether their modest income could be stretched to buy shares, but fortunately, her pig gave birth to ten piglets; the sale of the piglets enabled her to pay for her children's school tuition and clothing and to buy two shares of *Sóng Thần*. These ardent letters and donations reflect not only people's desire for good governance but also their willingness to take action to make this a reality.

By August 20, 1971, the paper had received a little over 3.5 million dong from 209 people (averaging 17,000 dong per person, or US$43). Though this was less than the newspaper organizers had hoped to raise, it was still a substantial and impressive amount of money. This would not be the last time the newspaper relied on readers for support. As the next chapter shows, in 1972 *Sóng Thần* once again had to mobilize its readers to survive a financial crisis brought on by the government's new press law.

True to its goal, *Sóng Thần* made exposing malfeasance in high places its mandate. Although the paper also covered major news events, its focus was investigating and reporting cases of bribery, embezzlement, and the general abuse of power throughout Vietnam. For example, one exposé concerned the misuse of public funds in Quảng Ngãi province in central Vietnam. In the summer of 1972 the local youth group raised more than 3 million dong to repair a stadium, but the head of the Youth Office awarded the contract to someone who had no experience or expertise in construction. As a result, the stadium remained in a state of disrepair.[75] The paper also alleged that officials in the Social Welfare Office in Ninh Thuận, a south-central province, had stolen donated goods, such as sewing machines and cooking oil, and sold them for their own profit.[76]

One of the paper's high-level investigations was conducted by journalist Lê Thị Bích Vân. It focused on Brigadier General Nguyễn Văn Toàn, who was known as the "Cinnamon General" because he allegedly got rich by pilfering from the state's cinnamon forest in Quảng Ngãi. *Sóng Thần*, however, accused him of another crime: sexual assault of a fifteen-year-old girl. To cover up this crime,

Toàn took the girl to court and charged her with prostitution. He also tried to silence *Sóng Thần* by offering Uyên Thao a bribe; when that did not work, Toàn threatened the paper and began a smear campaign.[77] The general also sued *Sóng Thần* for slander and managed to win the case, although the paper was fined only 1 dong.[78] In the end, the government tried to defuse the scandal by transferring Toàn to another military district. When that military district protested vociferously, the government was forced to move him again. Ironically, because of these reassignments, the Cinnamon General ended up in a more powerful position than before the sexual assault scandal.[79]

As expected, *Sóng Thần*'s penchant for investigating officials did not endear the paper to local or national authorities. In addition to highlighting corruption, the paper did not hesitate to point out the government's failings. During the Easter offensive, *Sóng Thần* and several other newspapers were frequently found to be in contravention of the press law for their candid coverage of the battles. As a result, many papers were confiscated. *Sóng Thần* was confiscated five times in April 1972, causing significant financial losses.[80] *Sóng Thần*'s relationship with the government worsened in subsequent months when President Nguyễn Văn Thiệu, citing the Easter offensive as justification, declared martial law, expanded his executive power, and promulgated a more restrictive press decree. These new measures drove *Sóng Thần* and other oppositional papers to become even more critical and vocal in their demands for freedom of the press, a topic examined in the next chapter.

Though at loggerheads with the government for most of its publishing life, the paper was not against the war; nor was it sympathetic toward the NLF and DRV. In fact, *Sóng Thần*, particularly Uyên Thao and Chu Tử, strongly opposed communism and believed the paper's anticorruption efforts actually contributed to the RVN's fighting capability.[81] In this context, the paper's burial project could be interpreted as an oblique criticism of the government not only for being overwhelmed by the DRV's attack but also for neglecting its victims. According to Uyên Thao, someone close to Thiệu reported that the president was angry and considered the project a personal attack on him.[82] There is no documentary evidence to support this, but it is clear that neither Thiệu nor his government provided any official support to the recovery project. To be fair, the government was bogged down fighting the PAVN and trying to regain lost territory. However, *Sóng Thần* received help on an informal basis from local government officials and regional units of the ARVN. Their support, along with the participation of residents of Thừa Thiên province and donors throughout the country, demonstrated that this was a grassroots undertaking and a prime example of civil society in action.

## *Sóng Thần*'s Burial Project

The bold and iconoclastic *Sóng Thần* was within its purview when it embarked on its recovery and burial project on July 9, six days after its first report about the grisly aftermath of the assault. The RVN was still defending itself on multiple fronts, so the government had not had time to collect and bury the corpses. *Sóng Thần* stepped in and spearheaded this work for Quảng Trị victims. The paper began by soliciting donations to cover expenses, such as the cost of plastic body bags, coffins, and transportation. It would cost about 2,000 dong to collect and bury one corpse.[83] The response from readers was heartening. Within just one month, the paper had received 1.8 million dong. By August 8, it had raised 2.9 million dong; by the end of August, when the total reached 3 million dong (US$7,634), the paper announced that it had enough funds and would stop taking donations.[84] By the end of the project, *Sóng Thần* had a surplus of 500,000 dong, which it used to build a stele and a shrine to honor the victims.[85]

Donations came from all sectors of society, from wealthy to poor. Some people gave as individuals, while others organized through their social networks. A teacher in Quảng Ngãi led his students and the local Boy Scouts to canvass for donations.[86] The Philanthropic Association for Maternal Care of Đà Nẵng raised 20,000 dong.[87] A group of market women made a collective donation. In one extraordinary example, an illiterate woman who had heard about the campaign walked nearly four kilometers to *Sóng Thần*'s office to donate 1,000 dong in person.[88]

In addition to financial aid from readers, the local community in the Huế area—including individuals, Buddhist groups, and disabled veterans' associations—provided logistical support, a place to identify the dead, and land for a cemetery.[89] *Sóng Thần*'s staff in Huế and Quảng Trị, particularly Huế office director Nguyễn Kinh Châu, were most directly involved with the work. As the project's de facto manager, Châu had detailed knowledge of the initiative from start to finish. In 2009 he could still clearly recall the many people who contributed.[90] For example, the chair of the Provincial Council, who also owned a jewelry store, lent the group 50,000 dong so they could start making coffins. Major Nguyễn Văn Cơ, head of the military hospital in Military Region I, initially donated two hundred nylon body bags; later, as more bodies were recovered, the hospital provided more bags.

*Sóng Thần*'s project also received support from local ARVN forces in Thừa Thiên and Quảng Trị provinces, which lent them several military trucks to transport workers and corpses.[91] Individual volunteers were also helpful. Buddhist monk Thích Đức Tâm was in charge of getting coffins made; Tôn Nữ Mộng Nhiên's house became the project's headquarters and a temporary home for those participating. Nhiên and her sister also accompanied the group to the highway, where they kept records of the dead and their belongings.[92]

To publicize the project, publisher Trùng Dương spent a week with the crew in Quảng Trị and wrote a series of articles describing the physical and emotional difficulties of the work.[93] According to her report, every day the crew traveled to the highway, where they tried to identify each body before bagging it. Each corpse was numbered, briefly described, and then brought to Phong Điền primary school (Phong Điền district) in Thừa Thiên-Huế province. People gathered there at the end of the day to see whether the bodies of their loved ones had been recovered. In addition to seeing, smelling, handling, and identifying hundreds of corpses on a daily basis, volunteers had to dodge occasional mortar attacks and unexploded ordinance, as the battle for Quảng Trị province was still active. In fact, one member of the *Sóng Thần* work crew was killed in a shelling attack.[94]

Some people in the Huế area had helped collect corpses after the 1968 Tet offensive, which left an estimated two thousand civilians dead in Huế. *Sóng Thần* hired some of these people, who were already experienced in the task of body collection. Trùng Dương remembers that these experienced workers brought whiskey to help calm their nerves and to disinfect their hands before eating lunch.[95] Other workers brought shrimp paste (*mắm ruốc*), hoping its pungent smell would mask the odor of decomposing corpses.[96] These workers not only knew the tricks of the trade but also told stories of their personal encounters with the unquiet spirits of the Tết offensive. These spirits occasionally tried to guide the workers in their search for bodies. For example, a nighttime visit from two female ghosts helped one worker recover the bodies of two sisters the next morning. In another case, a dead man came back to tell his mother and wife that the skull they had buried with his body was not his.[97] The workers' spectral encounters underscore the spiritual and psychological importance of *Sóng Thần*'s burial project to Vietnamese society.

Almost a month after beginning its work, *Sóng Thần* had recovered 202 bodies, 74 of which had been claimed and buried by their families.[98] The first collective funeral ceremony was held on August 1 for the 128 unclaimed bodies. The second round of recovery began on August 8. By then, the work was becoming more difficult because the bodies had sunk deeper into the sand. Digging had to be done with extra care to avoid compromising the corpses.[99] By November 22, the number of people buried totaled 580.[100] The work took about seven months to finish, and in the end, according to Nguyễn Kinh Châu, 1,841 bodies were recovered.[101]

A cemetery for these victims was established in Hội Kỳ commune in Phong Điền district, Thừa Thiên-Huế province. Unfortunately, after the war, the cemetery and the stele were both destroyed.[102] In an effort to control the people's collective memory of the war, the victorious communist government demolished many public monuments and grave sites of the old regime.[103] Cemetery land was sometimes claimed by the state for other uses, in which case those who were able to do so moved their loved ones' remains to some other site.[104] Unclaimed bodies were typically moved elsewhere and buried in a mass grave.[105] It is unclear when and for what official reason the cemetery created for the Quảng Trị victims was eradicated. It is also unclear where the victims' mass grave is currently located because the remains were moved not once but twice.[106]

Considering the importance Vietnamese tradition places on burial practices, the destruction of the cemetery and the multiple relocations of the bodies into mass graves undoubtedly caused anguish for the families and the community. One could consider these acts another injustice perpetrated on the victims. As mentioned earlier, many Vietnamese believe that proper burial rituals are essential to ensure the deceased person's safe passage into the afterlife. Otherwise, their souls are condemned to relive the painful trauma that caused their violent deaths.[107]

Although the idea of noncombatant immunity in wartime is widely accepted, civilians are rarely spared.[108] The Vietnam War, infamous for surpassing World War II in total tonnage of bombs dropped, produced untold numbers of civilian casualties in Vietnam (both DRV and RVN), Cambodia, and Laos. This chapter examines just one group of victims among many. Largely overlooked by historians, the killing along Highway 1 is an example of Vietnamese-on-Vietnamese violence, a phenomenon that also receives little scholarly attention.[109] Nevertheless, this was an important incident that underscores the conflict's characterization as a civil war, reminding readers that while the Cold War powers were involved, the brunt of the fighting on both sides was done by Vietnamese.

The Quảng Trị killing is also significant because it illuminates how civilians respond to the violence of war. When news spread about the unburied corpses along the highway, ordinary people acted. Rather than waiting for the government, Sóng Thần initiated a burial project, and people participated with enthusiasm. From the perspective of those who contributed to the burial project, this was not just a civic duty; it had spiritual ramifications for both the dead and the living. This chapter shows that the Vietnamese were victims of the war, but they were also their own rescuers and the perpetrators of violence. As subjects with agency, the Vietnamese have the capacity for both altruism and atrocity, as do all people.[110] As Avery Gordon reminds scholars, "even those who live in the most dire circumstances possess a complex and oftentimes contradictory humanity and subjectivity that is never adequately glimpsed by viewing them as victims or, on the other hand, as superhuman agents." In other words, by seeing them only as victims or superheroes, scholars deny them the "right to complex personhood."[111] Moreover, the complexity of their existence pertains not only to the material world but also to the afterlife, which is always relevant and present, even in its absence.

The burial project and *Sóng Thần*'s history are also noteworthy because they provide insight into the RVN's civil society and public sphere. *Sóng Thần*'s endeavors clearly indicate the existence of a socially conscious public willing to engage with issues in the public sphere and participate in collective actions. When they donated money to establish *Sóng Thần*, readers were expressing their support for the paper's anticorruption campaign. More than that, however, their support reveals a deep desire for an independent, activist press that works for social justice and government accountability. *Sóng Thần* consciously portrayed itself as the people's paper, particularly in its decision to operate as a cooperative. The burial project certainly bolstered this image. The project relied on grassroots support and volunteers and tried to assuage one of the most troubling aspects of war for the Vietnamese population: the trauma of violent death. It is even more impressive that this burial project took place during a militarily and politically difficult period. The RVN had been attacked on multiple fronts and was initially overwhelmed, losing territory to the DRV. Despite the precarious situation and wartime restrictions on freedom, the RVN's civil society remained active and dynamic. Concerned citizens articulated collective concerns and worked together to solve them. From taking down corrupt politicians to bringing peace to the spirits of the dead, these people were civically engaged.

# THE FIGHT FOR RIGHTS AND FREEDOMS IN THE 1970S

On the afternoon of September 19, 1974, paperboys waiting patiently outside Tân Minh printing house for their allotment of *Sóng Thần* newspapers witnessed a fiery display of civil disobedience.[1] *Sóng Thần* had allegedly contravened the press law, and police officers were about to execute a confiscation order. Rather than handing over copies of the paper, *Sóng Thần* staff decided to destroy the entire print run that had just come off the press. The news spread rapidly, Soon, prominent members of Saigon's civil society and the local and international press, including reporters from Associated Press, UPI, and Reuters, crowded in front of the printing house to witness the showdown. As Hà Thế Ruyệt, deputy manager of *Sóng Thần*, torched the freshly printed pages, some staff members had to turn away, unable to watch the destruction. After thousands of issues were reduced to ashes, the staff erected a large sign that read "Freedom or Death." Similar acts of defiance took place at the newspaper offices of *Điện Tín* (Telegraph) and *Đại Dân Tộc* (Great Nation). *Đại Dân Tộc* staff even tossed hundreds of copies of the banned newspaper onto the street, distributing it freely to the crowd. These dramatic actions were among many that unfolded in Saigon in the latter half of the Second Republic. What was behind the tense confrontation between the press and RVN authorities? This chapter examines the relationship between the government and the press and considers what it reveals about the state of civil society in the RVN.

By the early 1970s, the military situation in South Vietnam had become increasingly perilous. The Easter offensive of 1972 had overwhelmed the RVN, and although the ARVN regained control of most of the areas taken by PAVN forces, it did so only with massive airpower provided by the US military. This suggests that Vietnamization, the US policy implemented in 1969 to gradually transfer control of the fighting to the ARVN, had not yet achieved its goal. On the sociopolitical front, it was a challenging time for South Vietnam and the government of Nguyễn Văn Thiệu. The US military withdrawal that accompanied Vietnamization had a negative impact on the economy. As a result, ordinary Vietnamese, particularly those living in the cities, had to cope with high rates of inflation and unemployment. By 1973, these economic troubles were exacerbated by the global oil crisis. Furthermore, the Paris peace agreement, signed on January 27, 1973, put South Vietnam in a precarious military situation. Against South Vietnam's protests, the agreement allowed nearly 300,000 PAVN troops to remain in the south.[2]

The early 1970s was a period of high anxiety that led to an explosion of political activism and antigovernment protests. Student demonstrations against the war, US involvement, and social injustice grew more radical. While university and high school students were at the forefront of activism and street demonstrations, nonstudent organizations and movements were also fully engaged in fighting for various causes. Some groups fought for prison reform, human rights, freedom of the press, and an end to corruption. Some of these movements were led by left-wing or communist sympathizers, while others were spearheaded by liberal democrats, anticommunists, and right-wing activists.

In examining the social protest movements for rights and freedoms, this chapter illustrates that South Vietnam's public sphere was pluralistic and robust, and its civil society was effective in ensuring that this realm of public discourse remained free and open. As a result, a high level of engagement was maintained, even though Thiệu's government restricted the press and imposed fines, prison terms, or both on those who allegedly broke the law. Before delving into the various social movements, I first provide a brief sketch of the political situation of the Second Republic, particularly the contentious period beginning with the 1971 presidential election. It could be argued that Thiệu's decision to run unopposed for a second term ignited a maelstrom of antigovernment responses, even from those on the right.

## Political Background

After the overthrow of Ngô Đình Diệm and the tumultuous transition period of military rule (1963–67), South Vietnam's politics achieved some measure of stability. In 1966 the military junta that took power after Diệm was assassinated was pressured to fulfill its promise to establish democratic and free elections. As some scholars have argued, this promise might have been put off longer had it not been for the Buddhist struggle movement, which the military government violently suppressed in the spring of 1966. As a gesture of compromise, and in response to US pressure, the junta agreed to organize Constituent Assembly elections.[3] The elections were held on September 11, 1966, and on April 1, 1967, a new constitution for the Republic of Vietnam was promulgated, ushering in the Second Republic.

In accordance with the new constitution, presidential and National Assembly elections were held in subsequent months. Though there were many irregularities and instances of tampering by the regime, such as introducing rules that disqualified as many presidential candidates as possible and sabotaging opponents' campaign tours, the 1967 elections were relatively clean, especially compared with the elections carried out under Diệm.[4] This was probably the result of the military junta's realization that there would be heavy international scrutiny of the electoral proceedings.[5] Unlike Diệm, who won the referendum in 1955 with 98 percent of the vote, the junta's presidential ticket, General Nguyễn Văn Thiệu and Air Marshal Nguyễn Cao Kỳ, won with only 35 percent of the vote. Trương Đình Dzu and his running mate Trần Văn Chiêu received 16 percent of the vote, even though they were considered the "peace ticket." After his candidacy had been approved, Dzu announced that he was in favor of direct negotiations with the communists, a stance that would have disqualified him had he revealed it earlier. Shortly after the election was over, Dzu was arrested for allegedly writing a bad check and illegal US currency transfer committed five years earlier. It appears that he was being punished for coming in second with his pro-peace platform.[6]

Though there were problems with the 1967 elections, they paled in comparison to the blatant tampering and manipulation in the presidential election held four years later. The most conspicuous problem was that Thiệu was the only candidate. Kỳ had wanted to run for president in 1967 but had been pressured to take a secondary role to Thiệu, so he was especially keen to run in 1971. However, through adept maneuvering, Thiệu got the National Assembly to pass a new law that made many candidates ineligible to run. The law stipulated that each presidential candidate needed the endorsement of either forty members of both houses of the National Assembly or one hundred municipal or provincial councilors.[7] According to political observers at the time, Thiệu was mainly concerned with getting one of his two main rivals, Kỳ and General Dương Văn Minh, disqualified from the race. He correctly estimated that he could not win in a race against both of them.[8] Kỳ's candidacy would have split the military and conservative votes, while Minh, with Ấn Quang Buddhist support, would have won the left and antiwar votes.

As Thiệu had hoped, Kỳ was unable to get the required number of signatures because many of his would-be supporters had already pledged to endorse Thiệu and were not permitted to support another candidate. Dương Văn Minh had no trouble getting enough signatures, but given Thiệu's overt manipulation,

Minh's Buddhist supporters decided it would be better if he dropped out, thereby exposing the election as a farce. According to one of Minh's supporters, Professor Lý Chánh Trung, US ambassador Ellsworth Bunker did little to promote a fair election and instead tried to bribe Minh into running, knowing he would lose the election.[9] Not wanting to be part of an election that could not be guaranteed as fair or democratic, Minh withdrew his candidacy.[10] Within days of his announcement, the South Vietnamese Supreme Court, in an unexpected move, reversed its earlier decision that had disqualified Kỳ. However, Kỳ knew he would lose in a two-way race against Thiệu and so declined to run.[11] Thiệu could have postponed the election to allow other candidates to emerge, but he went ahead with a one-man race, despite severe domestic and international criticism.[12] In the end, Thiệu and his running mate Trần Văn Hương won the election with 91.5 percent of the votes, drawing accusations of electoral fraud.[13] Given Thiệu's interference with the election, it was no wonder that Kỳ supported the radical students protesting the election (see chapter 5).

In addition to Thiệu's manipulation of the presidential campaign, the opposition accused him of tampering with elections for the lower house (August 29, 1971) and the senate (August 26, 1973) in order to stack the National Assembly with his own supporters.[14] Consequently, both houses were dominated by Thiệu's allies, who used this advantage to pass bills that gave him more power and control. Some of the new laws clamped down on freedom of the press, outlawed most political parties except for the government's Dân Chủ (Democracy) Party, eliminated elections for hamlet chiefs and administrators, and amended the constitution to enable Thiệu to run for a third term.[15] Following the devastating Easter offensive, the government declared martial law and reversed some democratic reforms that had been implemented earlier.[16] Not surprisingly, Thiệu's attitude and actions fueled resentment and increased the size of the opposition.

## Campaigns for Prison Reform and the Right to Live

Thiệu's adoption of more repressive measures starting in 1971 not only incited his political rivals but also alienated his supporters and radicalized the opposition. This period saw the emergence of many organizations and movements that were highly critical of the government and its war policy; two notable groups were the Committee for Prison Reform and the Women's Movement for the Right to Live.

The Committee for Prison Reform was concerned with the rise in the illegal imprisonment and mistreatment of political prisoners, particularly students. As discussed in chapter 5, starting in the mid-1960s, communist-affiliated students infiltrated the student movement and encouraged more violent and provocative protest actions. One of their major grievances was the introduction of compulsory military training for students.[17] Consequently, the government began to crack down on student activists and arrest them. Some students had no doubt committed criminal and terroristic acts, such as attempting to blow up a police station, but others were just voicing their political concerns. There was strong public criticism of the government's tough actions against students.

Spearheading the prison reform movement were a number of Catholic priests and left-wing academics such as Father Chân Tín, Father Huỳnh Công Minh, and Professor Lý Chánh Trung. Together, they founded the Committee for Prison Reform in October 1970.[18] The committee worked on many fronts to call attention to illegal arrests and detention, poor prison conditions, and the use of torture. South Vietnamese prisons for political prisoners were already infamous for their brutality, and their reputation worsened after *Life* magazine published photographs of the "tiger cages" found at the Côn Sơn Island prison. Don Luce, executive secretary for the World Council of Churches and former head of International Voluntary Service in Vietnam, and Tom Harkin, a congressional aide, helped expose these small underground cells where political prisoners were held.[19] The photographs and article in *Life* suggested that torture and mistreatment were commonplace. According to the article, more than half the prisoners were women, some only in their teens. The article also described cruel punishments such as dousing prisoners with limewater from overhead through the bars of their cells.[20]

Like the exposé in *Life*, the work of the Committee for Prison Reform revealed that prison conditions in South Vietnam were appalling and inhumane. The committee conveyed this message through print media and street demonstrations. It also published a monthly paper *Lao Tù* (Prison) and a newsletter (*Bản Tin*) that reported cases of illegal imprisonment and poor treatment of prisoners. These publications also allowed prisoners to voice their grievances. Letters written by prisoners described unhealthy living conditions and inhumane treatment.[21]

Father Chân Tín also promoted prison reform through his political journal *Đối Diện* (Face-to-Face), which was established in 1969 to inform readers about pressing issues, particularly those related to the war.[22] The journal encouraged dialogue between people of different faiths, politics, and philosophies and promoted activism against illegal detention and the mistreatment of political prisoners. A relentless advocate of justice, Father Chân Tín taught at the Redemptorist seminary in Đà Lạt after receiving his PhD in Rome. In 1963 he managed the monthly newspaper *Our Lady of Mercy* (*Đức Mẹ Hằng Cứu Giúp*), which in the spirit of Vatican II reforms, encouraged the clergy and laity to work for democracy, equality, and justice.[23] This movement built on the foundation of the

Catholic action movement, which inspired Catholic social activism in Vietnam (see chapter 3).

The Committee for Prison Reform was adept at attracting media attention, particularly foreign media. Major US newspapers frequently reported on Father Tín and the committee's work. The committee also had links with international prison rights organizations such as Amnesty International, which relied on the committee for information about prisoners in Vietnam.[24]

Not surprisingly, the Thiệu government did not welcome this negative attention, and government repression began immediately after the committee's formation. Its opening ceremony, planned for November 11, 1970, had to be canceled because the police did not allow the guests, reportedly numbering in the thousands, to attend.[25] Prison reform activists were harassed and imprisoned. Both Fathers Tín and Trương Bá Cần were jailed for nine months in 1971 and fined; Father Phan Khắc Từ and two other YCW chaplains were held without trial in November 1971 for their prison reform work.[26] Father Tín's journal *Đối Diện* was officially banned in 1972, but it continued to circulate underground. To avoid censorship, it was published under different names, but always with the same initials: *Đồng Dao* (Children's Song) or *Đứng Dậy* (Stand Up).[27]

Other groups worked closely with the Committee for Prison Reform to call attention to injustice in South Vietnam. One vocal group was the Women's Movement for the Right to Live (Phong trào phụ nữ đòi quyền sống). The leader of this group was Phạm Thị Thanh Vân, better known by her husband's name, Ngô Bá Thành. An accomplished woman with two doctorates in law from universities in Paris and Barcelona and a master's degree in comparative law from Columbia University, Vân identified herself as a member of the Third Force.[28] This loosely knit group of activists and politicians, which included Hồ Ngọc Nhuận of the New Life Development Project, advocated for a negotiated end to the war and the withdrawal of US troops. Other prominent members of the women's movement were Buddhist nun Huỳnh Liên and lower house member Kiều Mộng Thu, both of whom were also associated with the Third Force. The Women's Movement for the Right to Live was officially founded on August 2, 1970.[29] In addition to the main group based in Saigon, local branches formed in Gia Định, Chợ Lớn, and Cần Thơ.[30]

Besides focusing on women's socioeconomic conditions and calling for an end to the war, which the group believed was the main cause of poverty, the movement advocated for prisoners.[31] Like the Committee for Prison Reform, members of the Women's Movement for the Right to Live were skilled at getting domestic and international media attention and were often willing to carry out dramatic public acts. Vân was particularly creative in her protest activities. For example, on one occasion, when the police had cordoned off the area around her house to stop her from joining a demonstration, she and a few supporters lay down in the street in protest.[32] Even when she was imprisoned, which happened on numerous occasions, Vân did not stop her political activism. She continued to write open letters, make demands, and raise awareness of social injustice.[33] More innovatively, while in jail, she continued to voice her concerns by "speaking the news" (*làm nói báo*). She did this daily from her jail cell, using just her voice to "broadcast" critiques of the current sociopolitical situation in three languages: Vietnamese, English, and French.[34]

When not in prison, Vân and members of the Third Force spoke the news in small-town marketplaces, where they hoped to raise awareness about the war and social issues. To avoid arrest, the group kept the time and location of their broadcast a secret and always had a getaway plan in place. Hồ Ngọc Nhuận was credited with coming up with this "guerrilla" style of political discourse.[35] In trying to inform and stimulate discussion, these activists were in fact expanding the public sphere to include the masses.

The Women's Movement for the Right to Live was ubiquitous in South Vietnam. Members of this movement could be found at rallies for a variety of causes. From their perspective, poverty intersected with other sociopolitical issues such as the ongoing war, corruption, political repression, and prison reform. When Thiệu won the one-candidate presidential race in 1971, the women's movement was there with other groups to protest.[36] The women collaborated with and provided support to other opposition groups. Student leader Huỳnh Tấn Mẫm credited Vân's intervention at several protests for saving student demonstrators from police brutality.[37]

Because these activists were against the war and US intervention, the Saigon authorities suspected they were affiliated with communist organizations. And indeed, some activists were working as communist or NLF agents. Others, however, were not. In his last letter before his death in 2012, Father Tín addressed this suspicion directly. He stated unequivocally that he had never been a communist and had never worked with any communist organizations.[38] Similarly, Vân, in a 1992 interview with the *Los Angeles Times*, denied ever being a communist and insisted that she was only a peace activist.[39] While their declarations might have been true, the government of the new Socialist Republic of Vietnam (SRV) appreciated their views and their activism. As a result, Father Tín and Vân were not sent to reeducation camps and were given roles in the new government instead.[40] Father Tín became a member of the Central Committee of the Fatherland Front, and Vân was elected to the National Assembly four times. Both, however, eventually fell out of favor when they criticized the new regime. In 1990 Chân Tín was arrested and held for three years under house arrest for criticizing the government's human rights and religious rights abuses.[41]

Though he was not a communist, Father Tín admitted that some of the students he lobbied for had been working with communist organizations.[42] Moreover, some of the student activists had committed crimes and, in some cases, terrorist acts as secret communist agents. For example, the Committee for Prison Reform had lobbied vigorously for the freedom of Huỳnh Tấn Mẫm, Nguyễn Ngọc Phương, and his wife Cao Thị Quế Hương, who were members of the People's Revolutionary Party, the southern branch of the Lao Động Party.[43] In 1965 Phương, whose undercover name was Ba Triết, was assigned to work directly with university students and with the Saigon Student Union. In this capacity, he collaborated closely with Mẫm. Despite the committee's efforts, Nguyễn Ngọc Phương died in prison in 1973 after staging a fourteen-day hunger strike.

Another story involves Thiều Thị Tạo and her younger sister Thiều Thị Tân, whom Don Luce and Tom Harkin met during their visit to Côn Sơn prison. Tân was the youngest inmate to spend time in the infamous tiger-cage cells. The teenaged sisters were students at the prestigious Marie Curie Private School in Saigon. A close friend of the family had recruited them into the communist movement. Tân was the leader of an agitation and propaganda unit, and both girls were tasked with transporting ten kilograms of explosives into the national police headquarters. However, someone who was supposedly helping them with the assignment had betrayed them, leading to their arrests.[44] Like these sisters, many communist youths were given undercover terrorist assignments, such as bombing government buildings and "punishing" members of the state security forces.[45] The backstory of these sisters, who are still celebrated in memory of the revolution in Vietnam, was not mentioned in the Life article. The article claimed they were kept in the tiger cages because of their refusal to salute the RVN flag, a morning ritual at the prison.[46]

Torture and inhumane treatment are not acceptable under any circumstances, but it is important to acknowledge that many secret agents and operatives were trying to overthrow the South Vietnamese government. It is now known that some high-profile members of the intelligentsia were covertly working for the communists. Besides famous Time correspondent Phạm Xuân Ẩn, other writers and journalists were members of the NLF or the Lao Động Party, including writer Vũ Hạnh (Nguyễn Đức Dũng), journalist Nguyễn Văn Hồng, and cartoonist Huỳnh Bá Thành (pen name Ớt).[47] Communism was outlawed in the RVN, and authorities considered communist activists agents of the RVN's enemy. After all, South Vietnam was at war against communist North Vietnam and the north's allies in the south. At the same time, however, many inmates were not affiliated with communism; they were democrats like Father Tín who were working for peace or were nonpartisan.

Evidently, the South Vietnamese government found it challenging to deal with opposition movements. Some of them were genuine members of civil society who sought reform and change, while others used violence and secretly sought to overthrow the entire sociopolitical system in favor of communism. The mistake made by Nguyễn Văn Thiệu, and by Ngô Đình Diệm before him, was that he did not make much of a distinction between legal and illegal opposition. Instead of allowing the public sphere to thrive and nurture constructive opposition, Thiệu, especially from 1971 onward, tried to curb all political contenders and opposing views. In so doing, he just produced more resentment. As Father Tín tried to warn him, illegal imprisonment was hurting the government in the political and ideological war. He cautioned that by locking up innocent people with communists, the government was giving communists the opportunity to indoctrinate and recruit more followers. Father Tín wrote that the "prison camps of the South are training schools for communist cadres."[48] Indeed, resentment against the government grew to such an extent that even supporters of the regime eventually became more critical and radical.

## Press Censorship

Press restriction was not unfamiliar to journalists and writers in Vietnam. There was strict censorship during the French colonial era, but as Shawn McHale argues, the colonial government's control was not airtight or uniform: "While the French colonial state repressed 'subversive' publications, it cared little about the vast majority." As a result, Vietnamese could carve out autonomous zones for public engagement.[49] Philippe Peycam's research also suggests that Cochin China, Vietnam's southern region during the French colonial period, had a robust public sphere. One factor that gave it more freedom than the rest of Indochina was that the colonial government needed the cooperation and support of Cochin China's diverse population, which included a significant number of French citizens. This in turn allowed the emergence of Vietnamese political journalism with a penchant for opposing the state.[50]

During the First Republic, Diệm significantly limited press freedom. The government controlled access to subsidized newsprint and the distribution of publications. The restrictions were so severe that by 1956, only one opposition paper existed; the rest either toed the government line or focused on entertainment news.[51] Even the one opposition daily, *Thời Luận* (Current Discussion), folded in 1958.[52] It appears that any critical journalism of the colonial period was effectively snuffed out during Diệm's regime.

With the overthrow of Diệm in 1963, there was a burst of excitement as the new ruling military junta cast itself as the antithesis of his authoritarianism and disavowed the rigid censorship of the ancien régime. Accordingly, freedom of the press was affirmed, and censorship of newspapers was suspended by a decree issued on July 20, 1964.[53] Freedom of the press was guaranteed in the Second Republic's constitution. The press law promulgated in 1969 (referred to as Law 019/69) further reduced some restrictions of the First Republic. For example, publishers could distribute their newspapers and periodicals independently from the government.[54]

However, there were still hurdles and de facto censorship. According to Law 019/69, before newspapers or periodicals could be distributed, copies had to be submitted to various government offices: ten copies to the Ministry of Information, two copies to the prosecutor's office, two copies to the Ministry of the Interior, and two copies to the National Archives.[55] For daily newspapers, this process was burdensome. Publishers had to take their galley proofs to the censor's office in the late morning, where one of the dozen censors would review them.[56] Articles that violated the press law either were removed in their entirety or had the offending sections cut. Once the issue was approved, it was sent to the printing press and prepared for distribution in the afternoon.[57] As there was usually no time to fill in the blanks or adjust the layout, blocks of empty space were common, sometimes with the ironic explanation "voluntarily removed."[58] However, the censors could still find fault with an issue after it was printed. In that case, the censors would send the police to confiscate the papers from news outlets and newsstands. In addition, the paper's publisher would have to go to court to answer the government's charges regarding the alleged offense.[59] Confiscation was costly because the paper had to pay court fees and lawyers' fees, in addition to the cost of printing and the loss of revenue for that day.[60] Nghiêm Xuân Thiện, former publisher of the opposition paper *Thời Luận* during the Diệm period, provided a rough estimate of the cost of confiscation for a medium-sized paper like his, which had a daily run of fifteen thousand copies.[61] Production costs, including salaries, totaled 393,000 dong per issue. In addition, the loss of advertising revenue amounted to approximately 50,000 dong. In total, confiscation might cost an average paper close to 500,000 dong, even before court expenses. As discussed later, confiscation became even more problematic for newspaper publishers after the promulgation of Decree 007 in 1972.

Despite state control, there was still a great deal of diversity in political views, criticisms, and opinions in the RVN's public sphere. Writers and publishers did not surrender to censorship easily or quietly. For example, when the political weekly journal *Sống* (To Live) was shut down in 1968 for allegedly misleading the public by reporting erroneous economic news, there was a great deal of protest in the public sphere. Critics of the shutdown voiced their opposition in the print media as well as in the National Assembly. The director of the government's press office was surprised at the widespread uproar, especially since it came from people who had no personal connection to the publication.[62] Similarly, when the publisher of *Tự Do* (Freedom) newspaper was fined and jailed for four months in 1969, PEN Vietnam, a branch of PEN International that was established in Vietnam in 1957, lobbied the government on his behalf.[63] *Tự Do*'s publisher, Phạm Việt Tuyền, was a member of PEN Vietnam and by 1970 had become its secretary-general. In addition to PEN Vietnam, the newspaper publishers association and three organizations for journalists protested the imprisonment of *Tự Do*'s publisher.[64]

Some publishers resisted censorship, while others found creative ways to evade it. It appears that many newspapers disregarded the requirement to send two copies to the Ministry of the Interior before distribution. As a result, ministry officials felt compelled to send reminders to newspaper publishers in July 1972.[65] Moreover, even when found to be in violation of the press law, some newspapers still managed to get the offending issue to readers. Ministry officials warned the mayor of Saigon and provincial chiefs of this problem and requested that they check all news outlets and shops for banned issues. One problem was the time lag between the issuance and execution of a confiscation order, which allowed publishers to get their papers to market.[66] Lý Quí Chung, who worked for several opposition papers in the 1970s, disclosed that the *Điện Tín* staff used to smuggle copies of banned issues to a neighboring house through the attic before the police could act.[67]

Government officials were certainly aware of newspapers' strategies to bypass confiscation. Huỳnh Ngọc Diệp, director of the office of the Ministry of the Interior, alerted the Ministry of Information about this problem and provided an example: although *Đông Phương* (The East) usually produced 27,000 copies daily, when the newspaper was confiscated, only 14,128 copies were seized.[68] Newspaper publishers were not the only ones who flouted the law. Diệp reported on the case of Vũ Văn Qũy, a member of the House of Representatives, who bought three hundred copies of a banned issue of *Sóng Thần* before seizure and sent them to his constituents in Phước Tuy province. He stamped each copy with the words: A gift from your Representative.[69]

These examples suggest that although the state attempted to restrict the public sphere, people continually worked to thwart state control. Compared with North Vietnam, where the Lao Động Party maintained tighter control over society, the RVN government was not as successful at muting opposition voices.[70] David Marr points out that there were many issues the RVN government did not care to control, and South Vietnamese intellectuals, unlike their counterparts in the north, did not have to "affirm the political line to retain access to food and housing."[71]

Although southern intellectuals did not depend on the state for their livelihood, they did depend on the forces of the capitalist market. Papers in the RVN had to compete for and cater to a small population of literate consumers to survive.[72] South Vietnamese readers expected not only news reports but also entertainment. Even the more serious newspapers typically included incisive editorials or satirical columns. Readers expected journalists to take a critical stance, and the most popular papers were those that dared to challenge, provoke, and satirize those in power. Consequently, when a paper was confiscated for infringing on the censorship law, illegal sales of that issue skyrocketed.[73] The authorities were certainly aware of this correlation, as evidenced by a report from the minister of information to the prime minister, in which he noted that confiscation not only increased the public's desire to read the paper but also increased advertising revenue.[74]

Confiscation might boost a paper's reputation, but a newspaper was unlikely to go out of its way to provoke the censors to the point of confiscation. Confiscation was costly in terms of both money and time, so most papers tried to strike a balance by delivering criticism in an indirect, satirical, or tongue-in-cheek way.[75] To this end, most had a satirical commentary column; some of the favorites were those written by Tiểu Nguyên Tử in Tiếng Chuông (Bell's Chime), Chu Tử of Sống, and Father Nguyễn Quang Lãm in Xây Dựng (To Build).[76]

Some newspapers in the RVN had more freedom than others. Because parliamentary immunity allowed members of the National Assembly more freedom of expression, it was common for senators and lower-house members to serve as publishers of dailies and periodicals. Some prominent examples were senators Đặng Văn Sung and Tôn Thất Đính and representatives Lý Quí Chung and Võ Long Triều (founder of the New Life Development Project). The newspapers published by these politicians had more freedom to express political opinions, but their immunity lasted only as long as they were members of the National Assembly. For instance, Ngô Công Đức, publisher of Tin Sáng (Morning News), had to go into exile when he lost his seat in the lower house in 1971. Đức, a prominent member of the Third Force, had used his paper to criticize Thiệu and to advocate for US withdrawal and a negotiated settlement.[77] Undercover communist agent and Time correspondent Phạm Xuân Ẩn was the one who warned Đức of the president's plan to arrest him.[78] It did not take much to convince Đức to flee; his newspaper office had already been firebombed twice and his press set on fire, probably by agents of the state.

Although the government had a powerful role in delineating the boundaries of the public sphere in the RVN, the NLF-communist side also played a part. In addition to infiltrating the press, communist operatives carried out acts of intimidation, harassment, and terrorism. One of the most respected newspapers in South Vietnam, *Chính Luận* (Political Discussion), and its publisher, Senator Đặng Văn Sung, routinely received threats for the paper's pro-American and anticommunist editorials. On December 30, 1965, *Chính Luận*'s editor Từ Chung was shot and killed in front of his house by communist assassins.[79] Although impeded by both government restrictions and communist intimidation, publishers and journalists continued to fight for their right to report the news and voice their opinions.

## Decree 007

Although the 1969 law imposed some limitations on the press, Decree 007, introduced on August 4, 1972, further reduced freedom of expression. Writers and publishers complained that Decree 007 enacted a level of censorship not seen since the days of Ngô Đình Diệm. The People's Bloc (Khối Dân Tộc), a political alliance in the legislature, went further and called it backward and more oppressive than French law, which to Vietnamese nationalists was a stinging insult.[80] It should be noted that the new press restrictions came in the wake of the Easter offensive. Martial law had been imposed in late June when the ARVN was still struggling to gain control over lost territories. While some observers considered press restriction an appropriate response to a precarious military situation, publishers of opposition papers believed the new law, particularly the requirement of a hefty deposit for each publication, was formulated to reduce the number of opposition papers and to muzzle the press.[81]

From the government's perspective, restrictions were necessary to stop communist infiltration of the press and, ultimately, for national security.[82] Moreover, according to Hoàng Đức Nhã, former press secretary for Thiệu and the minister of mobilization and open arms, the law's purpose was to weed out irresponsible newspapers that published misleading and slanderous information for profit or political purposes. As the minister in charge of implementing the law, Nhã maintained that he was flexible in enforcing it. He even waived the deposit requirement for a handful of publications deemed "respectable" from the government's point of view if they could not afford to pay.[83]

The law's requirement of a large deposit was clearly its most onerous aspect. Each daily paper had to deposit 20 million dong (approximately US$46,000) in the government's treasury.[84] Periodicals had to pay 10 million dong.[85] This money was intended to act as a guarantee against possible future violations of the press law. More specifically, it would be used to pay court fees resulting from either

violations of the press law or civil lawsuits against the newspaper.[86] Before Decree 007, publications were required to pay only 500,000 dong—one-fortieth the
amount required by the new regulation.[87] Publications had up to thirty days to
pay; those that could not or did not comply would be considered to have voluntarily suspended publication (*tự ý đình bản*).[88] On August 28, 1972, twenty-four
days after the issuance of the decree, no paper had complied with the new regulation. This led the government to extend the deadline to September 15.

Even with the extension, many papers had to close because they could not
raise enough money.[89] Before the new decree, there had been twenty-seven
Vietnamese-language and fourteen Chinese-language daily newspapers in the
RVN. Eleven of the Chinese-language newspapers survived, but only seventeen
Vietnamese papers did so.[90] The situation was just as dire for periodicals. Before the decree, there were 145 weekly and monthly publications. Of these, only
four were able to pay the deposit: *Phụ Nữ Mới* (New Woman), *Phụ Nữ Tân-Tiến*
(Trendy Women), *Văn Nghệ Tiền Phong* (Vanguard Arts), and *Sân Khấu Mới*
(New Stage).[91] The government waived the fee for thirty-eight publications that
were considered educational, religious, or scientific. Twenty-eight publications
applied to be recategorized as special arts publications (*giai phẩm đặc san*), which
meant they would not be subject to the new law and could avoid paying the deposit.[92] The other seventy-five periodicals presumably had to cease operation.

The minister of information confessed to the prime minister that he was sympathetic to the publishers' plight and was keen to help the periodicals recatego-
rize. However, he acknowledged that he was, in effect, helping them circumvent
the law.[93] Although the recategorization meant the publications did not have to
pay the deposit, it created other problems. According to a joint statement from
the Giai Phẩm (Arts) Collective and the Association of Periodical Publishers,
many of these publications encountered financial difficulties. Because special
arts publications were not produced on a regular schedule, it was difficult for
them to maintain readership. As a result, by the fall of 1972, only twelve special
arts publications still survived, but they were struggling.[94]

Some newspapers managed to keep operating through a variety of ways.
Some, such as *Hòa Bình* (Peace), borrowed money to pay the deposit. *Sóng Thần*
took a more innovative approach: it appealed to its readers and supporters. As
discussed in chapter 6, *Sóng Thần* was unique in that it was a cooperative paper;
the daily had raised its start-up capital by selling shares. To raise funds for its
deposit, the paper once again called on shareholders to increase their contributions and for regular readers to provide loans.[95] According to the paper, its plan
was to contribute 2 million dong from its own coffers, borrow 10 million, and
raise 8 million through readers. On August 7 the paper called for donations, and
within one week it had raised a little over 4 million dong. By August 28, *Sóng*

*Thần* had received more than 7 million dong, with individual donations rang-ing from 10,000 to 1 million dong.[96]

Decree 007 also increased the penalty for violating press regulations. Fines grew substantially, as did the length of prison terms.[97] Penalties for some viola-tions were particularly harsh. For example, publications found to be promoting communist ideas could be fined 1 million to 5 million dong, and their publish-ers could be sentenced to jail terms of two to five years (Article 47).[98] When a paper or periodical was confiscated for infringement of the press law, the gov-ernment seized not only copies of the issue but also the printing plates. Papers that had been confiscated more than once for publishing material that endan-gered national security and public order would be temporarily shut down, pend-ing the court's decision (Article 19).[99]

To make matters worse for publishers, the authorities became more assiduous in enforcing the law. According to Lý Quí Chung, onetime editor of *Điện Tín*, before 1972 the authorities were less likely to penalize papers found to be in contravention of the law.[100] In addition, censors had apparently taken a broader interpretation of the law. Like Law 019/69, Decree 007 banned works that were considered harmful to the national security, social order, Vietnamese customs, or an individual's reputation (Articles 23, 25, 27, and 29).[101] The decree did nothing to clarify the vagueness of these stipulations, but it seemed to be applied more often after 1972 for a wide range of situations. According to government records for 1974, the most violated aspect of the law was Article 28A, which forbade the publication of news, however truthful, that could harm national security or pub-lic order.[102] The broad interpretation of what constituted national security and public order caused many problems for newspapers. It was so difficult to discern that *Sóng Thần* surreptitiously hired someone from the Ministry of Information to inspect its galleys before sending them out for formal review.[103]

Not surprisingly, the media's reaction to the new decree was strongly criti-cal. Three days after Decree 007 was issued, members of the Association of News-paper Owners met to voice their concerns. The president of the association, Senator Tôn Thất Đính, owner of the newspaper *Công Luận* (Public Discussion), and Senator Hồng Sơn Đông of the newspaper *Điện Tín* declared that the new decree was unconstitutional and unlawful. They asked Thiệu to reconsider, as the changes would make it difficult for newspapers to operate or survive.[104]

Although the impact of Decree 007 was most immediate on those newspa-pers that could not come up with the 20 million dong deposit and were forced to close, the papers that survived felt the effects of the stringent press regula-tions over the next two years. By 1974, oppositional newspapers were finding it increasingly difficult to navigate the vague press regulations, and numerous is-sues had been confiscated because of alleged violations of Decree 007. It was not uncommon to see notices in papers such as *Sóng Thần* and *Hòa Bình* apologizing to readers about the previous day's confiscated issue. *Hòa Bình* was confiscated five times within a seventeen-day period in August 1974.[105]

# The Fight against Government Corruption

*Hòa Bình*'s numerous skirmishes with state censors were undoubtedly related to its unabashed support of an anticorruption movement that emerged in the summer of 1974. Led by right-wing, anticommunist priest Trần Hữu Thanh, this movement accused Thiệu's government and his family of corruption. The government's heavy-handed response to this movement galvanized the press and led to an explosion of antigovernment activities, joining the two causes of anticorruption and freedom of the press into one potent movement.

The economic, political, and military context of this period played an important role in the emergence of this anticorruption movement. US withdrawal and the global oil crisis in 1973 created widespread and profound economic problems for South Vietnam. The military situation for South Vietnam was also perilous. In March 1974 communist troops, bolstered by renewed Soviet military aid, were preparing for another general offensive and uprising.[106] With US president Richard Nixon's resignation in August over the Watergate scandal, any hope of US intervention against a massive communist offensive was snuffed out. The situation was desperate for the RVN government and those who wanted to prevent a communist takeover.

Given this situation, it was not surprising that government corruption aroused intense resentment and anger in the media and in society. Corruption had plagued the RVN throughout its history, but by 1974, rumors of scandal had reached the highest level of government, implicating the president's family and those around them. It had become difficult for even government supporters to overlook the serious scandals that emerged. For example, in late January 1974 the Long An scandal broke, revealing a high-level smuggling operation that involved Thiệu's wife and her family.[107] The Vietnamese media covered the story, confirming what many had suspected: the president's in-laws had been using convoys of military vehicles to transfer smuggled goods. Although some of those who were directly involved were punished, Thiệu was able to protect high-ranking officials and his own family members. To show that the regime was cracking down on corruption, in February the minister of veterans affairs was fired for running a gambling den at his home. In addition, top-ranking police officers were charged with smuggling electronics and luxury goods.[108] This massive scale of corruption at the highest levels and during an economically difficult period enraged the public.[109]

Not surprisingly, there was a groundswell of opposition against official malfeasance. On June 18, 1974, more than three hundred Roman Catholic priests signed a petition calling for an end to corruption. These priests later founded the People's Movement against Corruption, led by Father Trần Hữu Thanh.[110] A Redemptorist priest from Huế, Father Thanh was known for his strong anticommunist stance and involvement in politics. He shared the Ngô brothers' enthusiasm for personalism, a humanist social philosophy with roots in the French Catholic Left. His 1955 book proposed the application of personalism as a way to unite noncommunist nationalists and build a viable nation.[111] Father Thanh was also a strong advocate for an honest and scrupulous government. During the First Republic under Diệm, he had exposed corruption in the central region, leading to the demotion of half a dozen provincial heads.[112] His anticorruption activism in 1974 was therefore not out of character, but it was much more daring, as the People's Movement against Corruption was targeting not provincial-level leaders but national leaders, including the president and his family.

As a result of Father Thanh's prominent stance against communism, Thiệu could not dismiss him as a communist agent or left-wing sympathizer, as he had done with other Catholic priests who opposed his policies.[113] For example, left-leaning Fathers Chân Tín and Nguyễn Ngọc Lan were discredited by Thiệu as communist sympathizers and were frequently targeted for arrest and harassment.[114] Many Catholic priests and laypeople, who might have shied away from the activism of Chân Tín and Nguyễn Ngọc Lan because of their politics or fear of state persecution, were more likely to join Father Thanh's campaign. Consequently, the People's Movement against Corruption became popular, spreading to many parishes throughout Vietnam.[115] Anticorruption street rallies consistently attracted hundreds and sometimes thousands of people. For example, two demonstrations in Huế in September attracted several thousand people each and on November 17 an anticorruption meeting at Tân Chí Linh church in Saigon drew two thousand participants. Approximately five thousand people gathered to hear Father Thanh on December 8 in a Catholic village outside of Cần Thơ.[116]

The centerpiece of Father Thanh's anticorruption campaign was his Public Indictment No. 1 (Bản Cáo Trạng số 1), which consisted of six serious allegations against the president's family. The first two accusations alleged that Thiệu had illegally amassed substantial wealth in real estate. The third allegation implicated Thiệu's brother in-law, Nguyễn Xuân Nguyên, in a fertilizer speculation scandal. Thiệu was linked to this scandal because he had stopped a senate committee from investigating. The fourth allegation claimed that Vì Dân hospital (a charity hospital founded by Thiệu's wife) had been misused. The fifth allegation accused both the president and Prime Minister Trần Thiện Khiêm of protecting high-ranking officials who smuggled and distributed heroin throughout South Vietnam. According to the indictment, the person responsible for this smuggling operation was General Đặng Văn Quang, the president's special assistant for national security and military affairs and also a close personal friend. The last allegation charged Thiệu's aunt and Phạm Sanh, the president of Nam Việt Bank, for failing to deliver rice to central Vietnam, even though they had accepted payment of 1billion dong in advance. Their action had a grave impact on the rural population, which had been experiencing a rice shortage for over a year.[117]

According to anticorruption activists, corruption was not only hurting the people and society, it was also negatively affecting the RVN's prosecution of the war. Father Thanh argued that the war against communism could not be won with Thiệu at the helm because, by allowing corruption to fester, Thiệu was weakening South Vietnam's ability to fight communism. In other words, Father Thanh's motivation for indicting Thiệu was to strengthen South Vietnam in its fight against communism. By November, Father Thanh made his message more explicit by criticizing how Thiệu was waging the war and calling for his resignation. However, he later revised his position and suggested the formation of a National Leadership Committee to help guide the president.[118]

Because of Father Thanh's prowar stance, the DRV also saw his movement as a problem. According to the Lao Động–controlled daily newspaper *Nhân Dân* (The People), despite Father Thanh's opposition to Thiệu, his message was vague and, more importantly, he did not question the war's premise or US intervention in it.[119] In fact, Hanoi accused Thanh of working with the Americans.[120] According to the senior spokesperson for the NLF, Colonel Võ Đông Giang, Father Thanh's idea of a National Leadership Committee was a ploy to help Thiệu stay in power by spreading the "illusion that the Thiệu regime can be transformed."[121] The DRV's strong condemnation of Father Thanh and its effort to discredit him suggest that communist leaders felt threatened by the growing mass movement inspired by the priest.

Contrary to Hanoi's allegation of collusion between the United States and Father Thanh, the US embassy's assessment of the anticorruption movement was decidedly negative. Characterizing the movement as radical and its indictment of Thiệu as "sensationalized," the embassy's reports emphasized the lack of cooperation and support for the movement outside the core group.[122] In other words, embassy officials did not foresee this movement evolving into a sustained or effective political force. Embassy reports also stressed the lack of support from the Catholic hierarchy. The bishop of Saigon, Nguyễn Văn Bình, was "mildly supportive" at first but soon distanced himself.[123] The bishops of Qui Nhơn and Đà Nẵng were also against this movement, according to US officials.[124]

The Thiệu government was unsure how to react to this anticorruption movement. At first, the authorities responded harshly. On September 8, 1974, at Father Thanh's first mass anticorruption demonstration, the police ordered the people to disperse, claiming the organizers had not received permission for the event. When people did not leave the area, the police used force and pepper spray on the crowd, resulting in ten injuries, including two children, one lower house member, and one disabled veteran.[125] Public outcry against this heavy-handed response made the central government retreat, calling on local authorities to refrain from using force against anticorruption demonstrators. Going even further, the government dismissed Colonel Tôn Thất Khiên, province chief of Thừa Thiên and mayor of Huế, for mishandling the September 8 rally.[126] Although the next few rallies were peaceful, without any clashes, violence broke out on October 31 when police tried to stop Father Thanh and his supporters from marching outside the Tân Sa Châu parish neighborhood in Saigon. In the melee, approximately seventy-five people were hurt, including Father Thanh, who was punched in the face by a plainclothes police officer.[127]

Although Thiệu insisted that Father Thanh's accusations were false, he never charged the priest with slander. It is possible that Thiệu did not want to give Father Thanh a chance to denounce him in open court. Thiệu instead forbade the publication of the indictment against him and banned any mention that Thiệu was the target of these accusations. The publication ban backfired, however, and brought even more attention and support to Father Thanh's cause. In fact, the anticorruption march on October 31 had been organized to support three daily newspapers (*Sóng Thần, Đại Dân Tộc, and Điện Tín*) that were on trial for publishing Father Thanh's indictment.[128] As the anticorruption movement gained momentum and attention, the press became more resentful about its inability to fully report Father Thanh's grievances and, more specifically, his six-point indictment. The press's mounting indignation had already led to the founding on September 6, 1974, of the Committee for Freedom of the Press.[129] Members included newspaper publishers and journalists with divergent political views, including the anticommunist papers of Father Nguyễn Quang Lâm (*Xây Dựng* daily) and Nguyên Tu (*Chính Luận*), the Third Force publication of Hồng Sơn Đông (*Điện Tín*), and the opposition paper of Võ Long Triều (*Đại Dân Tộc*).[130] Other members included the Newspaper Owners Association, PEN Vietnam, and two major journalist associations, one of which was known to be dominated by communist-affiliated members. Many senators and elected lower house representatives from the opposition Quốc Gia (Nationalist) and Dân Tộc Xã Hội (Socialist People's) blocs also participated.[131] In short, the Committee for Freedom of the Press brought together various political factions and included many left-wing and antiwar activists as well as anticommunist nationalists.

The Committee for Freedom of the Press organized dramatic public protests, such as the burning of Decree 007 and the older Law 019/69 in the senate chamber, with three hundred members and supporters in attendance.[132] More daringly, on September 19 three dailies, *Sóng Thần*, *Đại Dân Tộc*, and *Điện Tín*, decided to print Father Thanh's indictments, in defiance of Thiệu's ban. As expected, a confiscation order was issued for all three papers. But the publishers had coordinated with supporters to turn this event into a dramatic protest, which resulted in the torching of the papers.[133] These three papers received a great deal of sympathy and support from civil society. More than two hundred lawyers volunteered to defend them against the government's charges of violating the publication ban.[134] However, their trials were postponed several times, and the charges would eventually be dropped in February 1975.[135]

While the three daily newspapers awaited their trials, protest actions continued into October, until Thiệu finally offered to compromise. On October 24, 1974, Hoàng Đức Nhã, the minister of mass mobilization and open arms, resigned. Because his ministry was responsible for censorship, and because many journalists and publishers believed he was overly draconic in applying the law, his resignation was a clear sign of the government's attempt to appease the protesters. Nhã, however, maintains that his resignation was more about a conflict between himself and Prime Minister Trần Thiện Khiêm, rather than pressure from the press.[136] Although there might have been more than one reason for his resignation, the timing suggests that the press outcry against him was a strong factor. Moreover, Thiệu made other changes in response to criticism. He dismissed 377 military officers on charges of corruption.[137] Since these were mostly lower-ranking officers, the critics were not satisfied. Six days later, the government relented and announced that three military corps commanders would be transferred elsewhere.[138] Thiệu did not, however, address any of the accusations against him and his family.

The government also made some compromises on the issue of freedom of the press. On September 23, near the start of the press crisis, the ministers of mobilization and open arms, interior, and justice met with members of the senate and house of representatives to discuss making changes to the press law. By November, the house and senate were writing draft bills to soften some of the more burdensome impacts of Law 019/69 and Decree 007.[139] On November 14 the lower house approved revisions to the press law in response to protesters' demands. Penalties were reduced, trials for violations of the law would be held in civilian rather than military court, and the 20 million dong deposit was abolished.[140] Even though the revised law barred the minister of mass mobilization from seizing a paper after two consecutive confiscations without a court order, the practice of confiscating papers was not outlawed. This was a defeat for the press because confiscation could easily lead to bankruptcy. Despite the government's efforts to compromise with the protesters, some in the press were not happy with the proposed amendments. Moreover, the gains achieved came at a great cost to the newspapers, many of which had to close shop because the struggle had been so financially burdensome.

In the 1970s South Vietnam clearly had a vibrant and plural public sphere. Activists, journalists, and writers with different political standpoints jostled to make their concerns heard. To voice their views, activists skillfully used the press, established associations and networks, organized street demonstrations, and held public rallies. Their public activities were pursued to inform and mobilize support from the people, both inside and outside the country. These were self-confident, media-savvy, informed activists who were not cowed by a repressive state.

Opposition to the government came from both the right and the left. While some demanded an end to the war, prison reform, and improved living conditions, others campaigned against corruption and censorship. By 1974, issues such as corruption and freedom of the press united people at both ends of the political spectrum. For the Left and liberals, these were important issues because freedom and good governance form the foundation of a just society. For the staunchly anticommunist activists, these issues were important because they impeded South Vietnam's ability to fight against the DRV and its organizations in the south.

The government tried its best to rein in elements of the public sphere and control civil society. It is evident that the authorities treated those suspected of working with communists more harshly; imprisonment without trial and the use of torture were common. In such instances, vocal members of civil society lobbied for their release and for their rights to be respected. Although they did not always succeed in getting political prisoners released or stopping the abusive treatment of dissidents, the relentless public pressure and attention marshaled by these activists undoubtedly helped curb state repression.

For political moderates and anticommunist opponents and critics, the government was more likely to follow due process. Some in the government recognized the need to compromise and be lenient with the politically moderate press to achieve hegemonic influence. To this end, in 1969 the director of the Office of the President criticized the Ministry of the Interior for being too strict when dealing with politically moderate newspapers such as *Hòa Bình*. He noted that their real enemies were communists, not democratic critics.[141] The director's attitude mirrors that of some officials when deliberating about Chinese mutual-aid associations after the Tet offensive. As discussed in chapter 2, pragmatists within the bureaucracy advocated leniency in allowing Chinese-only organizations to form because, in the war against communism, winning Chinese loyalty was more imperative than achieving cultural assimilation. It appears that, in the case of moderate newspapers in 1974, Thiệu eventually adopted a conciliatory approach. In the end, the government made concessions. It softened and loosened the press law, removed some offending officials and senior military officers, and eventually dropped the cases against the three newspapers that had published Father Thanh's banned indictment.

After 1975, it became clear that the new socialist government was even more parsimonious with press freedom. Journalists and publishers, especially those who had remained in Vietnam and endured years of imprisonment, expressed a new appreciation for the freedom they had enjoyed under the Second Republic. Reflecting on his fifteen years as a journalist in the RVN, one writer said he had not encountered any difficulties and "was never ordered to write by anybody."[142] Trùng Dương, the publisher of *Sóng Thần*, noted that despite the hardship of the press law and the many times she had to go to court for alleged violations, the South Vietnamese press at least had legal recourse that could be used to defend their rights.[143]

# CHALLENGES AND POSSIBILITIES IN COMPARATIVE CONTEXT

Although the historiography of South Vietnam has become richer, more nuanced, and grounded in rigorous research, this was not the case some fifteen years ago when I was casting about for book topics. The South Vietnam I consumed through both popular media and scholarship contained a limited assortment of people: corrupt and bumbling military generals, traumatized Vietnamese women and children, hard-core Viet Cong fighters, and exotic bar girls. This stereotypical presentation of the RVN did not correspond with the personal accounts and memories of those who lived there. The discrepancy inspired me to dig deeper, to examine how ordinary people experienced their lives in wartime South Vietnam. How did residents of South Vietnam cope with the ravages of war? How did they navigate government repression, communist terrorism, and US intrusion? To gain some insight, I chose to focus on voluntary associations and the public sphere. I wanted to see what collective actions people took to protect themselves, improve their lives, and assist others.

From this vantage point, I discovered that, contrary to the familiar depictions, South Vietnamese society was teeming with ordinary people from different walks of life, many of whom voluntarily participated in public life. They participated for diverse and multiple reasons. Some sought to boost their social status, widen their social network, or enrich their social lives. Others participated for religious, altruistic, or patriotic reasons. These motives were not mutually exclusive or fixed throughout time. It was likely that people had multiple reasons for joining a group or raising funds for a cause. No doubt, these reasons changed over time as well. The Vietnam War provided the context for a large part of people's associational lives, but the war certainly did not define them. People were organizing to shelter refugees, take care of war orphans, and bury victims of military massacres. But they were also organizing for social, religious, recreational, intellectual, and cultural purposes.

Even though people had agency in their associational lives, there were larger forces at work, shaping and delineating their public experiences and access. Like the many historical examples of associational life found in the West, as opposed to its idealized iteration, civil society in the RVN was not completely open and free to all. As is the case in many societies, money, politics, and status played a determining role in a group's ability to operate and an individual's ability to join. For the laboring class, some organizations' entrance and membership fees were significant barriers. Similarly, status and politics affected an individual's ability to participate. The political orientation or affiliation of a group could lead to intense state scrutiny or, worse, the inability to obtain official status.

However, as illustrated throughout this book, although the state controlled the parameters of civil society, determining the limits of the public sphere and its associated activities, its hegemony was not complete. This was true for all periods, including the First Republic under Ngô Đình Diệm, the interim period under military rule, and the Second Republic. Even during the First Republic, which was reputedly more repressive than later eras, the authorities did not have complete control over civil society. Despite the law, many groups did not register before they began operating. Moreover, with the increased US and communist presence from the mid-1960s onward, public life became more contested. The US government, along with many private agencies, attempted to extend its influence by providing aid, support, and advice to select Vietnamese groups and individuals. To this end, US officials and aid agencies promoted groups such as the Library Association, the Popular Culture Association, and the summer youth program. The Lao Động Party, through its many organizations in the south—the NLF, the PRP, and the Alliance of National, Democratic, and Peace Forces—also sought to shape civil society. Communist agents operated secretly in South Vietnamese society; some of them infiltrated voluntary organizations, while others were active in the public sphere as journalists, publishers, and activists.

These competing forces might have been challenging for civil society participants to navigate, but they could also provide an advantage, especially for groups with counterhegemonic views. Because this was a highly competitive arena, the state did not have a monopoly on coercive power. Therefore, to maintain its influence, the state sometimes needed to accommodate groups and limit its use of violence. Moreover, when besieged by state restrictions or repression, groups made alliances, appealed to the domestic and international public, and used street protests to dramatize their concerns.

This pattern of state accommodation was also prevalent in the French colonial era. Under colonial rule, the state placed limits on people's associational lives. However, as several scholars have observed, the French colonial government negotiated and accommodated some constituents of civil society to strengthen state control and its moral authority. The state supported philanthropic endeavors initiated by the Catholic Church and the elite Vietnamese to ease its own burden of providing social welfare and to stem the tide of radicalism.[1] To this end, colonial officials even supported the Vietnam Confederation of Workers, which did not have legal status, in an effort to forestall the growth of a communist-led labor movement in Vietnam.[2]

The continuity from the colonial to the postcolonial period also extended to participation in and organization of associational life. As discussed in chapters 2 and 3, colonial-era social and civic groups were active in both periods; some moved their organizations south after the Geneva Accords. In the RVN, many continued to expand mass education, take care of orphans, and provide rudimentary health care. Their work in the RVN continued to be shaped by an array of philosophies, ideologies, and worldviews, which included religious morality as well as Confucian ethics and a republican sense of citizenry. In the republican period, new ideas such as modernization theory and community development provided inspiration for participants to conceptualize their work.

Despite the similarities, there were significant differences between the two periods. The Cold War made the public sphere and civil society more contested in the RVN. The competition for influence was no longer just between society and state. Actions of the United States and the DRV and its southern allies had a palpable impact on associational life.

A discussion about South Vietnam inevitably invites questions about the north. Although my focus is the RVN, I will comment briefly on the DRV's associational life. The existence of numerous voluntary organizations in South Vietnam stands in stark contrast to the public life in North Vietnam. During the war, the ruling Lao Động Party effectively restricted activities by funneling citizens into associations controlled by the party and state. The Fatherland Front (Mặt Trận Tổ Quốc) was established in 1957 to act as an umbrella organization for multiple groups such as the Women's Union, the Youth Union, and the General Confederation of Labor. Professionals and intellectuals were encouraged to join various organizations such as the Historical Association, the Writers Union, or the General Association of Medical and Pharmaceutical Studies.[3] At the national and provincial levels, each major religion in North Vietnam—Catholic, Buddhist, and Protestant—was permitted to establish an official organization. By law, North Vietnamese were allowed to organize associations, but they had to "have a legitimate purpose and contribute to the construction of the 'people's democratic regime.'"[4] Consequently, very little associational life existed outside of party and state control, with the exception of elderly women's local Buddhist prayer groups, which seemingly posed little threat to the party.[5] The various groups under the control of the Fatherland Front participated in spreading the state's messages and promoting various state campaigns. The Peasants Union, for example, helped promote land reform and collectivization.[6] The Women's Union was at the forefront of the state's campaign to encourage women to participate in building socialism.[7]

Although the party and state exerted enormous control over associational life in the DRV, there is still much to be learned about state-society dynamics in North Vietnam, as this is an understudied topic. As such, it would be premature to assume that the state completely dominated society, quashing any possibility of state-society compromise and negotiation. Deeper research into how groups within the Fatherland Front operated and how they interacted with local and national governments is required to ascertain how much latitude there was for negotiation and compromise. From what we have learned about civil society during the French colonial period and during the RVN, we could surmise that the DRV's need to mobilize support for the war might have required the state to be more tolerant and compromising in some instances. Research on the DRV's attempts to revolutionize culture and social practices suggests that the state's ability to impose its will was far from all-encompassing. Shaun Malarney's research into North Vietnamese village customs and rituals during the war, for example, illustrates how the state had to accommodate, to some extent, people's spiritual and social needs.[8] Ashley Pettus's research shows that, by the early 1970s, inconsistencies and contradictions in the DRV's messaging about gender and socialist modernity allowed young women to defy the socialist feminine ideal. These examples of small compromises and fissures in state control suggest that associational life might have had more leeway to maneuver.

Research on contemporary Vietnam similarly suggests that civil society has been successful in eking out space and compromises, despite the one-party rule that has existed since the end of the war. Following the implementation of liberal economic reforms (đổi mới) starting in 1986, Vietnam has seen a resurgence of civil society and a proliferation of a multitude of diverse voluntary organizations. The country's shift toward a market economy, coupled with the state's retreat from social service provision, prompted and perhaps even required voluntary groups to step in to fill the gaps. In villages, many kinship and communal-based associations sprang up to assist people in their social, cultural, and spiritual lives.[9] These informal and localized organizations, which tended to operate without legal status, were also active in addressing government corruption and other larger socioeconomic issues. In urban areas, both officially recognized and unrecognized civil society organizations also emerged during the period of reform. Some were religious based, focusing on charity and philanthropy, while other tackled development, health, and environmental issues.[10] Both domestic and foreign donors played a critical role in providing much-needed aid to these organizations.

Although civil society groups have been able to operate outside of state- or party-directed organizations since the mid-1980s, the field of action available for nonstate groups remains limited. The state and the Vietnamese Communist Party maintain tight control over what kind of issues or activities voluntary groups can pursue. Moreover, as state-endorsed mass organizations continue to be prevalent in all aspects of society, there is a large overlap between state and party agents and civil society participants. This makes it difficult to discern between state and nonstate activities and to determine whether civil society organizations are acting independently.[11] Because of these restrictions and blurred boundaries, which are seen as deviations from the dominant idealized model, Vietnam scholars have suggested alternative ways to identify and understand civil society.[12] Some have proposed a focus on actual state-society conflict, dialogue, and negotiation and on processes and actions rather than on groups' organizational structures or ideation. Other scholars have found that civil society groups have been able to advance their interests by circumventing and navigating the system to achieve their goals.[13] In doing so, these scholars have identified significant collective actions carried out for an array of pressing issues.

This brief discussion of civil society in contemporary Vietnam suggests that to operate in an authoritarian political environment, voluntary groups need to strategize carefully. Groups may try to collaborate with or work around state and party agencies. In many cases, groups must make alliances with other sectors within the ruling elite or leverage their connections with domestic and foreign supporters. Similarly, in the RVN, those voluntary groups whose goals and outlook aligned with the objectives of the government in power had the best chance of success and survival. Organizations with less favorable standing with the authorities did their best to cultivate domestic and foreign support when faced with state restriction or repression. In their maneuvering and strategizing, voluntary organizations in both historical and contemporary periods demonstrate agency, suggesting that even in challenging circumstances, civil society can be resilient, creative, and consequential.

# Notes

## INTRODUCTION

1. Nguyễn Hữu Châu, minister of the interior and government representative (*đại biểu chánh phủ*), January 8, 1956, Records of the President's Office, First Republic, National Archive of Vietnam, No. 2, Ho Chi Minh City, 16200 (hereafter cited as PTTD1). Châu was also the minister of state at the prime minister's office. See Tran, *Disunion*, 174.

2. See tables in PTTD1 16200.

3. Two exceptions are books by Sophie Quinn-Judge and Heather Stur, which examine aspects of civil society. Quinn-Judge focuses on the Third Force and the antiwar movements, while Stur examines political activism in Saigon. Covering the French colonial period, Charles Keith writes about Catholic organizations, both Shawn McHale and Philippe Peycam examine the public sphere, and Martina Nguyen writes about the Tự Lực Văn Đoàn's League of Light housing project. Quinn-Judge, *Third Force in the Vietnam War*; Stur, *Saigon at War*; Keith, *Catholic Vietnam*; McHale, *Print and Power*; Peycam, *Birth of Vietnamese Political Journalism*; Nguyen, "French Colonial State, Vietnamese Civil Society."

4. Many historians consider the beginning of the Vietnam War, also known as the Second Indochina War and the American War, to have occurred in 1965, when the United States sent combat troops to South Vietnam. I suggest that from South Vietnam's perspective, the war started in 1960 with the formation of the National Liberation Front and the movement of supplies and people from North Vietnam to the south to support this insurgency.

5. For critical overviews of the historiography, see Catton, "Refighting Vietnam in the History Books"; Miller and Vu, "Vietnam War as a Vietnamese War."

6. Notable examples of monographs include Catton, *Diem's Final Failure*; Elliott, *Vietnamese War*; Brigham, *ARVN*; Hunt, *Vietnam's Southern Revolution*; Wiest, *Vietnam's Forgotten Army*; Veith, *Black April*; Miller, *Misalliance*; Chapman, *Cauldron of Resistance*; Stewart, *Vietnam's Lost Revolution*; Tran, *Disunion*.

7. Books on South Vietnamese society include Dror, *Making Two Vietnams*; Quinn-Judge, *Third Force in the Vietnam War*; Vu and Fear, *Republic of Vietnam*; Stur, *Saigon at War*.

8. Wiktorowicz, "Civil Society as Social Control," 43.

9. Habermas, "Further Reflections on the Public Sphere," 421–61.

10. Bratton, "Beyond the State," 418.

11. Wiktorowicz, "Civil Society as Social Control," 45; Bratton, "Beyond the State," 411.

12. Kerkvliet, "Approach for Analysing State-Society Relations in Vietnam," S159. See also Hannah, "Local Non-Government Organizations in Vietnam."

13. Weller, *Alternate Civilities*, 35.

14. Madsen, "Public Sphere, Civil Society and Moral Community," 189–90. See also Koo, "Origins of the Public Sphere and Civil Society," 381–86.

15. Putnam, *Making Democracy Work*, 88.

16. Putnam, "Bowling Alone," 67.

17. Ryan, "Civil Society as Democratic Practice," 559–84.

18. Bourdieu, "Forms of Capital," 241–58.

19. Gramsci, *Selections from the Prison Notebooks*, 12–13, 261–63; Femia, *Gramsci's Political Thought*, 24–29.

20. Alagappa, "Civil Society and Political Change," 29.

21. Gramsci, *Selections from the Prison Notebooks*, 263.

22. Landau, "Law and Civil Society in Cambodia and Vietnam," 244.

23. Alagappa, "Civil Society and Political Change," 33.

24. Landau, "Law and Civil Society in Cambodia and Vietnam"; Bui, "Development of Civil Society," 77–93.

25. Habermas, "Further Reflections on the Public Sphere," 453; Habermas, *Structural Transformation of the Public Sphere*, 1417.

26. Fraser, "Rethinking the Public Sphere," 109–42; Ryan, "Gender and Public Access," 259–88; DeVido, "Buddhism for This World," 253–54.

27. Berry, "Public Life in Authoritarian Japan," 133–65; McHale, *Print and Power*; Peycam, *Birth of Vietnamese Political Journalism*.

28. Berry, "Public Life in Authoritarian Japan," 139.

29. Berry, 133.

30. McHale, *Print and Power*, 11.

31. Through personal introductions and the snowball method, I was able to interview past participants of civil society. Interviews were conducted in Vietnamese and took place in person, by telephone, or email.

32. Baker, *Fraternity among the French Peasantry*; Munck, "Mutual Benefit Societies in Argentina."

## 1. THE HISTORICAL AND POLITICAL LANDSCAPE

1. Except for a short period in the early nineteenth century, the name Vietnam was not used until 1945. For simplicity, I use the term Vietnam even when discussing the period before 1945. The term Viet refers to the ethnic group while Vietnamese is a general term for the population of Vietnam, of which the Viet comprised the majority.

2. Taylor, *History of the Vietnamese*, 400; Dutton, Werner, and Whitmore, *Sources of Vietnamese Tradition*, 259.

3. This section is based on the research of Li, "Alternative Vietnam?," 111–21; Cooke, "Regionalism and the Nature of Nguyen Rule," 122–61; Whitmore and Zottoli, "Emergence of the State in Vietnam," 197–233.

4. The classic work on this topic is Woodside, *Vietnam and the Chinese Model*; see also Whitmore and Zottoli, "Emergence of the State in Vietnam."

5. For more on the Nguyễn's relationship with Christianity, see Ramsay, *Mandarins and Martyrs*.

6. For more on the Cần Vương and other early anti-French activities, see Marr, *Vietnamese Anticolonialism*.

7. Marr, chaps. 6, 7.

8. Goscha, *Penguin History of Modern Vietnam*, 102–9.

9. Marr, *Vietnamese Anticolonialism*, 136.

10. Marr, 164–68.

11. Marr, *Vietnamese Tradition on Trial*, chap. 1.

12. Asselin, *Vietnam's American War*, 35.

13. Bernal, "Nghe-Tinh Soviet Movement," 158.

14. Chapman, *Cauldron of Resistance*, 16–17.

15. Goscha, *Penguin History of Modern Vietnam*, 140–41.

16. Rettig, "French Military Policies," 316.

17. Bernal, "Nghe-Tinh Soviet Movement," 150.

18. Truong and Vo, *Peasant Question*, 13–14.

19. Holcombe, *Mass Mobilization*, 65–66.

20. Vu, "'It's Time,'" 534.

21. Vu, "Other Side," 297.

22. Huff, "Causes and Consequences," 181.

23. Vu, "Other Side," 307–8.

24. Guillemot, "Lessons of Yên Bái," 45–47.

25. Tonnesson, *Vietnam 1946*, 18.

26. Vu, "'It's Time,'" 523; Goscha, *Penguin History of Modern Vietnam*, 204.

27. Tonnesson, *Vietnam 1946*, 22.

28. Vu, "'It's Time,'" 523–24.

29. Guillemot, "'Be Men!'" 185.

30. Goscha, *Penguin History of Modern Vietnam*, 238–42.

31. Guillemot, "Autopsy of a Massacre," 229–36.

32. Reilly, "Sovereign States of Vietnam," 117–18.

33. Goscha, *Penguin History of Modern Vietnam*, 266.

34. Goscha, 265.

35. Asselin, *Vietnam's American War*, 67.

36. Hansen, "Bắc Di Cư," 180.

37. Asselin, *Hanoi's Road to War*, 18–19.

38. For more on land reform in the early years, see Vo, "Nguyễn Thị Năm and Land Reform."

39. Hess, "Educated Vietnamese Middle Class," 90.

40. Hoang, "Ideology in Urban South Vietnam," 213–14.

41. Keith, *Catholic Vietnam*, chaps. 1, 2.

42. Hansen, "Bắc Di Cư," 181; Hardy, *Red Hills*, 156–57.

43. Vu and Fear, introduction to *Republic of Vietnam*, 2–3.

44. Jacobs, *Cold War Mandarin*, 20.

45. Catton, Diem's Final Failure, 41–43; Stewart, Vietnam's Lost Revolution, 95–100.

46. Jacobs, *Cold War Mandarin*, 22.

47. Miller, "Vison, Power and Agency," 442–45.

48. Vu, "Other Side," 300.

49. Goscha, *Penguin History of Modern Vietnam*, 310.

50. Jammes, "Caodaism in Times of War," 257–58; Tran, "Beneath the Japanese Umbrella," 71.

51. Jammes, "Caodaism in Times of War," 265.

52. Chapman, *Cauldron of Resistance*, 75.

53. Li, "Partisan to Sovereign," 144.

54. Chapman, *Cauldron of Resistance*, 74.

55. Miller, *Misalliance*, 109, 6.

56. Asselin, *Hanoi's Road to War*, 18.

57. Tran, *Disunion*, 95.

58. I concur with Andrea Kathryn Talentino's suggestion that nation building consists of two interrelated aspects, one that creates state apparatus and the other that builds social solidarity and collective identity. Thank you to Edward Miller for pointing me to Talentino's "Two Faces of Nation-Building."

59. Republic of Vietnam, *Cuộc Di Cư Lịch Sử Tại Việt Nam*, 127.

60. Hansen, "Bắc Di Cư," 177.

61. Republic of Vietnam, *Cuộc Di Cư*, 212.

62. Hansen, "Bắc Di Cư," 209–10n72.

63. Republic of Vietnam, "Decree 48," *Pháp-Lý Tập San* (1956): 123–24; letter from Nguyễn Văn Vàng to the Province Heads, November 6, 1958, PTTD1 6580.

64. Report from Nguyễn Ngọc Lễ, General Director of Police and Security, to Minister of Internal Affairs and Minister of the President's Office, v/v Phản- ứng của Hoa-Kiều về hai Dụ 48 và 53, Oct 22, 1956 (Hoa Kiều opposition against decrees 48 and 53, October 22, 1956), PTTD1 6579.

65. Vu, "Other Side," 308–9.

66. Goscha, *Penguin History of Modern Vietnam*, 402–3.

67. Elkind, *Aid under Fire*, 173–74.

68. Elkind, 176.

69. Elkind, 176.

70. Tonnesson, *Vietnam 1946*, 1.

71. Nguyen, *Hanoi's War*, 59–60.

72. Truong, *Viet Cong Memoir*, chap. 7.

73. Pike, *Viet Cong*, 244–47.

74. Asselin, *Vietnam's American War*, 102.

75. Nguyen, *Hanoi's War*, 59.

76. Asselin, *Hanoi's Road to War*, 94–96.

77. Catton, *Diem's Final Failure*, 14.

78. Catton, 33.

79. Catton, "Counter-Insurgency and Nation Building."

80. Vu and Fear, introduction to *Republic of Vietnam*, 2–3.

81. Quoted in Catton, *Diem's Final Failure*, 59.

82. Catton, 190–91.

83. Miller, "Religious Revival."

84. Miller, 1923.

85. Herring, *America's Longest War*, 192.

86. Smith et al., *Area Handbook of South Vietnam*, 59.

87. Wiesner, *Victims and Survivors*, 90–91.

88. Tait, *Devil's Snare*, 43.

89. Stur, *Saigon at War*, 40–51.

90. Nguyen, *Hanoi's War*, 59–60.

91. Nguyen, 113.

92. Nguyen, 196.

93. Cosmas, *MACV*, 348.

94. Cosmas, 353.

95. Brigham, *ARVN*, 101.

96. Asselin, *Vietnam's American War*, 202.

97. For more detail, see Asselin, 208–9.

98. Goscha, *Penguin History of Modern Vietnam*, 367.

99. Asselin, *Vietnam's American War*, 220–21.

100. Veith, *Black April*, 39–41.

## 2. SOCIABILITY AND ASSOCIATIONAL LIFE IN SOUTH VIETNAM

1. Baker, *Fraternity among the French Peasantry*; Munck, "Mutual Benefit Societies in Argentina."

2. Ainslie, "Harnessing the Ancestors"; Rodima-Taylor, "Passageways of Cooperation."

3. Putnam, *Making Democracy Work*, 88.

4. Weller, *Alternate Civilities*.

5. Weller, 33.

6. Luong, "State, Local Associations," 124.
7. Luong, 123.
8. Luong, "Social Capital Configuration Variation," 284.
9. Bùi, *Lệ Làng Phép Nước*, 45.
10. *Phe* is translated as "faction" or "side," while *hội* is translated as "association."
11. Nguyễn, "Traditional Viet Village in Bac Bo," 108–10.
12. Nguyễn, 112.
13. Nguyễn, 113.
14. Nguyễn, 108–13.
15. Luong, "State, Local Associations," 126.
16. Nguyen-Marshall, *In Search of Moral Authority*, 23–26.
17. Nguyen-Marshall, "Ethics of Benevolence," 164.
18. Nguyễn, *Niên-Lịch Công Đàn*, 1; Woodside, "Development of Social Organizations," 50.
19. Nguyễn, *Niên-Lịch Công Đàn*, 367.
20. Nguyen-Marshall, "Ethics of Benevolence," 172–73.
21. Lê, "Những 'hội tương trợ' ở thôn quê."
22. Woodside, "Development of Social Organizations." This theme is examined in detail in Woodside, *Community and Revolution in Modern Vietnam*.
23. Woodside, "Development of Social Organizations," 43–49.
24. Kohn, "Panacea or Privilege?" 290.
25. Kohn, 296.
26. Munck, "Mutual Benefit Societies in Argentina," 575.
27. Munck.
28. Trần, *Ties that Bind*.
29. Trần, 24–25; Wehrle, "'Awakening the Conscience of the Masses,'" 16.
30. Wehrle, "'Awakening the Conscience of the Masses,'" 17–19. Note that the Vietnamese rendition of this organization's name (Tổng Liên Đoàn Lao Công Việt Nam) did not include the word "Catholic," and after 1964, it was dropped from the French version of the name as well. This was probably done to reflect the fact that the majority of members were not Catholic. Trần Quốc Bửu was in fact Buddhist. To avoid confusion, I refer to this organization throughout the book as the Vietnam Confederation of Workers (VCW). In other publications and in government documents, it is identified by its French acronyms CVTC before 1964 and CVT after 1964.
31. Nguyen-Marshall, *In Search of Moral Authority*, 43–52.
32. Nguyễn Hữu Châu, minister of the interior, to mayors and provincial heads, January 8, 1956, PTTD1 16200.
33. The minister of the interior's letters of approval can be found in President's Office, Second Republic, National Archives of Vietnam, No. 2, (hereafter cited as PTTD2) 4412. Some of the organizations had submitted their applications many months before, but they were not processed until the spring and summer of 1971.
34. Nguyễn Xuân Liêm to office director of the General Secretariat of the Presidency, July 10, 1969, PTTD2 4265.
35. Charter of the Friends and Family Mutual-Aid Society (Hội gia-hữu tương-tế), January 30, 1969, PTTD2 4265; charter of the Society for the Worship of National Saints and Heroes (Tổng hội phụng tự thánh thần và anh-hùng dân tộc), Prime Minister's Office, National Archives of Vietnam II, Ho Chi Minh City, 28771 (hereafter cited as PTT). Dollar equivalents are based on exchange rates provided by Dacy, *Foreign Aid*, 190, table 9.5. Following his suggestion, I used the black-market currency exchange rate for the years 1969–1974.

36. Charter of the Society of Engineers and Technicians of Vietnam (Hội kỷ sư và thuật gia Việt Nam), 1954, PTT 29237.

37. Calculated from data provided by Dacy, *Foreign Aid*, 118, table 5.2.

38. Nguyễn, *Niên-Lịch Công Đàn*, 371, 373.

39. Letter from Hội ái hữu cựu sinh viên các trường kỹ thuật to President Thiệu, January 20, 1970, PTTD2 4353. See also letter from the association to President Thiệu, February 5, 1971, PTTD2 4421.

40. The Confucius Studies Society published the journal *Minh Tân Nguyệt San*, PEN Vietnam published *Tin Sách*, and the Alumni Society of the Faculty of Pedagogy of Saigon University published *Nghiên Cứu Văn-Hoá Giáo Dục*.

41. "Foreword," *Luận Đàm* 1, no. 1 (December 1960): 2.

42. *Luận Đàm* 1, nos. 1–4 (1960).

43. Wiesner, *Victims and Survivors*, xviii.

44. Lê Văn Khoái, cabinet chief of the Ministry of the Interior, to office director of the General Secretariat of the Presidency, January 31, February 6 and 14, 1969, PTTD2 4256.

45. Nguyễn Xuân Liêm, cabinet chief of the Ministry of the Interior, to office director of the General Secretariat of the Presidency, March 28, 1969, PTTD2 4256. Liêm became cabinet chief in March 1969.

46. Applications for these groups can be located in files PTTD2 4423, PTTD2 4256, and PTTD2 4265.

47. Nguyễn Xuân Liêm to Mai Quốc Đống, June 13, 1969, PTTD2 4256.

48. Mai Quốc Đống to Nguyễn Xuân Liêm, June 19, 1969, PTTD2 4256.

49. Barrett, "Transnational Webs," 13–14.

50. Tsai, *Les Chinois*, 105; Purcell, *Chinese in Southeast Asia*, 215.

51. Republic of Vietnam, *Pháp Lý Tập San*; Luong, "Chinese in Vietnam"; Nguyễn Văn Vàng to province heads, November 6, 1958, PTTD1 6580.

52. Report for the President from the Research Secretariat of the Presidency, March 12, 1969, PTTD2 4364.

53. Nguyễn Văn Vàng to mayors and province chiefs, December 28, 1959, PTTD1 6580.

54. Nguyễn Văn Vàng to administrative director of the Labor Ministry, July 12, 1960, PTTD1 6580.

55. The clubs in question were Đồng hương hội Huê-Huyện and Hội thể dục tam-dân. Nguyễn Văn Vàng to interior minister, October 20, 1962, PTTD1 7927.

56. Vàng to mayor of Saigon, December 29, 1962, PTTD1 7927.

57. Smith et al., *Area Handbook for South Vietnam*, 89.

58. PTTD2 4364 Trình Tổng Thống VNCH về các chánh sách đối với người Việt gốc Hoa, 1969–1970.

59. Mai Quốc Đống to Nguyễn Xuân Liêm, June 13, 1969, PTTD2 4256.

60. The Vietnamese names of these groups are Hội tương-tế Triều-Châu Vĩnh Long and Hội phước-lợi Mai-Huyện.

61. Đống to Liêm, May 9, 1969, PTTD2 4256.

62. Liêm to Đống, June 25, 1969, PTTD2 4256.

63. Gramsci, *Selections from the Prison Notebooks*, 12–13, 261–63.

64. Elkind, *Aid under Fire*, 176.

65. Their applications are in folders PTTD2 4265 and PTTD2 4412.

66. Nguyễn Xuân Nhẫn, association president, to President Thiệu, March 14, 1969, PTTD2 4265; minutes of general meeting, February 2, 1969, PTTD2 4265.

67. Nguyễn Xuân Nhẫn to President Thiệu, March 14, 1969.

68. For more on this institute and Michigan State University, see Elkind, *Aid under Fire*, chap. 2.

69. Hội cựu sinh viên quốc gia hành chánh, *Bản Tin*, August–September 1969, 1.

70. Nguyễn Châu, "Lịch-sử trường Quốc-học Huế," *Đặc San Ái Hữu Quốc Học*, April 26, 1970, 7–12.

71. The seven chapters were in Da Nang, Saigon, Dalat, Quang Tri, Nha Trang, Hue, and Qui Nhon. The association was planning to establish chapters in Phan Rang, Tuy Hoa, and Hoi An.

72. Nguyễn Đình Hàm (president of Quốc Học Alumni Association) to President Thiệu, April 1, 1971, PTTD2 4422.

73. Nguyễn Đình Hàm to President Thiệu, April 1, 1971.

74. Nguyễn Xuân Liêm to Mai Quốc Đống, March 13, 1969, PTTD2 4265.

75. Mai Quốc Đống to Nguyễn Xuân Liêm, March 17, 1969, PTTD2 4265.

76. Nguyễn Xuân Liêm to Mai Quốc Đống, March 22, 1969, PTTD2 4256.

77. Goodman, *Politics in War*, 254–55.

78. Charter of hội chuyên viên và kỹ sư nông nghiệp, PTT 29881.

79. The association's charter is in PTTD2 4256.

80. "Điều Lệ Hội Thư-viện Việt-Nam," *Thư Viện Tập San* [*Library Review*, hereafter cited as *TVTS*] (1960): 29.

81. "Biên Bản của Hội Thư Viện," *TVTS* (1960): 39–41.

82. When the country was divided, some material from the General Library (Tổng Thư Viện) in Hanoi was moved and stored in the Southern Library (Thư Viện Nam Phần).

83. This building is now the Social Science Library, 34 Lý Tự Trọng Street. "Thư Viện Quốc Gia," *TVTS* (1960): 10–16.

84. *TVTS* (1960): 54–55.

85. Phan Vô Ky, "Hội thư viện và ước-vọng thiết-tha của nó," *TVTS* (1960): 6.

86. La Văn Thu, "Hướng về Thư-viện Quốc-Gia," *TVTS* (1960): 7.

87. "Phi Lộ," *TVTS* (1960): 3.

88. Phan Vô Ky, "Báo Cáo" *TVTS* (1960): 36.

89. Phan, 34.

90. Phan, 38.

91. *Bản Tin. Hội thư viện Việt Nam* 2 (April 1974): 4.

92. Barnett, Michener, and Stone, *Developmental Book Activities*, 75.

93. Bush, "Political Education of Vietnam Christian Service"; Flipse, "Latest Casualty of War."

94. Elkind, *Aid under Fire*, 173.

95. Chou, "Cultural Education," 23.

96. Chou, 23; Chester, *Covert Network Progressives*, 165–78; McGarr, "'Quiet Americans in India,'" 1046–47.

97. Phan, "Báo Cáo," 35.

98. *Bản Tin* 1 (March 1974): 2–8.

99. Phan, "Báo Cáo," 37.

100. Nguyễn Thị Cút translated Richard Gardner, *The Cataloguing and Classifying of Books* (Saigon: Asia Foundation, 1966). *TVTS* 1 (1968).

101. Toan Ánh's book was *Người Việt Đất Việt* (The Vietnamese and Their Land).

102. The association was able to publish three issues of *TVTS* annually from 1968 to 1974.

103. Wehrle, "'Awakening the Conscience of the Masses,'" 18.

104. Trần, *Ties that Bind*, 73–77.

105. This is one of the main arguments in Wehrle, *Between a River and a Mountain*.

106. Wehrle, 33–34.

107. Wehrle, 18.

108. Wehrle, "'Awakening the Conscience of the Masses,'" 20.

109. Tran, *Disunion*, 38, 85.

110. Wehrle, *Between a River and a Mountain*, 70.

111. For more on the National Revolutionary Movement, see Tran, *Disunion*, 85.

112. Wehrle, *Between a River and a Mountain*, 69.

113. Wehrle, 70.

114. Wehrle, "'Awakening the Conscience of the Masses,'" 20–23.

115. Trần, *Ties that Bind*, 75.

## 3. PERFORMING SOCIAL SERVICE IN SOUTH VIETNAM

1. Berquist, "Operation Babylift or Babyabduction?"

2. Susan Aasen and Sadie Bass, "Betty Tisdale's Heroic Orphan Airlift," ABC News, April 30, 2010.

3. Richard Hyatt, "Rescued Vietnamese Orphan Remembers 'Angel of Saigon,'" *Ledger-Enquirer*, August 20, 2015.

4. Only later in the essay does Tisdale mention that Madam Ngãi "collected the abandoned and neglected children and cared for them with the help of Dr. Dooley." Tisdale, "Helping and Loving Orphans," 332–33.

5. Ryan, "Civil Society as Democratic Practice"; Bourdieu, "Forms of Capital."

6. Nguyen-Marshall, *In Search of Moral Authority*, 25–26.

7. Nguyen et al., *History of Vietnamese Buddhism*, 172.

8. Bùi, *Lệ Làng Phép Nước*, 57.

9. Keith, *Catholic Vietnam*, 31.

10. Keith, 60; Firpo, *Uprooted*, 22.

11. Keith, *Catholic Vietnam*, 30–32.

12. Nguyễn, "Nguyên Nhân," 49, For the care of Métis children during the French colonial period, see Firpo, *Uprooted*.

13. Keith, *Catholic Vietnam*, 68.

14. Beaudoin, "'Without Belonging to Public Service,'" 673.

15. Beaudoin, 676.

16. Keith, *Catholic Vietnam*, 154.

17. Phan, *Việt-Nam Giáo-Sử*, 487–518.

18. Keith, *Catholic Vietnam*, 155.

19. Keith, 155–60; Phan, *Việt-Nam Giáo-Sử*, 487–518.

20. Woodside, *Community and Revolution*, 192–200; McHale, *Print and Power*, chap. 5; DeVido, "Influence of Chinese Master Taixu."

21. DeVido, "Buddhism for This World," 251–52.

22. Nguyen, "Vietnamese Buddhist Movement," 103.

23. DeVido, "Eminent Nuns," 71–81.

24. Thompson, "Setting the Stage," 45–46.

25. Nguyen, "Vietnamese Buddhist Movement," 102.

26. Goscha, *Penguin History of Modern Vietnam*, 102–9, 489–96.

27. Zinoman, *Vietnamese Colonial Republican*, 5.

28. Nguyen-Marshall, *In Search of Moral Authority*, chaps. 4, 5.

29. The owners and publishers of *Women's News* were Cao Thị Khanh and her husband, Nguyễn Đức Nhuận. For more on the periodical, see Marr, *Vietnamese Tradition on Trial*, 220–28; Thiện, *Phụ-nữ*, 62–70. For more on the Dục Anh Society, see Nguyen-Marshall, *In Search of Moral Authority*, 88–91.

30. Nguyễn Đức Hiệp, "Đời sống kinh tế và xã hội ở Saigon 1930–1945," Diễn Đàn Forum, March 11, 2018, https://www.diendan.org/phe-binh-nghien-cuu/doi-song-kinh-te-va-xa-hoi-o-saigon-1930-1945.

31. In 1922 the Association for Intellectual and Moral Formation for the Annamites established charitable day-care centers, but this initiative was led by Louis Marty, head of the French Sûreté.

32. Nguyen, "French Colonial State," 20.

33. Nguyen, 32–33.

34. Dương, "Ba Phụ Nữ."

35. Dooley, *Deliver Us from Evil*, chap. 14.

36. Dooley, 112.

37. Tisdale, "Helping and Loving Orphans."

38. Vũ Quốc Thông, head of Ministry of Society and Health, to Prime Minister, September 23, 1955, PTTD1 16,188.

39. *Bản Thông Tin* (Saigon: Hội Đồng Cơ Quan Từ Thiện tại Vietnam, [1971]), 49–50 (pt. 2).

40. *Bản Thông Tin*, 1 (pt. 2).

41. *Bản Thông Tin*, 24–25 (pt. 2).

42. Lê, "Các tổ chức," 20.

43. Nguyen, "Vietnamese Buddhist Movement," 111–12.

44. Nguyen, 113.

45. Nguyễn, "Nguyên Nhân," 55–56.

46. Traditionally, married Vietnamese women were known by their husbands' full names; therefore, use of the title "Mrs." is important.

47. *Bản Thông Tin*, 44.

48. Lê, "Các tổ chức," appendix "Danh Sách các tổ chức từ thiện tôn giáo"; Nguyễn, "Nguyên Nhân," 55.

49. Nguyễn, "Nguyên Nhân," 55.

50. Miller, "Religious Revival."

51. Pham, "Socio-political Philosophy," 14.

52. Thích Thiên Minh's speech at the Congress, Biên Bản Đại Hội Thống Nhất Phật Giáo (Saigon: n.p., 1964), 25–26.

53. *Bản Thông Tin*, 47–48.

54. The storms were Violet (September 14–15), Iris (November 2–4), and Joan (November 6–8). US Weather Bureau, *Climatological Data: National Summary, 1964* (Asheville, NC: US Department of Commerce, 1965), 74–78.

55. The official name of the committee was the Inter-Ministry Committee for Assisting Flood Victims of the Central Region. It produced a news bulletin: *Bản Tin Tức: Tương trợ và tái thiết Miền Trung* 1–15 (1964–1965).

56. The mobilization material is in Office of Prime Minister, National Archives of Vietnam, No. 2, [hereafter cited as PPT], 29473 Cứu trợ đồng bào nạn lụt miền Trung năm 1964–5 (folder 2).

57. "Việt-Cộng phục kích bắn giết những đoàn cứu-tế," *Dân Chủ*, November 13, 1964, 1, 4. Note that this is not the same *Dân Chủ* newspaper established in 1973 to be a mouthpiece for President Nguyễn Văn Thiệu.

58. "Reds Seize Flood-Relief Goods in Vietnam, US Aides Report," *New York Times*, November 14, 1964; Peter Grose, "Saigon's Premier to Spur Flood Aid," *New York Times*, November 12, 1964. See also Đường Thiên Lý, "Miền Trung ngập lụt," *Chính Luận*, December 5, 1964, 2.

59. *Bản Thông Tin*, 47–48; Nguyễn, "Nguyên Nhân," 55.

60. Nguyễn, "Nguyên Nhân," 46–48.

61. "Hội Bảo Trợ Gia Đình Binh Sĩ," *Bản Thông Tin*, 9–10.

62. Nguyễn Thị Thương, "Hội bạn trẻ em và nữ nạn nhân chiến cuộc," *Nguyệt San Xã Hội* (School of Social Work,) 3 (1972): 49–50.

63. Nguyễn, "Hội bạn trẻ em," 51–54.

64. "Hội cứ trợ xã hội thống nhất Việt Nam," *Bản Thông Tin*, 43.

65. Thu-Huong Nguyen-Vo, personal interview, Saigon, April 10, 2020.

66. For example, the society to help poor students was headed by Mrs. Vũ Bá Hùng. Mrs. Trần Ngọc Oanh led both the Friends of People with Leprosy and the Friends of People with Mental Illness in 1971. Danh Sách Cơ Quan Tư Thiện Xã Hội, 1971, PTTD2 3661.

67. Koven and Michel, "Womanly Duties," 1077; Morgan, "'Sort of Land Debatable,'" 185.

68. Koven and Michel, "Womanly Duties," 1076–108.

69. Fraser, "Rethinking the Public Sphere," 109–42; Morgan, "'Sort of Land Debatable.'"

70. Habermas, "Further Reflections on the Public Sphere," 453; Habermas, *Structural Transformation of the Public Sphere*, 14–17.

71. Ryan, "Gender and Public Access"; DeVido, "Buddhism for This World,'" 253–54.

72. Fraser, "Rethinking the Public Sphere," 114.

73. Nguyễn, *Niên-Lịch Công Đàn*, 371; Đào, "Khảo Luận."

74. Marr, *Vietnamese Tradition on Trial*, 214.

75. Their Vietnamese names are Tập Đoàn Phụ nữ Văn Hóa Xã Hội, Hội Phụ nữ Thiện Chí Việt Nam, Hội Bảo Trợ Phụ nữ, Hội Phụ nữ Phật Tử, Hội Quả Phủ Tự Sĩ Việt Nam, and Hội Phụ nữ Quốc Tế.

76. The founders of this organization (Hội Phụ Nữ Cấp Tiến) were Trần Thị Công and Trần Thị Tích. The former was the publisher and editor of the periodical *Phụ nữ Việt Nam*, and the latter was a businesswoman. Lê Văn Khoái to Mai Quốc Đống, November 15, 1968, PTTD2 4152.

77. Their newspapers were *Sài Thành* (1929–1931), *Sài Gòn* (1932–1945), and *Sài Gòn Mới* (1948–1972).

78. Trần Nhật Vy, *Ba Nhà Báo Sàigòn* (Ho Chi Minh City: Văn Hóa-Văn Nghệ, 2015), 217–49; "Nữ chủ bút tài ba chưa từng viết báo," *Phụ Nữ Vietnam*, June 21, 2017.

79. Nguyễn, *Niên Lịch Công Đàn*, 381.

80. Dương, "Ba Phụ Nữ."

81. Lê, *Hồi ký*, 244.

82. Lê, *Hồi ký*, 244–46; Trần, *Ba Nhà Báo*, 248.

83. Lê Quang Kim was her husband's name. I do not know her maiden name, so I refer to her as Mrs. Lê Quang Kim.

84. Lê, *Hồi ký*, 244.

85. Tran, *Disunion*, 127.

86. Embassy in Saigon, Foreign Service Dispatch to Department of State, March 22, 1962, Confidential US State Department Central Files, Vietnam, 1960–January 1963: internal affairs, 12199, reel 22; Demery, *Finding the Dragon Lady*, 125–26.

87. Bui, "Reporting on Madame Nhu," 858.

88. According to Lê Thị Bạch Vân, she was invited even though she was not a member of the economic or political elite, although she was a popular writer with some social prominence. Lê, *Hồi ký bà Tùng Long*, 246.

89. Miller, "Buddhist Revival Movement," 1943.

90. PTTD2 4427, The Organization and Activities of the Vietnam Women's Association for Social Service.

91. Della Denman, "Women of Vietnam: Some Grew Strong in Face of War," *New York Times*, February 28, 1972, 46.

92. Also known as Pauline Nguyễn Văn Thơ.

93. Tan Nguyen, "Một Thoáng Hương Xưa: Bà Thượng Nghị Sĩ Phan Nguyệt Minh," *Người Việt*, August 27, 2015, https://www.nguoi-viet.com/amp/nhin-tu-hoa-ky/Mot -Thoang-Huong-Xua-Ba-Thuong-Nghi-Si-Phan-Nguyet-Minh-2855/.

94. George McT. Kahin, "Biographies of Prominent Vietnamese," n.d., Collection on the Origins of the Vietnam War, #4251, Division of Rare Books and Manuscripts, Cornell University.

95. *Bản Thông Tin*, 57 (pt. 2).

96. PTTD2 3655 regarding the organization of the One Heart (Đồng Tâm) Charity Fair, 1971.

97. "Phiếu Trình [memo]," (n.d. [1971]), PTTD2 3668.

98. "Statement of Robert Nooter, Assistant Administrator, Bureau for Supporting Assistance, Agency of International Development," in *Relief and Rehabilitation of War Victims in Indochina, Part II: Orphans and Child Welfare. Hearing before the Subcommittee to Investigate Problems Connected with Refugees and Escapees* (Washington, DC: US Government Printing Office, 1973), 30. 2390916001, Douglas Pike Collection: Unit 11—Monographs, Vietnam Center and Sam Johnson Vietnam Archive, Virtual Vietnam Archive, Texas Tech University.

99. Wells Klein, "The Special Needs of Vietnamese Children: A Critique, Appendix IV, February 1972," in *Relief and Rehabilitation of War Victims in Indochina, Part II*, 85.

100. Dự án thành lập cô-nhi-viện Quốc Gia Thủ Đức, 1956, PTTD1 16,178.

101. Using the black-market rate of 439 dong per US$1. Dacy, *Foreign Aid*, 190.

102. Minh, "Bộ Xã Hội," 17–32.

103. Đào, "Khảo Luận," 25–28.

104. Vũ Quốc Thông to Prime Minister, September 23, 1955, 2–6.

105. Trần Ngọc Liễng, official of Ministry of Social Welfare, to director of Dục Anh Society, August 27, 1966, PTT 29881.

106. Trần Ngọc Liễng to Special Commissar of Administration, September 14, 1966, PTT 29651.

107. Lý Kim Huỳnh (special aide) to cabinet chief of chair of Central Executive Committee, January 3, 1967, PTT 29828. For more about gambling at fairs, see PTT 29651.

108. Huỳnh Thao Lược to Special Commissar of Administration, October 2, 1967, PTT 29828.

109. Nguyễn, *Hồi Ký*.

110. "The Association of (Vietnamese) Professional Social Workers," *Bulletin of the Council of Voluntary Agencies in Vietnam*, Spring 1970, 21.

111. Nguyễn, "Historical Development," 85–86; Nguyễn, "School of Social Work," 41–42.

112. Gardner Munro, "Vietnamese Voluntary Agency Staff Development Program," in *Relief and Rehabilitation of War Victims in Indochina, Part II*, 77.

113. Đào, "Khảo Luận," 25.

114. Walkowitz, *Working with Class*, 13.

115. Nguyễn, *Hồi Ký*, 27–28; Nguyễn, "School of Social Work," 42.

116. "Association of (Vietnamese) Professional Social Workers," 21–23.

117. Nguyễn, "Historical Development," 88.

118. Nguyễn, "Viên Trợ Nhân Đạo," 107–8.

119. Nguyễn, "Historical Development," 86–87.

120. Interview with Bạch Công An, Mississauga, Ontario, Canada, June 23, 2010.

121. Đoàn, "Hồi tưởng—Quận 8 (bài 2)."

122. Interview with Bạch Công An.

123. Kohn, "Panacea or Privilege?" 290–96.

124. Nguyễn, "Viên Trợ Nhân Đạo," 97.
125. Landau, "Law and Civil Society," 246.

## 4. VOLUNTARY EFFORTS IN SOCIAL AND COMMUNITY DEVELOPMENT

1. Trần Quang Thuận, "Công Tác Xã Hội với Sinh Viên," in *Đặc San Trại Hè Công Tác Hội Thảo* (Saigon: Liên Đoàn Sinh Viên Phật Tử Vietnam, 1964), 26–29.
2. Nguyễn, *Viên Trợ Nhân Đạo*, 107–8.
3. *12 năm*, 8–9.
4. For example, founding member Huỳnh Văn Lang received graduate-level training in econometrics at the University of Chicago, and Đỗ Trọng Chu had an MA in international relations from Georgetown University. Nguyễn Thái had an MA from Cornell and later worked with the USOM government liaison office and the Ministry of Construction and Plans. Huỳnh, "Món nợ"; Nguyễn Ngọc Ngạn, "Nhớ một người," *Thời Báo Online*, March 21, 2014.
5. Huỳnh, "Món nợ."
6. Marr, *Vietnamese Anticolonialism*, 164, 182.
7. Miller, *Misalliance*, 135–36.
8. Nguyễn, "Nhớ một người."
9. According to the report presented to the General Assembly by Lê Thành Cường, chair of the Provisional Administrative Committee, on June 5, 1955 (PTT 29237), Đinh Quang Chiêu of the foreign aid office helped secure this funding from the Department of Education Services. However, Huỳnh Văn Lang explained in his memoir that in 1954, when he was working for the Ministry of Finance, he found the unused fund of 50,000 dong in the national budget under the title "popular university program" (chương trình đại học bình dân). Lang was able to persuade minister Trần Hữu Phương to give the money to the group. Huỳnh, *Ký Ức*, 484.
10. Nguyễn Hữu Châu to Minister of Education and Youth, July 15, 1955, PTT 29237.
11. Edgar N. Pike, "Adult Education in Vietnam," *Asia Foundation Newsletter*, September 1959, 1–3, Douglas Pike Collection, Unit 06—Democratic Republic of Vietnam, 2322002008, Vietnam Center and Sam Johnson Vietnam Archive, Virtual Vietnam Archive, Texas Tech University.
12. Miller, *Misalliance*, 281.
13. Nguyễn Đức Hiệp, "Vài kỷ niệm về anh Cung Đình Thanh," April 20, 2006, http://www.vanchuongviet.org/index.php?comp=tacpham&action=detail&id=5459.
14. Huỳnh, *Ký Ức*, 491.
15. The association held other concerts, including one by renowned cellist Gregor Piatigorsky. International Rescue Committee, "Quarterly Report of the Saigon IRC Office," September 1956, Pike Collection, Other Manuscripts—American Friends of Vietnam, 1781048001.
16. Lê Thành Cường, "Phúc trình hoạt động," June 5, 1955, PTT 29237, 2.
17. Pike, "Adult Education," 1–3.
18. Lê, "Phúc trình," 2–3.
19. "Story on Literacy Center in Saigon," Pike Collection, Other Manuscripts—American Friends of Vietnam, 1780935069.
20. *12 năm*, 40.
21. *12 năm*, 10.
22. Bách Khoa chapters were founded in Huế, Biên Hòa, Bảo lộc (in Lâm Đồng province), Darlac (Ban Mê Thuột), Chợ Lớn, Ba Xuyên, Nha Trang, Đà Lạt, Long Khánh, Vịnh Long, Kiến Hoa, Quảng Đức, and Gia Định. *12 năm*, 13–21.
23. *12 năm*, 43.

24. Võ, *Văn Học Miền Nam*, 240; Vũ, "Tạp chí Bách Khoa."

25. *12 năm*, 43–44.

26. Chester, *Covert Network Progressives*, 160–62.

27. International Rescue Committee, "Memorandum to the Foreign Operations Administration," April 23, 1955, 8, Pike Collection, Other Manuscripts—American Friends of Vietnam, 1781048026.

28. International Rescue Committee, "Memorandum," 5.

29. International Rescue Committee, 5.

30. International Rescue Committee, "Thirty Years of The International Rescue Committee (1933–1963), 1933–1963," 27–28, Pike Collection, Other Manuscripts—American Friends of Vietnam, 1781048022.

31. Nguyen, "Vietnamese Buddhist Movement," 123–24.

32. Thích Nhất Hạnh quoted in Nguyen, "Vietnamese Buddhist Movement," 175–76.

33. Thích Nhất Hạnh, *Basic Concepts*, 23–25.

34. Thích Nhất Hạnh, *Fragrant Palm Leaves*, 184–87.

35. Chan, *Learning True Love*, 90–92.

36. Immerwahr, *Thinking Small*, 4.

37. Miller, *Misalliance*, 69; Stewart, *Vietnam's Lost Revolution*, 68.

38. For more information on these programs, see Miller, *Misalliance*; Stewart, *Vietnam's Lost Revolution*.

39. Thích Thanh Văn, "The School of Youth for Social Service and Its Concepts on Rural Social Activities." 35.

40. Thích Nhất Hạnh, *Basic Concepts*, 22–23.

41. Chan, *Learning True Love*, 90–92.

42. Chan, 70–71. See also Chan's online memoir, *52 năm*, chap. 9; Thích Nhất Hạnh, *Basic Concepts*, 17–18.

43. Thích Nhất Hạnh, *Basic Concepts*, 19–20. Chan provides higher numbers of applicants (1,000) and enrollment (3,000) in *Learning True Love*, 70.

44. Thích Nhất Hạnh, *Basic Concepts*, 19.

45. Chan, *Learning True Love*, 57, 89. See also Chan, *52 năm*, chap. 9.

46. Chan, *52 năm*, chap. 9.

47. Chan, *Learning True Love*, 86.

48. CIA memorandum, "The Organization, Activities, and Objectives of the Communist Front in South Vietnam," September 7, 1965, Central Intelligence Agency Collection, Vietnam Center and Sam Johnson Vietnam Archive, 04108114005.

49. Citing David Wurfel, an American academic working in Vietnam, Sophie Quinn-Judge suggests that right-wing war hawks were responsible. Quinn-Judge, *Third Force*, 100. However, Đoàn Thanh Liêm, a lawyer and leader of the New Life Development Project, suggests that the assassins were communist affiliated. According to his source, who was a former SYSS student, one communist officially reported his involvement in the attacks at an August Revolution celebration in the early 1980s. Đoàn, "Chuyện vui buồn."

50. Stur, *Saigon at War*, 25, 44.

51. Thích Thanh Văn, "School of Youth for Social Service," 34.

52. Toner, "Life and Death of Our Republic," 43–44.

53. These included Võ Long Triều, Hồ Văn Minh, Mai Như Mạnh, Đoàn Thanh Liêm, Hồ Ngọc Nhuận, Uông Đại Bằng, Võ Văn Bé, Hồ Công Hưng, Nguyễn Phúc Khánh, Dương Văn Long, Nguyễn Ngọc Thạch, Đặng Kỳ Trân, Nguyễn Đức Tuyên, Nguyễn Ngọc Phan, and Phạm Duy Tuệ. Hồ Ngọc Nhuận, *Đời Hồi Ký*, chap. 9, p. 2; Đoàn, "Hồi tưởng—Quận 8 (bài đầu)"; see also Nguyễn, *Buddha's Child*, 137–38.

54. Quinn-Judge, *Third Force*, 94.

55. As cited in Charles Sweet, "Experiment in District Eight" (graduate economics term paper, Harvard University, 1970), 8–9, John Donnell Collection, 0720616012, Vietnam Center and Sam Johnson Vietnam Archive, Virtual Vietnam Archive, Texas Tech University.

56. Võ, *Hồi Ký*, 252.

57. Võ, 286.

58. Sweet, "Experiment," 2.

59. Goodman, *Politics in War*, 167–68; Sweet "Experiment," 4.

60. Quoted in Goodman, *Politics in War*, 168.

61. Sweet, "Experiment," 5–7.

62. Đoàn, "Câu chuyện."

63. Dror, *Making Two Vietnams*, 54.

64. Đoàn, "Câu chuyện."

65. Hồ, *Đời Hồi Ký*, chaps. 9, 4, 13.

66. Hồ Công Hưng, "Quá Trình Hình Thành Trường Trung Học Cộng Đồng Quận 8 (Establishing the District 8 Public High School)," Lương Văn Can Alumni Site. "https://luongvancan.avcyber.com/p29a12549/luoc-su-truong-luong-van-can-quan-8-qua-50-nam.

67. Goodman, *Politics in War*, 169–70.

68. Hồ, *Đời Hồi Ký*, chap. 9, p. 31.

69. Đoàn, "Thanh Thiếu Niên (bài 3)."

70. Sweet, "Experiment," 11. The average wage for skilled workers from 1956 to 1974 was 98.7 dong per day. Dacy, *Foreign Aid*, 118.

71. Đoàn, "Hồi tưởng—Quận 8 (bài đầu)."

72. Đoàn, "Làm Men trong Bột."

73. Đoàn, "Chuyện vui buồn."

74. Hồ, *Đời Hồi Ký*, chap. 9, p. 3.

75. Võ, *Hồi Ký*, 260–82.

76. Võ, 254–55.

77. Võ, 256.

78. Đoàn, "Hồi tưởng–Quận 8 (bài đầu)."

79. See Đoàn, "Làm Men trong Bột"; Sweet, "Experiment," 17.

80. Đoàn, "Hồi tưởng–Quận 8 (bài 2)."

81. Carroll Kilpatrick, "Humphrey Makes Wide Saigon Tour," *Washington Post*, February 12, 1966, A1, A12; Hồ, *Đời Hồi Ký*, chap. 9, p. 27.

82. Sweet, "Experiment," 25.

83. Võ, *Hồi Ký*, 285.

84. The original song begins: "Cái nhà là nhà của ta / Công khó ông cha lập ra / Cháu con hãy gìn gữi lấy / Muôn năm với nước non nhà." Hồ, *Đời Hồi Ký*, chap. 9, p. 9.

85. Võ, *Hồi Ký*, 287.

86. After 1975, Hồ Ngọc Nhuận was able to confirm that these death sentences were indeed true. Hồ, *Đời Hồi Ký*, chap. 9, p. 27.

87. Paget, *Patriotic Betrayal*, 305, 324–25.

88. Boot, *Road Not Taken*, 505–6.

89. Sweet, "Experiment," 29–30.

90. Charles Sweet to his family, February 24, 1966, box 3, folder 16, Charles F. Sweet Papers, 1953–1990, Cornell University Library Division of Rare and Manuscript Collections.

91. McAllister, "Lost Revolution," 12.

92. McAllister, 9.

93. McAllister, 9.

94. The New Life Project started August 15, 1965; Lansdale returned to Vietnam in late August. Hồ, *Đời Hồi Ký*, chap. 9, p. 4.

95. Charles Sweet, "A Vietnamese Revolution," speech at Kennedy School of Government, Harvard University, October 23, 1968, 4, Glenn Helm Collection, 1070319001, Vietnam Center and Sam Johnson Vietnam Archive, Virtual Vietnam Archive, Texas Tech University.

96. Sweet to family, October 17, 1965, box 3, folder 15, Sweet Papers.

97. Sweet, "Experiment," 28.

98. Charles Sweet, "SEADAG Discussion Paper Political and Social Development in Saigon: Implications for American Communities," May 1, 1969, 9, Donnell Collection, 0720706008.

99. Võ, *Hồi Ký*, 294.

100. Sweet, "Experiment," 31–32.

101. Hồ Ngọc Nhuận mentions in his memoir that he had contact with NLF members (Hồ, *Đời Hồi Ký*, chap. 4, pp. 3, 11). See also his colleagues' accounts of his activities. Lý, *Hồi Ký*, 428–29; Võ, *Hồi Ký*, 344–53.

## 5. SOCIAL AND POLITICAL ACTIVISM OF STUDENTS IN SOUTH VIETNAM

The core argument for this chapter was previously published in *Journal of Vietnamese Studies* 10, no. 2 (Spring 2015): 43–81.

1. *Ý Hướng* 1, new series (Spring 1971): 29; my translation.

2. For a discussion of this literature, see Klimke, *Other Alliance*, introduction.

3. Phung, *South Vietnam's Women in Uniform*.

4. Brigham, *ARVN*, chap. 1.

5. Brigham, chap. 1.

6. The requirement to serve in the People's Self-Defense Force applied to all males aged sixteen to fifty who were not already serving in the ARVN. General Mobilization Law 003/68, June 19, 1968, Về Chương Trình công tác huấn luyện quân sự học đường 1969–71, PTT 17100.

7. Communiqué, Ministry of Defense, September 3, 1970, v/v huấn luyện quân sự học đường, PTT 17100.

8. *Đối Thoại* 1, 15–38.

9. *Đối Thoại* 1, interview with Tuyết Nga, 17.

10. *Đối Thoại* 1, interview with Tôn Ngọn Sum, 17–18.

11. *Đối Thoại* 1, interview with Phạm Vân Phải, 18.

12. *Đối Thoại* 1, interview with Bách Ái Tâm, 30–32.

13. It is likely that the USIA and *Đối Thoại* surveys came from the same study: "University Students in Saigon: Personal Aspirations vs National Development," Confidential US State Department special files Vietnam Working Group, 1963–1966, film 12947, reel 7.

14. Marks to Secretary of State Dean Rusk, December 21, 1966, Confidential US State Department special files Vietnam Working Group, 1963–1966, film 12947, reel 7.

15. "University Students in Saigon."

16. Telegram from American Embassy in Saigon to Department of State, #5548, June 15, 1966, Confidential US State Department central files, Vietnam, February 1963–1966, film #13039, reel 37; Lê and Trần, "Sinh Viên."

17. Marr, "Political Attitudes," 250.

18. Nguyễn, "Hiện trạng," 11.

19. US Department of Labor, *Labor Law*, 21–22.

20. The nine cities with populations over fifty thousand were Saigon–Chợ Lớn, Đà Nẵng, Huế, Đà Lạt, Nha Trang, Phan Thiết, Cần Thơ, Mỹ Tho, and An Lộc. US Department of Labor, *Labor Law*, 21–22.

21. Nguyễn, "Hiện trạng," 12–13.

22. Morris, "Voluntary Societies"; Sutherland, "Voluntary Societies."

23. *Đặc-san tổng-kết hoạt-động*; various reports in PTT 29870, "Về tổ chức và hoạt động của tổng sinh viên Sài Gòn, năm 1964–7"; Nguyễn, "Hiện trạng," 14.

24. Other universities each had between two thousand and three thousand students in 1970. CIA, "Weekly Summary and Special Report: The Thieu Government and Students Militant," No. 44, December 18, 1970, no. 0401/70A. Freedom of Information Act Electronic Reading Room, https://www.cia.gov/readingroom/document/cia-rdp85t00875r001500020059-6.

25. Nguyễn, "Hiện trạng," 11. According to Marr, there were about three thousand in the mid-1960s. Marr, "Study of Political Attitudes," 27.

26. Phạm, "Phong trào," 34, 40.

27. Telephone interview with Trần Trí.

28. In the 1940s this organization was known as the Buddhist Youth Family Movement. Nguyen, "Vietnamese Buddhist Movement," 103.

29. Marr, "Study of Political Attitudes," 31.

30. Marr, 33.

31. Keith, *Catholic Vietnam*, 156–60; Phan, *Việt-Nam Giáo-Sử*, 487–518.

32. Interview with Father Phan Khắc Từ; interview with former priest Nguyễn Văn Nghị.

33. Nguyễn, *Hồi ký*, 12.

34. Interview with Trần Thị Nên.

35. Interview with Trần Thị Nên.

36. Interview with Nguyễn Văn Nghị.

37. Trần, *Ties that Bind*, 81–85.

38. Its official name was Thanh Niên Thiện Chí Công Tác và Nghị Luận Hội (The Youth of Goodwill Work Camp and Seminar Association). Trần Văn Phước, "Hội Thanh Niên Thiện Chí Công Tàc và Nghị Luận," excerpted from *Báo Thanh Niên Phụ Nữ*, Saigon, n.d., http://tuongniem.multiply.com/journal/item/14/14.

39. Trần, "Hội Thanh Niên."

40. Trần, "Hội Thanh Niên."

41. Nguyễn, "Vài nét về hoạt động của đời tôi"; interview with Trần Khánh Tuyết.

42. Interview with Trần Khánh Tuyết.

43. Interview with Trần Khánh Tuyết.

44. Đoàn, "Thanh Thiếu Niên (bài 1)."

45. There were three major storms that year: Violet (September 14–15), Iris (November 2–4), and Joan (November 6–8). US Weather Bureau, *Climatological Data: National Summary, 1964* (Asheville, NC: US Department of Commerce, 1965), 74–78.

46. Charles Sweet, "The 1965 Summer Youth Program," March 26, 1965, box 3, folder 45, SYP 1965 Background, Charles F. Sweet Papers, collection 4827, Cornell University Library Division of Rare and Manuscript Collections.

47. Pham Huu Quang, *Final Report of the Flood Relief 1964*, submitted to President Suu on March 8, 1965, trans. Charles Sweet. box 2, folder 2, Student Flood Relief, Sweet Papers.

48. For criticisms of the relief effort, see Người Xứ Quảng, "Nói Chuyện Cứu Trợ," *Sinh Viên Huế* 5 (December 17, 1964): 6, 5.

49. Đoàn, "Thanh Thiếu Niên (bài 2)."

50. Writers such as Ngô Nhân Dụng depict this as an idealistic and patriotic time for youths. "Ai Cũng có Một Thời Tuổi Trẻ," http://thongtinberlin.de/diendan/aicungcomothtoituoitre.htm.

51. John Donnell, "Vietnam's Youth Associations—Social Commitment and Political Promise 1969," report commissioned by Simulmatics Corp., 1969, 24–25, John Don-

nell Collection, 0721005002, Vietnam Center and Sam Johnson Vietnam Archive, Virtual Vietnam Archive, Texas Tech University.

52. Britton, "Vietnamese Youth," 16–18.

53. Đoàn, "Mấy nét chính yếu."

54. Trần Tiên Tự, "Hoạt động sinh viên quốc nội," *Chuông Việt* 144 (December 1965): 8–9. See also Marr, "Study of Political Attitudes," 38–39.

55. Charles Sweet to his family, January 13, 1965, box 3, folder 14, Sweet Papers.

56. Paget, *Patriotic Betrayal*, 305.

57. Paget, 325.

58. Charles Sweet to family, February 24, 1965, box 3, folder 14, Sweet Papers.

59. Paget, *Patriotic Betrayal*, 325.

60. South Vietnam, Assistance Programs of U.S. Non-Profit Organizations, American Council of Voluntary Agencies for Foreign Service Technical Assistance Information Clearing House, 1971, 3, Douglas Pike Collection, Unit 03—US Economy and US Mission (Saigon), 2274212005, Vietnam Center and Sam Johnson Vietnam Archive, Virtual Vietnam Archive, Texas Tech University.

61. Nguyễn, "Vài nét về hoạt động của đời tôi," 1.

62. US Embassy in Saigon to Department of State, telegram 3725, section 1 of 2, August 17, 1966, 2, US State Department, Confidential US State Department central files Vietnam, February 1963–1966, film 13039, reel 4.

63. Rodell, "International Voluntary Services."

64. Interview with Trần Khánh Tuyết.

65. Britton, "Vietnamese Youth," 17.

66. Charles Sweet to family, March 31, 1965, box 3, folder 14, Sweet Papers.

67. Interview with Trần Khánh Tuyết.

68. Interview with Nguyễn Huỳnh Tân.

69. Dung [no family name], "Lá Thư Sài Gòn," *Chuông Việt* 144 (December 1965): 10–12.

70. Nguyễn, *Will of Heaven*, 9.

71. Người, "Nói Chuyện," 6, 5.

72. Bourdieu, "Forms of Capital"; Ryan, "Civil Society."

73. Interviews with Nguyễn Huỳnh Tân, Nguyễn Vân Hạnh, and Trần Khánh Tuyết.

74. Trần, "Hội Thanh Niên."

75. "University Students in Saigon," 3.

76. For more on youth political activism, see Tai, *Radicalism*; Lessard, "Colony Writ Small."

77. Marr, "Study of Political Attitudes," 33–34.

78. Marr, 32–33.

79. Marr, 40–41.

80. Nguyễn, *Việt Nam Phật Giáo Sử Luận*, chap. 40.

81. Nguyễn, chap. 40. See also Nguyễn, "Sinh viên," 17. A day after its founding, this committee changed its name to Ban Chỉ Đạo Sinh Viên Và Học Sinh (the Steering Committee for University Students and Pupils).

82. Nguyễn, *Việt Nam Phật Giáo Sử Luận*, chap. 40.

83. Nguyễn, chap. 40.

84. CIA, "Weekly Summary and Special Report: Thieu Government," 3.

85. Minister of Security, Tôn Thất Đính, to Prime Minister, November 28, 1963, PTT 29.256.

86. Tôn Thất Đính to Prime Minister, November 28, 1963.

87. Topmiller, *Lotus Unleashed*, 19.

88. CIA, "Weekly Summary and Special Report: Thieu Government," 3.

89. The PRP was the southern branch of the Lao Động Party. Both the NLF and the PRP had a number of organizations that targeted youths and students.

90. PTTD2 819, "Hồ sơ về các hoạt động chống cộng sản của sinh viên Việt Nam, năm 1968."

91. Lê, *Sài Gòn Dậy Mà Đi.*

92. For example, Võ Như Lanh was the president of Vạn Hạnh in 1971.

93. Ministry of Education to office director of Central Executive Committee, September 15, 1967, PTT 2987. The permit for the SSU can be found in file PTTD2 4411.

94. Donnell, "Vietnam's Youth Associations," 19.

95. Correspondence and reports in PTT 29870.

96. Tôn Thất Đính to Prime Minister, January 30, 1964, PTT 29870.

97. Correspondence and reports in PTT 29870.

98. Stur, "'To Do Nothing,'" 289.

99. Interview with Lâm Thành Qúy.

100. *Sinh Viên*, new series, 1 (1968), published by the Federation of Sài Gòn University Students.

101. Marr, "Study of Political Attitudes," 17.

102. *Sinh Viên Huế*, new series, 5 (December 17, 1964): 1; *Sinh Viên Huế*, new series, 6 (January 5, 1965): 5. For a description of the student protest against the draft, see Stur, *Saigon at War*, 46–47.

103. Nguyễn Khải, "Chủ quyền quốc gia," *Diễn Đàn Sinh Viên* 4 (April 1966): 6–11. One of the student advisers for this journal was Nguyễn Tường Cẩm, an active member of the Voluntary Youth Association.

104. Mai Kim Đình, "Viện Trợ Mỹ và Chương Trình Phát Triển Kinh Tế Việt Nam," *Diễn Đàn Sinh Viên*, new series, 5 (December 1966): 51–65.

105. Trần Huyền, "Làm Thế Nào Kết Thúc Chiến Tranh Việt Nam?" *Chuông Việt* 146 (July 31, 1966): 22–24.

106. Robert Shaplen, *The Lost Revolution* (New York: Harper & Row, 1965), 343–45; Nguyen, "Vietnamese Buddhist Movements," 193.

107. Marr, "Study of Political Attitudes," 28–29.

108. "1 Nhóm Sinh Viên Tố Cáo," *Chính Luận*, November 21, 1968, 3. For more documents on anticommunist groups, see PTTD2 819.

109. Former SSU president Nguyễn Đăng Trừng was discovered to be a communist agent. "Sinh Viên Lập Văn Phòng Tạm Thời," *Chính Luận*, September 27, 1968.

110. Statement by Huỳnh Tấn Mẫm to National Assembly and members of the domestic and international press, July 2, 1971, Pike Collection, Unit 08—Biography, 2360502048.

111. Charles Sweet to family, March 14, 1965, box 3, folder 14, Sweet Papers.

112. Charles Sweet to family, May 29, 1965, box 3, folder 14, Sweet Papers.

113. Statement by Huỳnh Tấn Mẫm, July 2, 1971.

114. Lê, *Sài Gòn Dậy Mà Đi*, 36–37.

115. Hội Sinh Viện Việt Nam, *Sơ Thảo Lịch Sử*. For the event as told from the noncommunist side, see Phạm Tín An Ninh, "Tiễn Biệt Ký Giả Cao Sơn Nguyễn Văn Tấn," *Văn Nghệ Biên Khơi* (online arts magazine) 61, January 2014, www.bienkhoi.com/so-61/tien-biet-ky-gia.htm.

116. Hội Sinh Viện Việt Nam, *Sơ Thảo Lịch Sử*, 111.

117. UPI, "Hold Student for Murder," *Pacific Daily*, July 2, 1971, 28.

118. Nguyễn, "Sinh Viên," 22.

119. Vũ, "Phong trào," 17; Gareth Porter, "Vietnam Students Protest War," *Michigan Daily*, November 7, 1968, 3.

120. Chan, *Learning True Love*, 107.

121. Donnell, "Vietnam's Youth Associations," 4.

122. Trần, "Tay Nắm," 194–201; Hợp, "Trung Tâm," 202–6.

123. Nguyen, *Hanoi's War*, 65.

124. Nguyen, 65.

125. Porter, "Vietnam Students," 3.

126. Hợp, "Trung Tâm," 202–6.

127. CIA, "Weekly Summary and Special Report: Thieu Government," 5.

128. John A. Graham, "Radicalism in Hue: The Politics of Discontent. Civil Operations Revolutionary Development Support CORDS Report," November 1, 1971, 2, John Graham Collection, 0930101018, Vietnam Center and Sam Johnson Vietnam Archive, Virtual Vietnam Archive, Texas Tech University.

129. Interviews with Huỳnh Thị Ngọc Tuyết, Huỳnh Tấn Mẫm, and Thích Tâm Đức.

130. Lê, *Sài Gòn Dậy Mà Đi*, 27–28.

131. "PRP Political Work among Saigon Youth," 1, Pike Collection, Unit 05—National Liberation Front, 2311107002.

132. The student population of Saigon and Vạn Hạnh Universities in 1965 totaled around thirty-three thousand.

133. "PRP Political Work," 1.

134. Nguyễn, "Sinh Viên," 19.

135. Report from Nguyễn Lưu Viên, Vice Prime Minister and Minister of Education, to Prime Minister, July 24, 1970, v/v huấn luyện quân sự học đường trong niên học 1969–1970 (school military training in academic year 1969–1970), PTT 17100.

136. Minister of Defense, Nguyễn Văn Vỹ, to Prime Minister, May 31, 1971, PPT 17100.

137. Vũ Thị Dung, "Phong Trào Đấu Tranh SVHS Việt Nam," *Sinh Viên* 7 (November 1970): 4; Ralph Blumenthal, "Saigon Police Halt Protest Including US Marchers," *New York Times*, July 11, 1970, 3.

138. Diêu, *Huỳnh Tấn Mẫm*, 38.

139. Inteview with Huỳnh Tấn Mẫm.

140. Inteview with Huỳnh Tấn Mẫm; Diêu, *Huỳnh Tấn Mẫm*, 122, 132.

## 6. *SÓNG THẦN* NEWSPAPER AND THE "HIGHWAY OF HORROR" PROJECT

An abridged version of this chapter was published in *War and Society* 37, no. 3 (2018): 206–22.

1. According to Trùng Dương, when Ngy Thanh first reported the killing, he used the term the "Highway of Horror." "Đi nhặc xác đồng bào Q. Trị trên đường 'Kinh Hoàng," *Sóng Thần*, July 11, 1972, 1, 3.

2. Malarney, "'Fatherland Remembers'"; Gustafsson, *War and Shadows*; Kwon, *After the Massacre*; Kwon, *Ghosts of War*.

3. Kwon, *After the Massacre*, 123–25.

4. Kwon, 123–25.

5. Gustafsson, *War and Shadows*.

6. Ngo, *The Easter Offensive*, 11–12.

7. Turley, *Second Indochina War*, 186.

8. Herring, *America's Longest War*, 309.

9. Isaacs, *Without Honor*, 25.

10. The few books that discuss the killing include Isaacs, *Without Honor*, 24–25; Andradé, *Trial by Fire*, 141–44; Turley, *Easter Offensive*, 289–90.

11. Military History Institute of Vietnam, *Victory in Vietnam*, 292.

12. Major General Lê Mã Lương, "Quảng Trị-Thừa Thiên, năm 1972: Cuộc đụng đầu lịch sử, bài 2: Giải Phóng Quảng Trị," *Quan Doi Nhan Dan Online*, March 27, 2012, http://

www.qdnd.vn/quoc-phong-an-ninh/xay-dung-quan-doi/quang-tri-thua-thien-nam
-1972-cuoc-dung-dau-lich-su-bai-2-439588.

13. Military History Institute of Vietnam, *Victory in Vietnam*, 292.

14. Ministry of Foreign Affairs of the RVN, *The Communist Policy of Terror* (Saigon: n.p., 1972), 23–44, Douglas Pike Collection, Unit 05—National Liberation Front, 2311413025, Vietnam Center and Sam Johnson Vietnam Archive, Virtual Vietnam Archive, Texas Tech University.

15. "Defector Tells of Massacre by Enemy at Quang Tri," *New York Times*, September 9, 1972, 6; Tom Peterson, "Slaughter of Viet Civilians Described by Ex-Red Soldiers," *Pacific Stars and Stripes*, September 6, 1972, 6, Pike Collection, Unit 05—National Liberation Front, 2311413003.

16. "Defector Tells of Massacre," 6.

17. Turley, *Easter Offensive*, 281–89; Andradé, *Trial by Fire*, 141–44.

18. Turley, *Easter Offensive*, 41, 283.

19. Turley, 281.

20. Fox Butterfield, "Enemy Artillery Batters Quangtri as Ring Tightens," *New York Times*, April 30, 1972, 20.

21. Sydney Schanberg, "Convoys to Quang Tri Blocked: Refugees Crowd Hue," *New York Times*, April 30, 1972, 20.

22. Peter Braestrup, "Refugees and Hope Returning to Hue," *Washington Post*, May 19, 1972, A25.

23. Holger Jensen, "Quang Tri Refugee Path: A Scene of Gore, Defeat," *Boston Globe*, April 30, 1972, 19. See also "Quang Tri Is Encircled," *Chicago Tribune*, April 29, 1972, 1; "Reds Press Offensive in North," *Chicago Tribune*, April 30, 1972, 1.

24. Nguyễn Tú, "Quốc Lộ số 1 bắc Mỹ Chánh: Hành lang dẫm máu đầy sững sờ," *Chính Luận*, May 3, 1972, 1.

25. Mann, *1972 Invasion*, 41; emphasis added.

26. Sheridan was the senior adviser to the 369th Marine Brigade; Price was the senior adviser to the 5th Battalion, 369th Marine Brigade. Turley, *Easter Offensive*, 260.

27. As quoted in "N. Viet Massacre of Civilians Told: 1,000–2,000 Reported Killed Near Quang Tri," *Los Angeles Times*, August 8, 1972, A1. For more of Sheridan's description, see Turley, *Easter Offensive*, 290.

28. Lê, "Người đi trong," 410.

29. Lê, 411.

30. As recounted in Hà, *Thép và Máu*, 116–17.

31. As recounted in Hà, 116–17.

32. Ngy, "Đại Lộ," 57–59.

33. Ngy Thanh and Đoàn Kế Tường, "Xác dân tỵ nạn trơ xương nằm dài 2 cs trên quốc lộ 1m," *Sóng Thần*, July 3, 1972, 1. See also "Trên quốc lộ 1 nối Quảng Trí vời Huế: Đoạn đường kinh hoàng," *Sóng Thần*, July 5, 1972, 1.

34. Đoàn, "Mỹ Chánh, Quảng Trị," 40.

35. Đoàn, 40.

36. See, for example, Lê Văn Thiệp, "Những hình ảnh khủng khiếp trên Đại Lộ Kinh Hoàng," *Chính Luận*, July 4, 1972, 3.

37. Dương and Vũ, *Tình Yêu Ngục Tù*, 309–16.

38. Dương and Vũ, 313–15.

39. Isaacs, *Without Honor*, 25.

40. Among the most controversial mass killing in terms of disputed numbers is the Nanjing massacre. See Joshua Fogel, ed., *The Nanjing Massacre in History and Historiography* (Berkeley: University of California Press, 2000).

41. Holger Jensen, "No Signs of 'Civilian Massacre' in Quang Tri Slaughter," *Lakehead (FL) Ledger*, August 10, 1972, 11A; Dương and Vũ, *Tình Yêu Ngục Tù*, 315n3.

42. Andradé, *Trial by Fire*, 144.

43. Nicholas Ruggieri (IPS correspondent), "Witnesses Tell of N. Vietnam Massacre of Civilians," August 7, 1972, Pike Collection, Unit 05—National Liberation Front, 2311412029.

44. Interview with Nguyễn Kinh Châu.

45. Interview with Nguyễn Kinh Châu.

46. I used data published up to August 9; after that date, there are some inconsistencies. I am also missing data for three days (July 24 and August 4 and 5), so my calculation is short twenty-six bodies whose descriptions would have been printed in those issues.

47. Walzer, *Arguing about War*, 97.

48. Levene, "Introduction," 5; Sémelin, "From Massacre," 436.

49. Levene, "Introduction," 5.

50. For example, Major Robert Sheridan refers to this event as a massacre. "N. Viet Massacre of Civilians Told," *Los Angeles Times*, August 8, 1972, A1.

51. Jensen, "No Signs."

52. For a discussion of war atrocities, see Sleezer, "Atrocities."

53. Trùng Dương, "Vận động nghĩa cử đắp một nấm mồ yên nghỉ," *Sóng Thần*, July 20, 1972, 1.

54. US Embassy in Saigon, "Assessment of Easter Offensive, June 24, 1972," Pike Collection, Unit 01—Assessment and Strategy, 2122404016.

55. US Embassy in Saigon, "Assessment of Easter Offensive," 8.

56. "Dân Quảng Trị tràn ngập Huế, Đà Nẵng," *Chính Luận*, May 2, 1972, 3.

57. The first issue was published on September 25, 1971, and it ceased publication in February 1975. Uyên Thao, "Giấy bút."

58. Elliott, *Sacred Willow*, 376–77.

59. *Đời* 51 (September 24–October 1, 1970) contains many articles on Nhơn. Especially helpful is the one by Uyên Thao, "Hồ sơ vụ Hà Thúc Nhơn," 5–9. See also Bích Nguyên's serialized article "Hà Thúc Nhơn đã chết—Ai giết Hà Thúc Nhơn? Giết làm gì?" *Điện Tín*, September 3–20, 1970.

60. Bích Nguyên, "Hà Thúc Nhơn đã chết," *Điện Tín*, September 8, 1970, 1.

61. Trần Triệu Việt, "Một đoàn người lên đường chống tham nhũng," *Đời* 59 (November 19–26, 1970): 15.

62. "Bạn đời viết về Hà Thúc Nhơn," *Đời* 59 (November 19–26, 1970): 42–43.

63. Mạc Lâm's interview with Trùng Dương, "Tự do báo chí của Miền Nam trước 1975," Radio Free Asia, October 31, 2015; Lê Quỳnh Mai's interview with Trùng Dương, "Phỏng Vấn Nhà Văn Trùng Dương," *Hợp Lưu*, December 26, 2010.

64. Email correspondence with Ngy Thanh.

65. Interview with Uyên Thao.

66. Chapman, *Cauldron of Resistance*, 75, 132–39; Donald Lancaster quoted by Chapman, 132.

67. Chapman, 132.

68. Interview with Uyên Thao.

69. "Thư ngỏ của nhóm chủ trương nhật báo *Sóng Thần*," *Đời* 98 (August 12–19, 1971): 1.

70. "Ngày anh em *Sóng Thần* họp mặt 5–9," *Đời* 99 (September 9–16, 1971): 52–53; "6 đặc điểm của nhật báo *Sóng Thần*," *Đời* 99 (September 9–16, 1971): 54.

71. In 1970, 393 dong were equivalent to US$1. Dacy, *Foreign Aid*, table 9.5, 190.

72. "Về việc góp vốn cho cơ sở nhân chủ và nhật báo Sóng Thần," *Đời* 92 (August 5–12, 1972): 54.

73. "Sóng Thần: Tiếng nói sau cùng của nhân dân ta," *Đời* 98 (September 2–9, 1971): 34.

74. "Sóng Thần," 35.

75. "Ông Trưởng Ty Thanh Niên và việc tu sửa sân Diên Hồng," *Sóng Thần*, July 5, 1972, 5; July 7, 1972, 4.

76. "Ty Xã Hội Ninh Thuận, miền đất máu nuôi tham nhũng mập," *Sóng Thần*, July 4, 1973, 5; July 5, 1972, 5.

77. "Gọt đầu 'Quế Tướng Công,'" *Sóng Thần*, January 2, 1972, 1; "Quân Khủng bố đe dọa phá toà soạn Sóng Thần," *Sóng Thần*, January 2, 1972, 1.

78. Email correspondence with Trùng Dương.

79. Interview with Uyên Thao. See also first-page articles in *Sóng Thần*, January 1, 2, 6, and 7, 1972.

80. *Tài liệu của bộ nội vụ v/v tịch thu và truy tố báo chí loan tin hại cho an ninh, tháng 4, 1972*, PTT 17579.

81. Interview with Uyên Thao.

82. Interview with Uyên Thao.

83. Dương, "Vận động nghĩa cử đáp một nấm mồ yên nghỉ"

84. "Sơ lược về việc chi tiêu sau hai đợt lượm xác," *Sóng Thần*, September 26, 1972, 11.

85. Nguyễn, "Bảy tháng giữa những xác người."

86. "Sống mái nhà, thắc nấm mồ," *Sóng Thần*, August 1, 1972, 1.

87. Trùng Dương, "Đắp một nấm mồ," *Sóng Thần*, July 20, 1972, 1, 3.

88. Trùng Dương, "Đi nhặt xác," *Sóng Thần*, July 22, 1972, 3; "Đi nhặt xác," August 3, 1972, 3.

89. Interview with Uyên Thao.

90. Nguyễn, "Bảy tháng giữa những xác người," 107–9.

91. Nguyễn, 107–9.

92. For other local supporters, see Trần Tường Trình, "Nỗi buồn của những người còn sống trên Đại Lộ Kinh Hoàng," *Sóng Thần*, September 26, 1972, 11.

93. Trùng Dương, "Nhật báo Sóng Thần và các thân hữu với chương trình: Đi nhặt xát đồng bào Q. Trị trên đường 'Kinh Hoàng,'" *Sóng Thần*, July 11, 1972, 1, 3. See also her articles on July 12–16, 1972.

94. Telephone interview with Uyên Thao.

95. Trùng, "Hốt xác," 105.

96. Nguyễn, "Bảy tháng," 109.

97. Trùng Dương, "Đi nhặt xác," *Sóng Thần*, July 14, 1972, 3.

98. *Sóng Thần*, August 3, 1972, 1.

99. "Nấm mồ yên nghỉ," *Sóng Thần*, August 14, 1972, 1.

100. "An táng đợt III," *Sóng Thần*, November 22, 1972, 3.

101. Interview with Nguyễn Kinh Châu.

102. The memorial still stands along the highway, however.

103. Tai, "Faces," 191; Nguyen-Vo, "Forking Paths," 160.

104. Schwenkel, *American War*, 99, 217n20.

105. Kwon, *After the Massacre*, 120–23.

106. Email communication with Ngy Thanh, who has been searching for the graveyard.

107. Kwon, *After the Massacre*, 120–23.

108. Michael Walzer, *Just and Unjust Wars*, 3rd ed. (New York: Basic Books, 2000), 135–37.

109. Guillemot, "Autopsy," 230.

110. Nguyen, *Nothing Ever Dies*, chap. 3.

111. Gordon, *Ghostly Matters*, 4. See also Nguyen, *Nothing Ever Dies*.

## 7. THE FIGHT FOR RIGHTS AND FREEDOMS IN THE 1970S

1. The description of these events comes from "Nhật Báo Sóng Thần tự thiêu để khỏi bị tịch thu," *Chính Luận*, September 21, 1974, 1, 9; "3 báo Sóng Thần, Điện Tín, Đại Dân Tộc, tung bê báo và đốt để khỏi bị tịch thu," *Chính Luận*, September 22–23, 1974, 1, 9.

2. Goodman, "South Vietnam," 71.

3. Kirk, "Thieu Presidential Campaign," 611; McAllister, "'Fiasco'"; Fear, "Ambiguous Legacy."

4. McAllister, "'Fiasco,'" 649.

5. Turley, *Second Indochina War*, 143–44.

6. Fear, "Saigon Goes Global," 20; Tom Buckley, "A Court Convicts Saigon Runner-up," *New York Times*, September 16, 1967, 1, 6.

7. Kirk, "Thieu Presidential Campaign," 616–17.

8. Kirk, 616–18.

9. Quinn-Judge, *Third Force*, 152–53.

10. Lý, *Hồi Ký*, 222.

11. Kirk, "Thieu Presidential Campaign," 618–19.

12. Gloria Emerson, "Thieu's Foes Trying to Unite to Defeat Him," *New York Times*, September 24, 1971, 10.

13. Kirk, "Thieu Presidential Campaign," 609; Lý, *Hồi Ký*, 229–30.

14. Lý, *Hồi Ký*, 212–13.

15. Isaacs, *Without Honor*, 105; Turley, *Second Indochina War*, 212.

16. Turley, *Second Indochina War*, 212–13.

17. Phúc, "Các Điểm Hẹn," 277.

18. "Ủy ban vận động cải thiện chế độ lao tù," *Đối Diện* 18 (December 1970): 103–8; Trần, "Challenge for Peace," 463.

19. Ralph Graves, "How They Unearthed the Tiger Cages," *Life* 69, no. 3 (July 17, 1970): 2A.

20. Limewater, which is a solution of diluted calcium hydroxide, is an irritant to the eyes, skin, and respiratory tract. Graves, 26–29.

21. See *Bản Tin* (of the Committee for Prison Reform)], December 7, 1970, 1–2, and December 17, 1970.

22. Chân Tín, "Trang viết cuối cùng."

23. Tôn, "Chân Tín"; Chân, "Trang viết cuối cùng"; Trần, "Challenge for Peace," 448; Bonner, Burns, and Denny, introduction to *Empowering the People*.

24. Tôn, "Chân Tín."

25. "Lễ ra mắt ủy ban vận động cải thiện chế độ lao tù," *Phong Trào Phụ Nữ Đòi Quyền Sống* 4 (December 2, 1970): 22.

26. Trần, "Challenge for Peace," 463.

27. Trần, 460.

28. Christine Courtney, "Profile: No Fear of Reform," *Los Angeles Times*, November 24, 1992. For more about Phạm Thị Thanh Vân (Mrs. Ngô Bá Thành), see Stur, *Saigon at War*, chap. 2.

29. "Phụ Nữ Đòi Quyền Sống: Hòa Bình và Chống Dự Luận Chương Trình," *Hòa Bình*, August 4, 1970, 1, 8.

30. Đông Thảo, "Tường thuận lễ ra mắt Phong Trào Phụ Nữ Đòi Quyền Sống tỉnh bộ Cần Thơ," *Phong Trào Phụ Nữ Đòi Quyền Sống* 4 (December 2, 1970): 3.

31. "UB Phụ nữ đòi quyền sống họp báo công bố kháng thơ," *Điện Tín*, August 20, 1970, 1.

32. James Markham, "Militants' Areas Are Cordoned off by Saigon Police: Lies Down on Street," *New York Times*, October 28, 1974, 12.

33. Phạm Vũ, "Bà Ngô Bá Thành 'Người đàn bà thép' đã ra đi," *Tuổi Trẻ Online*, February 6, 2004.

34. Lý, *Hồi Ký*, 232.

35. Lý, 234.

36. Lý, 229–30.

37. Phạm Vũ, "Bà Ngô Bá Thành."

38. Chân Tín, "Trang viết cuối cùng."

39. Courtney, "Profile: No Fear of Reform."

40. According to Lý Quí Chung, some peace activists such as Hồ Ngọc Nhuận, Dương Văn Ba, Đinh Văn Đệ, Phan Xuân Huy, Đinh Xuân Dũng, Nguyễn Phúc Liên Bảo, and Trần Bá Thành were given separate reeducation sessions and were not sent to the camps, as millions of South Vietnamese were. Lý Quí Chung himself was exempted from reeducation, but maintains that he does not know why. Lý, *Hồi Ký*, 427.

41. Tôn, "Chân Tín."

42. Chân, "Trang viết cuối cùng."

43. Interview with Huỳnh Tấn Mẫm; "Liệt Sĩ Nguyễn Ngọc Phượng," *CLB Sử Học Trẻ*, August 20, 2013; "Nguyễn Ngọc Phương—Người lãnh đạo kiên cường của phong trào thanh niên—sinh viên Sài Gòn," Thanh Doan (Revolutionary Youth Union), accessed August 29, 2020, http://www.thanhdoan.hochiminhcity.gov.vn/ThanhDoan/webtd/News/1991.

44. Võ Thu Hương, "Nữ tù nhân nhỏ tuổi nhất chuồng cọp," *Báo Phụ Nữ*, April 28, 2017; "Cựu nữ tù Côn Đảo 28 kg và tình đẹp cùng chàng trai Pháp," *Cảnh Sát Toàn Cầu*, August 28, 2011.

45. Hội Sinh Viên Việt Nam, *Sơ Thảo Lịch Sử*, 111–12.

46. Graves, "How They Unearthed Tiger Cages," 29.

47. Lý, *Hồi Ký*, 315.

48. Chân Tín, "Chế độ lao tù: Một hình thức đấu tranh chánh trị?" *Lao Tù* 3 (March 14, 1971): 2.

49. McHale, *Print and Power*, 8, 44.

50. Peycam, *Birth of Vietnamese Political Journalism*.

51. Phạm, "Life and Work," 117–18.

52. Picard, "'Renegades.'"

53. Nguyễn, *Lược sử báo chí*, 75.

54. Phạm, "Life and Work," 121.

55. *Quy Chế Báo Chí* (Press regulations) (Saigon: Ministry of Information, 1969).

56. Interview with Hoàng Đức Nhã.

57. Email correspondence with Trùng Dương.

58. Nghiêm Xuân Thiện, presentation to senate committee regarding changes to press law, November 30, 1974, PTT 31560, h/s v/v thực hiện quy chế báo chí, 1974–1975.

59. Email correspondence with Trùng Dương.

60. Telephone interview with Uyên Thao, June 9, 2015.

61. Nghiêm, presentation, November 30, 1974.

62. Report from director of the Press Office to the president, August 5, 1968, PTTD2 3451, Tài Liệu của phủ Tổng Thống thượng nghị viện v/v đình bản, đóng cửa báo chí vì phạm và khiếu nại của các chủ báo, 1968–1969.

63. Letter from Hội Văn Bút (PEN Vietnam) to the president, April 4, 1969, PTTD2 3451.

64. These organizations were Hội Chủ Báo, Nghiệp Đoàn Ký Giả Nam Việt, Hội Ái Hữu Ký Giả, and Nghiệp Đoàn Ký Giả Việt Nam. Phạm, "Life and Work," 123.

65. Letter to newspaper publishers from Ministry of the Interior, July 1, 1972, PTT 30912, Danh sách báo chí xuất bản ngày ban hành luật báo chí năm 1970–1972.

66. Letters from Huỳnh Ngọc Diệp to office director of Ministry of Justice, May 1, 1972; mayor of Saigon and provincial chiefs, May 4, 1972; commander of National Police, May [8], 1972, PTT 30914.

67. Lý, *Hồi Ký*, 209.

68. Letter from Huỳnh Ngọc Diệp to office director of Ministry of Information, October 10, 1972, PTT 30914.

69. Letter from Huỳnh Ngọc Diệp to cabinet director of Ministry of Justice and administrative assistant of Ministry of Mobilization and Open Arms, February 28, 1974, PTT 31322 h/s v/v tịch thu, truy tố, xử ly báo chí vi phạm luật năm 1974.

70. Ninh, *World Transformed*; Marr, "Passion for Modernity," 269–76; Zinoman, "Nhân-Văn-Giai Phẩm."

71. Marr, "Passion for Modernity," 275.

72. Nguyễn, *Lược sử báo chí*, 121.

73. Lý, *Hồi Ký*, 142.

74. Report from Ngô Khắc Tỉnh, minister of information, to the prime minister, April 16, 1970, 2, PTTD2 7772.

75. Interview with Trần Quang Lâm.

76. Lý, *Hồi Ký*, 142.

77. Quinn-Judge, *Third Force*, 145–47, 153.

78. Lý, *Hồi Ký*, 141.

79. CIA, "Weekly Report: The Situation in South Vietnam: Intelligence and Reporting Subcommittee of the Interagency Vietnam Coordinating Committee," January 5, 1966, Central Intelligence Agency Collection, 0410694007, Vietnam Center and Sam Johnson Vietnam Archive, Virtual Vietnam Archive, Texas Tech University.

80. Tuyên bố lập trường of Khối Dân Tộc, September 12, 1974, PTTD2 3455. See also Uyên Thao, "Giấy bút lấm than," *Cỏ Thơm*, December 2001. Uyên Thao paraphrased Ngọa Long's article, which compared Laws 1881 and 1898, promulgated during the French colonial period, with Decree 007. That article was published in *Sóng Thần*, August 30, 1974.

81. Nguyễn, *Lược sử báo chí*, 79.

82. Trùng, "Sóng Thần's Campaign," 144.

83. Interview with Hoàng Đức Nhã.

84. In 1972 the black market exchange rate was 439 dong to every US dollar. Dacy, *Foreign Aid*, 190.

85. Lý, *Hồi Ký*, 241; Nguyễn, *Lược sử báo chí*, 80.

86. Nguyễn, *Lược sử báo chí*, 78.

87. Phạm, "Life and Work," 122.

88. Việt Nam Tân Xã (VTX), August 28, 1972, PTT 30910.

89. Newspapers anticipated this problem when the decree was promulgated. "Nhiều tờ báo phải dẹp tiệm vì không có đủ tiền ký qũy," *Sóng Thần*, August 6, 1972, 1, 4.

90. Ministry of Information communiqué, September 16, 1972; report from minister of information to prime minister, September 16, 1972, PTT 30910. The ten dailies that had to close were *Xây Dựng, Đồng Nai, Tin Sớm, Saigon Mới, Đuốc Nhà Nam, Dân Chủ Mới, Thách Đố, Thời Đại Mới, Bút Thần,* and *Đuốc Miền Tây*. Of the five foreign-language papers, only the *Saigon Post* was able to continue operating. *Việt Nam Nhật Báo* also met the new requirement, but it was newly founded and had not received permission to publish; therefore, it was not counted in this tally.

91. "Tuyên Ngôn I: Tổ hợp giai phẩm Định kỳ VN Hội Báo Định Kỳ VN," n.d., (circa November 1972), PTTD2 7764.

92. Report from minister of information Trương Bửu Điện to prime minister, September 16, 1972, PTT 30912; Bộ Thông Tin, "Danh Sách," November 27, 1972, PTT 30910. The latter document stated that forty-two (not thirty-eight) periodicals were given waivers.

93. Report from minister of information Trương Bửu Điện to prime minister, November 27, 1972, PPT 30910.

94. "Tuyên Ngôn I." The surviving special arts publications were Khoa Học, Huyền Bí, Thời Nay, Tiếng Dân, Bách Khoa, Trường Sơn, Dân Mới, Tân Học, Dân, Tùng Uyên, Văn Phổ Thông, and Vì Dân

95. "Gọi thêm vốn và vay nợ để đóng ký qũy cho Sóng Thần," Sóng Thần, August 15, 1972, 4; "Sóng Thần đã nhận được 7,004,000 đ do các thân hữu gửi tới để ký qũy," Sóng Thần, August 28, 1972, 4.

96. "Sóng Thần đã nhận được 7,004,000 đ," 4.

97. Articles 42 and 43, Quy Chế Báo Chí. Sửa đổi bở sắc luật 007-TT/SLu, 13.

98. In the former regulation (Press Regulation 069), the fine ranged from 300,000 to 1.5 million dong, and the jail term was between one and five years.

99. Quy Chế Báo Chí 007-TT/SLu, 5–6; Nguyễn, Lược sử báo chí, 78.

100. Lý, Hồi Ký, 241–42.

101. Quy Chế Báo Chí 007-TT/SLu, 6–7; Nguyễn, Lược sử báo chí, 76.

102. Tập tài liệu của bộ nội vụ về danh sách báo chí vi phạm, 1974, PTT 31320.

103. Email correspondence with Trùng Dương.

104. "Hơn 30 chủ nhiệm kêu gọi triệu tập DH báo chí," Sóng Thần, August 9, 1972, 3.

105. Thanh Lãng (chairman of PEN Vietnam), "Trung Tâm Văn Bút ra tuyên bố," Chính Luận, September 3, 1974, 1.

106. Asselin, Vietnam's American War, 224–25.

107. Tâm Chung, "Tin thêm về vụ bắt được trăm triệu hàng lậu tại Long An," Chính Luận, February 9, 1974, 3; "Những bí ẩn ly kỳ quanh đoàn quân xa chở hàng lậu," Chính Luận, February 10, 1974, 3, 6; Mặc Lâm's interview with Trùng Dương, "Tự do báo chí của miền Nam VN trước 1975," Radio Free Asia, October 31, 2015.

108. UPI, "Viet Cabinet Quits in Wake of Drive to End Corruption," Boston Globe, February 17, 1974, 33.

109. Elliott, Sacred Willow, 377.

110. The group was officially inaugurated on August 18, 1974, in Tân Việt Cathedral in Saigon. The executive committee included Tran Huu Thanh; former senator Hoang Xuan Tửu; magistrate Tran Thuc Linh; deputies Nguyen Van Binh, Dan Van Tipp (sic), Do Sinh Tu, Nguyen Tuan Anh, Nguyen Trong Nho, Nguyen Van Cu, and Nguyen Van Kim; and engineer Tran Van Tri. Embassy Saigon's Mission Weekly for August 15–21, 1974, 1974 Saigon 11053, Saigon Embassy to State Department, August 21, 1974, Central Foreign Policy Files 1973–9, Electronic Telegrams, Group 59.

111. Trần Hữu Thanh, Cuộc cách mạng nhân-vị: Đối đáp (Saigon: Phan Thanh Giản, 1955). For more on his thoughts about personalism see, Nguyen, "Fighting the First Indochina War Again?"

112. Vũ Khởi Phụng, "Nhớ Cha Trần Hữu Thanh," Gia Đình An Phong, January 7, 2008.

113. James Markham, "A Large Protest Erupts in Saigon," New York Times, September 21, 1974, 11; Turley, Second Indochina War, 215.

114. Trần, "Challenge for Peace," 463.

115. "Danh sách 84 L.M. chống tham nhũng thuộc giáo phận Cần Thơ," Điện Tín, October 7, 1974.

116. "Vietnam Catholics Stage Hue Protest," New York Times, September 16, 1974, 7; US Central Foreign Policy Files (hereafter USCFPF), Activities of People's Anti-Corruption Movement in MR-1, 1974 Danang 00405, US Consulate in Danang to the

Embassy in Saigon, September 14, 1974; "Mít-tinh tại công trường Phủ Cam: cảnh sát không can thiệp như trước," *Chính Luận*, September 17, 1974, 1, 9; USCFPF, People's Anti-Corruption Movement Meeting in Saigon Area, 1974 Saigon Embassy to State, November 18, 1974. One rally at Lộc Hưng church in Saigon drew so many people that dozens had to climb onto rooftops to participate. "Mít-tinh chống tham nhũng tại nhà thờ Lộc Hưng," *Điện Tín*, October 8, 1974, 3; USCPF, Embassy Saigon's Mission Weekly for December 5–11, 1974, 1974 Saigon 15335, Saigon to State, December 11, 1974.

117. Father Trần Hữu Thanh, letter from Vietnam Indictment No. 1, September 8, 1974, Social Movements Collection, 14510325042, Vietnam Center and Sam Johnson Vietnam Archive, Virtual Vietnam Archive, Texas Tech University.

118. USCFPF, Embassy Saigon's Mission Weekly for November 14–20, 1974, 1974 Saigon 14511, Saigon to State, November 20, 1974.

119. "Nhan Dan Criticizes Anti-Thieu Movement's Political Indictment," February 9, 1975, Douglas Pike Collection, Unit 05—National Liberation Front, 2311415012, Vietnam Center and Sam Johnson Vietnam Archive, Virtual Vietnam Archive, Texas Tech University.

120. "Front Radio: US Directing Father Thanh's Actions—Liberation Radio in Vietnamese to South Vietnam," November 22, 1974, Pike Collection, Unit 08—Biography, 2361206084.

121. James Markham, "Viet Cong Assail Thieu Opponent," *New York Times*, November 24, 1974, 13.

122. USCFPF, Opposition Political Activity Seeks to Exploit Strains in the Body Politics, 1974 Saigon 12026, Saigon to State, September 16, 1974; Bases of People's Anti-Corruption Movement," 1974 Saigon 15885, Saigon to State, December 3, 1974.

123. USCFPF, Father Thanh Going Downhill, 1975 Saigon 1231, Saigon to State, January 31, 1975.

124. USCFPF, Activities of People's Anti-Corruption Movement in MR-1.

125. "Bửu tình ở Huế chống tham nhũng bị giải tán vì luật không cho phép," *Chính Luận*, September 10, 1974, 1, 9.

126. USCFPF, Embassy Saigon's Mission Weekly for September 12–18, 1974, 1974 Saigon 12142, Saigon to State, September 18, 1974.

127. James Markham, "Thieu Ousts 3 Army Aides in Seeming Bow to Protests," *New York Times*, October 31, 1974, 1; "More Critics Attack Thieu: He Says Foes Serve Reds," *New York Times*, November 2, 1974, 1.

128. "Bửu tình ở Huế," 1, 9.

129. Its Vietnamese name was Ủy ban tranh đấu cho tự do báo chí và xuấn bản.

130. "Thành lập ủy ban tranh đấu cho tự do báo chí và xuấn bản," *Chính Luận*, September 9, 1974, 1.

131. "Thành lập ủy ban tranh đấu," 1. Some of the participants were Trần Văn Tuyên, Nguyễn Văn Bình, Nguyễn Tuấn Anh, Kiều Mộng Thu, Nguyễn Trọng Nho, Nguyễn Đức Cung, Nguyễn Văn Hàm, and Senators Hà Thế Ruyệt and Dương Văn Long.

132. "Đốt sắc luật 007 và luật 019/69 tại Hạ Viện," *Chính Luận*, September 14, 1974, 1, 9.

133. *Chính Luận*, September 23, 1974, 1; *Hòa Bình*, September 22, 1974, 1; Markham, "Large Protest," 11; "Newspaper Battle Steps up in Saigon," *New York Times*, September 22, 1974, 19.

134. On the first day of the trial, October 31, Saigon was like a war zone. Defending lawyers met riot police and barbed wire as they tried to get into the courthouse. *Chính Luận*, November 2, 1974; *Đại Dân Tộc*, November 2 and 4, 1974.

135. Government officials claimed they had identified and rooted out several secret communist agents embedded in the press and could now show the newspapers some leniency. Report from Huỳnh Thới Tây, deputy commander of National Police, to

Combined Intelligence Committee, Office of the Prime Minister, February 23, 1975, PTT 31563.

136. Interview with Hoàng Đức Nhã.

137. James Markham, "Thieu Foes Shrug at Aide's Resignation," *New York Times*, October 26, 1974, 44.

138. The three generals were Lieutenant General Nguyễn Vĩnh Nghi (commander of 4th Corps in the Mekong Delta), Lieutenant General Phạm Quốc Thuần (commander of 3rd Corps around Saigon), and Lieutenant General Nguyễn Văn Toàn (commander of 2nd Corps of the Central Highlands). Markham, "Thieu Ousts 3 Army Aides." 1.

139. Reports of the discussion and consultation can be found in PTT 31560, Documents Regarding Revisions to Press Laws 019 and 007, 1974–1975.

140. Although the deposit requirement was abolished, the government apparently did not return the deposits to the publishers. Letter from Hồ Văn Châm, minister of mobilization and open arms, to prime minister, February 6, 1975, PPT 31560; USCFPF, Embassy Saigon's Mission Weekly for November 14–20, 1974, 1974 Saigon 14511, Saigon to State, November 20, 1974.

141. Nguyễn Văn Hướng (director of the Office of the President) to the president, March 5, 1969, PTTD2 3451.

142. Phạm, "Life and Work," 123.

143. Interview with Trùng Dương.

## CONCLUSION

1. Keith, *Catholic Vietnam*, 68; Nguyen, "French Colonial State," 32–33.

2. Wehrle, "'Awakening the Conscience,'" 17.

3. Luong, "State, Local Associations," 124–26.

4. Luong, 124.

5. Luong, 126.

6. Kerkvliet, "Approach for Analysing," S165.

7. Pettus, *Between Sacrifice and Desire*, chap. 1.

8. Malarney, *Culture*.

9. Luong, "State, Local Associations."

10. Marston, "Bauxite Mining"; Le, "Doing Bodhisattva's Work"; Swenson, "Affective Politics"; Dinh et al., "Historic and Contemporary Influences on HIV Advocacy."

11. Dalton and Ong, "Civil Society." See also Wischermann, "Vietnam in the Era of Doi Moi"; Gray, "Creating Civil Society?"

12. Kerkvliet, "Approach for Analysing"; Marston, "Bauxite Mining"; Hannah, "Local Non-Government Organizations."

13. Bui, "Development of Civil Society."

# Bibliography

**ARCHIVES**

Cornell University Library Division of Rare and Manuscript Collections
Charles F. Sweet Papers, 1953–1990. Collection Number 4827
George McT. Kahin, Collection on the Origins of the Vietnam War, Collection Number 4251.

General Sciences Library, Ho Chi Minh City, Vietnam
Restricted collection on the Republic of Vietnam

National Archives II (Trung Tâm Lưu Trữ Quốc Gia), Ho Chi Minh City, Vietnam
Presidential Office Document, First Republic, 1955–1963
Presidential Office Document, Second Republic, 1967–1975
Prime Minister's Office Document, 1954–1975

The Vietnam Center and Sam Johnson Vietnam Archive, Virtual Vietnam Archive, Texas Tech University
Central Intelligence Agency Collection
Douglas Pike Collection
Glenn Helm Collection
John Donnell Collection
John Graham Collection
Social Movements Collection

**US GOVERNMENT DOCUMENTS**

US Central Foreign Policy Files 1973–1979, Electronic Telegrams, Group 59, US National Archives. https://www.archives.gov/research/foreign-policy/state-dept/rg-59 -central-files/1973-1979.
US State Department. Confidential US State Department central files. Vietnam, 1960–January 1963. Internal affairs, decimal numbers 751K, 751G, 851K, 851G, 951K, 951G. Foreign affairs, decimal numbers 611.51K, 611.51G, 651K, 651G. Film 12199, Cornell Kroch Asian Library.
US State Department. Confidential US State Department central files. Vietnam, February 1963–1966. Subject-numeric categories: AID, CSM, DEF, POL. Film 13039, Cornell Kroch Asian Library.
US State Department. Confidential US State Department special files. Vietnam Working Group, 1963–1966. Lot files: Bureau of Far Eastern Affairs, subject files of the Vietnam Working Group, 1963–1966; Lot files 67D54, 68D84, 69D67, 70D102, 70D232, 70D233. Film 12947, Cornell Kroch Asian Library.

**PUBLICATIONS OF VIETNAMESE VOLUNTARY ASSOCIATIONS**

*Bản Tin. Hội Cựu Sinh Viên Quốc Gia Hành Chánh* [Bulletin of the Alumni Association of the National Institute of Administration], August–September 1969.
*Bản Tin. Hội Thư Viện Việt Nam* [Bulletin of the Library Association], March–April 1974.

*Bản Tin của ủy ban vận-động cải-thiện chế độ lao-tù* [Bulletin of the Committee for Prison Reform], 1970.

*Biên Bản Đại Hội Thống Nhất Phật Giáo* [Minutes from the general meeting of the Unified Buddhist Congregation], January 1963–December 1964.

*Chuông Việt* [Vietnamese bell]. Association of Vietnamese Students in the US, 1965–1966.

*Đặc-san tổng-kết hoạt-động* [Summary review of activities]. Tổng Hội Sinh Viên Quốc Gia Việt Nam [National Association of University Students]. Saigon, 1960.

*Đặc San Ái Hữu Quốc Học* [Special issue of the National School Friendly Society], 1970.

*Đại San Trại Hè Công Tác Hội Thảo.* [Summer work and conference camp]. Liên Đoàn Sinh Viên Phật Tử Vietnam [Federation of Buddhist University Students]. Saigon, 1964.

*Diễn Đàn Sinh Viên* [University student forum (of Đà Lạt University)], 1966.

*Đối Thoại* [Dialogue, produced by students of the Faculty of Letters, Saigon University]. Saigon, June 15, 1966.

*Luận Đàm* [Discussion]. Tổng Hội Giáo Giới Việt Nam [Association of Educators of Vietnam], 1960.

*Phong Trào Phụ Nữ Đòi Quyền Sống* [Women's Movement for the Right to Live], December 2, 1970.

*Sinh Viên* [University student], 1968.

*Sinh Viên Huế* [Huế University student], 1964–1965.

*Sinh Viên Vạn Hạnh* [Vạn Hạnh University student], 1971–1972.

*Thư Viện Tập San* [Library review]. Hội Thư Viện Việt Nam [Library Association], 1960–1971.

*12 năm hoạt động của Hội Văn Hóa Bình Dân* [12 years of activities of the Popular Culture Society]. Saigon: n.p., 1967.

*Ý Hương* [Intention]. Sinh Viên Dược Khoa [Pharmacy Student Association], 1971.

## VIETNAMESE NEWSPAPERS AND PERIODICALS

*Chính Luận* [Political discussion]
*Đại Dân Tộc* [Great nation]
*Dân Chủ* [Democracy]
*Điện Tín* [Telegraph]
*Đối Diện* [Face-to-face]
*Hòa Bình* [Peace]
*Sống* [To live]
*Sóng Thần* [Tsunami]

## INTERVIEWS

Bạch Công An, Mississauga, Ontario, June 23, 2010
Hoàng Đức Nhã, telephone, March 22, 2017
Huỳnh Tấn Mẫm, Ho Chi Minh City, May 4, 2010
Huỳnh Thị Ngọc Tuyết, Ho Chi Minh City, April 20, 2010
Lâm Thành Qúy, Ho Chi Minh City, May 4, 2010
Nguyễn Huỳnh Tân, telephone, October 19, 2010
Nguyễn Kinh Châu, telephone, June 29, 2016
Nguyễn Tường Cẩm, email, October 2, 2010
Nguyễn Vân Hạnh, telephone, October 27, 2010
Nguyễn Văn Nghị, Ho Chi Minh City, April 12, 2010
Ngy Thanh, telephone and email, 2015, 2016

Phan Khắc Từ (Reverend), Ho Chi Minh City, April 13, 2010
Thích Đồng Bổn, Ho Chi Minh City, April 26, 2010
Thích Tâm Đức, Ho Chi Minh City, April 21, 2010
Thu-Huong Nguyen-Vo, Ho Chi Minh City, April 10, 2020
Trần Khánh Tuyết, telephone, December 2, 2010
Trần Quang Lâm, telephone, July 27, 2017
Trần Thị Nên, Ho Chi Minh City, May 3, 2010
Trần Trí, telephone, October 19, 2010
Trần Văn Sơn, email, September 2015.
Triều Giang Nancy Bui, email, 2015
Trịnh Cung, Ho Chi Minh City, April 23, 2010
Trùng Dương (Nguyễn Thị Thái), email 2015–2017; Berkeley, California, October 17–18, 2016
Uyên Thao, telephone, June 9, 2015; Falls Church, Virginia, July 23, 2015.

## MEMOIRS, PUBLISHED PERSONAL ACCOUNTS, AND OTHER PUBLISHED WORKS

Alagappa, Muthiah. "Civil Society and Political Change: An Analytical Framework." In *Civil Society and Political Change in Asia*, edited by Muthiah Alagappa, 26–57. Stanford, CA: Stanford University Press, 2004.

Amer, Ramses. *The Ethnic Chinese in Vietnam and Sino-Vietnamese Relations*. Kuala Lumpur: Forum, 1991.

Anderson, David. *The Vietnam War*. New York: Palgrave Macmillan, 2005.

Andradé, Dale. *Trial by Fire: The 1972 Easter Offensive; America's Last Vietnam Battle*. New York: Hippocrene Books, 1995.

Ainslie, Andrew. "Harnessing the Ancestors: Mutuality, Uncertainty and Ritual Practice in the Eastern Cape Province, South Africa." *Africa* 84, no. 4 (2014): 530–52.

Asselin, Pierre. *Hanoi's Road to War*. Berkeley: University of California Press, 2013.

———. *Vietnam's American War: A History*. Cambridge: Cambridge University Press, 2018.

Baker, Alan. *Fraternity among the French Peasantry: Sociability and Voluntary Associations in the Loire Valley, 1815–1914*. Cambridge: Cambridge University Press, 1999.

Barnett, Stanley, Erroll Michener, and C. Walter Stone. *Developmental Book Activities and Needs in the Republic of Vietnam*. Washington, DC: USAID, 1966.

Barrett, Tracy. "Transnational Webs: Overseas Chinese Economic and Political Networks in Colonial Vietnam, 1870–1945." PhD dissertation, Cornell University, 2007.

Beaudoin, Steven. "'Without Belonging to Public Service': Charities, the State, and Civil Society in Third Republic Bordeaux, 1870–1914." *Journal of Social History* (Spring 1998): 671–99.

Bernal, Martin. "The Nghe-Tinh Soviet Movement 1930–1931." *Past and Present* 92, no. 92 (August 1981): 148–68.

Berquist, Kathleen. "Operation Babylift or Babyabduction? Implications of the Hague Convention on the Humanitarian Evacuation and 'Rescue' of Children." *International Social Work* 52, no. 5 (2009): 622–33.

Berry, Mary Elizabeth. "Public Life in Authoritarian Japan." *Daedalus* 127, no, 3 (Summer 1998): 133–65.

Bonner, Jeremy, Jeffrey Burns, and Christopher Denny. Introduction to *Empowering the People of God: Catholic Action before and after Vatican II*, edited by Jeremy Bonner,

Christopher Denny, and Mary Beth Connolly, 1–18. New York: Fordham University Press, 2014.

Boot, Max. *The Road Not Taken: Edward Lansdale and the American Tragedy in Vietnam*. New York: Liveright, 2018.

Bourdieu, Pierre. "The Forms of Capital." In *Handbook of Theory and Research for the Sociology of Education*, edited by John Richardson, 241–58. New York: Greenwood Press, 1986.

Bratton, Michael. "Beyond the State: Civil Society and Associational Life in Africa." *World Politics* 41, no. 3 (1989): 407–30.

Brigham, Robert. *ARVN: Life and Death in the South Vietnamese Army*. Lawrence: University Press of Kansas, 2006.

Britton, Edward C. "Vietnamese Youth and Social Revolution." *Vietnam Perspectives* 2, no. 2 (1966): 13–27.

Bui, Diem-My T. "Reporting on Madame Nhu in the Viet Nam War: Representing the Gendered Other." *Positions: East Asia Cultures Critique* 20, no. 3 (Summer 2012): 851–75.

Bui, Thiem. "The Development of Civil Society and Dynamics of Governance in Vietnam's One Party Rule." *Global Change, Peace and Security* 25, no. 1 (2013): 77–93.

Bùi Xuân Đính. *Lệ Làng Phép Nước* [Village customs and state law]. Hanoi: Phap Ly, 1985.

Bush, Perry. "The Political Education of Vietnam Christian Service, 1954–1975." *Peace and Change* 27, no. 2 (April 2002): 198–224.

Catton, Philip. "Counter-Insurgency and Nation Building: The Strategic Hamlet Programme in SVN, 1961–3" *International History Review* 21, no. 4 (December 1999): 918–40.

——. *Diem's Final Failure*. Lawrence: University Press of Kansas, 2002.

——. "Refighting Vietnam in the History Books: The Historiography of the War." *Magazine of History* 18, no. 5 (2004): 7–11.

Chan Khong [Cao Ngọc Phương]. *52 năm theo thầy học đạo và phụng sự—Hồi kí của Sư cô Chân Không* [52 years of following the master to study religion and perform service—memoir of Nun Chân Không]. https://langmai.org/tang-kinh-cac/vien-sach/tap-truyen/con-duong-mo-rong/loi-gioi-thieu/.

—— [Cao Ngọc Phương]. *Learning True Love: Practicing Buddhism in a Time of War*. Berkeley, CA: Parallax Press, 2007.

Chân Tín. "Trang viết cuối cùng của LM Chân Tín" [Last written page of Father Chân Tín]. Đàn Chiêm Việt [Flock of Vietnamese birds] online, December 16, 2012. http://www.danchimviet.info/archives/70543/trang-viet-cuoi-cung-cua-lm-chan-tin/2012/12.

Chapman, Jessica. *Cauldron of Resistance: Ngo Dinh Diem, the United States, and 1950s Southern Vietnam*. Ithaca, NY: Cornell University Press, 2013.

Chester, Eric. *Covert Network Progressives, the International Rescue Committee and the CIA*. Armonk, NY: M. E. Sharpe, 1995.

Choi Byung Wook. "The Nguyen Dynasty's Policy toward Chinese on the Water Frontier in the First Half of the Nineteenth Century." In *Water Frontier: Commerce and the Chinese in the Lower Mekong Region, 1750–1880*, edited by Nola Cooke and Li Tana, 85–99. Lanham, MD: Rowman and Littlefield, 2004.

Chou, Grace Ai-Ling. "Cultural Education as Containment of Communism: The Ambivalent Position of American NGOs in Hong Kong in the 1950s." *Journal of Cold War Studies* 12, no. 2 (Spring 2010): 3–29.

Cooke, Nola. "Regionalism and the Nature of Nguyen Rule in Seventeenth-Century Dang Trong." *Journal of Southeast Asian Studies* 29, no. 1 (March 1998): 122–61.

Cosmas, Graham. *MACV: The Joint Command in the Years of Withdrawal, 1968–1973.* Washington, DC: Center of Military History, US Army, 2006.

Council of Foreign Voluntary Agencies in Vietnam. *Bản Thông Tin* [Bulletin]. Saigon: Hội Đồng Cơ Quan Từ Thiện tại Vietnam [Council of Foreign Voluntary Agencies in Vietnam], [1971].

Dacy, Douglas. *Foreign Aid, War, and Economic Development: South Vietnam, 1955–75.* Cambridge: Cambridge University Press, 1986.

Dalton, Russel J., and Nhu-Ngoc T. Ong. "Civil Society and Social Capital in Vietnam." socialcapital.www.doc (uci.edu). Accessed April 12, 2008.

Đào Thị Kim Dung. "Khảo Luận Về Một Số Cô-Nhi-Viện Hoạt Động Tại Đô Thành Sài Gòn" [An examination of active orphanages in the capital city of Saigon]. Graduating thesis, National Institute of Administration, Saigon, 1973.

Demery, Monique. *Finding the Dragon Lady.* New York: Public Affairs, 2013.

DeVido, Elise. "Buddhism for This World: The Buddhist Revival in Vietnam 1920s–1951, and Its Legacy." In *Modernity and Re-enchantment: Religion in Post-revolutionary Vietnam*, edited by Philip Taylor, 250–96. Singapore: Institute of Southeast Asian Studies, 2007.

———. "Eminent Nuns of Hue, Vietnam." In *Eminent Buddhist Women*, edited by Karma Lekshe Tsomo, 71–81. New York: SUNY Press, 2014.

———. "The Influence of Chinese Master Taixu on Buddhism in Vietnam." *Journal of Global Buddhism* 10 (2009): 413–58.

Diêu Ân, *Huỳnh Tấn Mẫm: Một Đời Sôi Nổi* [Huynh Tan Mam: an exciting life]. Hanoi: Lao Động, 2008.

Dinh, Kathryn, Khuat Thu Hong, Bridget Haire, and Heather Worth. "Historic and Contemporary Influences on HIV Advocacy in Vietnam." *Voluntas* 32 (2021): 610–20.

Đoàn Kế Tường. "Mỹ Chánh, Quảng Trị: Chặng đường ngút ngàn tử khị" [My Chanh, Quang Tri: Barricaded road killed well over a thousand]. In *Những Ngày Dài trên Quê Hương: Bút Ký Chiến Trường* [The long days in the homeland: battlefield memoirs], 39–42. 1972. Reprint, Fort Smith, AR: Song Moi, 1980.

Đoàn Thanh Liêm. "Câu chuyện vận động thành lập trung học cộng đồng quận 8, năm 1965–1966" [The story of activism to build a public high school in District 8, 1965–1966]. http://www.luongvancancausa.com/vh-nt/vhnt/bk-nc/dtl/cau-chuyen-van-dong-thanh-lap-trung-hoc-cong-dong-quan-8-nam-1965-1966/.

———. "Chuyện vui buồn với anh chị em Phụng sự xã hội" [Sharing sad and happy stories with the participants of social service]. Việt Báo Online, 2011. http://vietbao.com/D_1-2_2-44_4-181996_5-15_6-4_17-131_14-2_15-2_10-909_12-1/.

———. "Hồi tưởng—Quận 8 (bài đầu)" [Remembering District 8 (first essay)]. Viet Bao Online, September 2015. https://vietbao.com/a242365/chuong-trinh-phat-trien-quan-8-sai-gon-ky-1-vai-cau-chuyen-dang-nho-tu-nhung-ngay-dau.

———. "Hồi tưởng–Quận 8 (bài 2)" [Remembering District 8 (second essay)]. Việt Báo Online, September 2015. https://vietbao.com/a232308/bai-2-ton-giao-cac-lop-day-nghe-o-quan-6-7-8-sai-gon.

———. "Làm Men trong Bột—Bài viết nhân kỷ niệm năm thứ 45 Ngày Thành Lập Chương Trình Phát Triển Quận 8 Saigon 1965–2010" [Fermenting dough—essay on the 45th anniversary of the development program for District 8, Saigon, 1965–2010]. Viet Bao Online, 2010. https://vietbao.com/a146950/lam-men-trong-bot.

———. "Mấy nét chính yếu về Xã hội Dân sự tại miền Nam Việt nam trước năm 1975" [Some main characteristics of civil society in South Vietnam before 1975]. Việt Báo Online, October 25, 2011. https://vietbao.com/D_1-2_2-44_4-182124_5-15_6-4_17-131_14-2_15-2_10-909_12-1/.

———. "Thanh Thiếu Niên Và Công Tác Xã Hội (bài 1)—Việc Trợ Giúp Nạn Nhân Bão Lụt Ở Miền Trung Năm 1964" [Youth and adolescents and social work (essay 1)—the work of helping flood victims in the central region, 1964]. Công Giáo Việt Nam.net. http://www.conggiaovietnam.net/index.php?m=module2&id=35.

———. "Thanh Thiếu Niên Và Công Tác Xã Hội (bài 2): Chương Trình Công Tác Hè 1965" [Youth and adolescents and social work (essay 2): summer workcamp program, 1965]. Cong Giao Viet Nam.net, March 19, 2010. http://www.conggiaovietnam.net/index.php?m=module2&v=detailarticle&id=35&ia=9003.

———. "Thanh Thiếu Niên và Công Tác Xã Hội (bài 3)—Chương Trình Phát Triển Quận 8 Saigon" [Youth and adolescents and social work (essay 3)—the development program of District 8, Saigon]. Cong Giao Viet Nam.net. http://www.conggiaovietnam.net/index.php?m=module2&v=detailarticle&id=35&ia=9011.

Dooley, Thomas. *Deliver Us from Evil: The Story of Viet Nam's Flight to Freedom*. New York: Signet Books, 1961.

Dror, Olga. "Foundational Myths in the Republic of Vietnam (1955–1975): 'Harnessing' the Hùng Kings against Ngô Đình Diệm. Communists, Cowboys, and Hippies for Unity, Peace, and Vietnameseness." *Journal of Social History* 49, no. 4 (2016): 1–36.

———. *Making Two Vietnams: War and Youth Identities, 1965–1975*. Cambridge: Cambridge University Press, 2018.

Dương Phục and Vũ Thanh Thủy. *Tình -Ngục Tù & Vượt Biển* [Love, prison and escape by sea]. Houston, TX: Saigon-Houston Publisher, 2016.

Dương Thái Bình. "Ba Phụ Nữ Trong Nghề Làm Báo" [Three women in newspaper publishing]. https://petruskyaus.net/ba-phu-nu-trong-nghe-lam-bao-thanh-binh.

Dutton, George, Jayne Werner, and John Whitmore, eds. *Sources of Vietnamese Tradition*. New York: Columbia University Press, 2012.

Eaton, David. "Education as an Aspect of Development: South Vietnam." *Southeast Asia* 1, no. 3 (1972): 257–74.

Elkind, Jessica. *Aid under Fire: Nation Building and the Vietnam War*. Lexington: University Press of Kentucky, 2016.

Elliott, David. *The Vietnamese War: Revolutionary and Social Change in the Mekong Delta 1930–1975*. Concise ed. Armonk, NY: M. E. Sharp, 2003.

Elliott, Duong Van Mai. *The Sacred Willow*. New York: Oxford University Press, 1999.

Fear, Sean. "The Ambiguous Legacy of Ngô Đình Diệm in South Vietnam's Second Republic (1967–1975)." *Journal of Vietnamese Studies* 11, no. 1 (2016): 1–75.

———. "Saigon Goes Global: South Vietnam's Quest for International Legitimacy in an Age of Détente." *Diplomatic History* 42, no. 3 (2018): 428–55.

Femia, Joseph. *Gramsci's Political Thought: Hegemony, Consciousness, and the Revolutionary Process*. Oxford: Clarendon Press, 1981.

Firpo, Christina. *The Uprooted: Race, Children and Imperialism in French Indochina 1890–1980*. Honolulu: University of Hawaii Press, 2016.

Fisher, Christopher T. "Nation Building and the Vietnam War: A Historiography." *Pacific Historical Review* 74, no. 3 (2005): 441–56.

Flipse, Scott. "The Latest Casualty of War: Catholic Relief Services." *Peace and Change* 27, no. 2 (April 2002): 245–70.

Fraser, Nancy. "Rethinking the Public Sphere: A Contribution to the Critique of Actually Existing Democracy." In *Habermas and the Public Sphere*, edited by Craig Calhoun, 109–42. Cambridge, MA: MIT Press, 1991.

Gadkar-Wilcox, Wynn. "Existentialism and Intellectual Culture in South Vietnam." *Journal of Asian Studies* 73, no. 2 (2014): 377–95.

Goodman, Allan. *Politics in War: The Bases of Political Community in South Vietnam.* Cambridge, MA: Harvard University Press, 1973.

———. "South Vietnam: War without End?" *Asian Survey* 15, no. 1 (January 1975): 70–84.

Gordon, Avery. *Ghostly Matters: Haunting and the Sociological Imagination.* Minneapolis: University of Minnesota Press, 2008.

Goscha, Christopher. "'Hell in a Very Small Place': Cold War and Decolonisation in the Assault on the Vietnamese Body at Dien Bien Phu." *European Journal of East Asian Studies* 9, no. 2 (2010): 201–23.

———. *The Penguin History of Modern Vietnam.* New York: Penguin, 2016.

———. "A 'Total War' of Decolonization? Social Mobilization and State-Building in Communist Vietnam (1949–54)." *War and Society* 31, no. 2 (2012): 136–62.

Gramsci, Antonio. *Selections from the Prison Notebooks.* Translated and edited by Quintin Hoare and Geoffrey Nowell Smith. London: Lawrence and Winhart, 1971.

Gray, Michael L. "Creating Civil Society? The Emergence of NGOs in Vietnam." *Development and Change* 30 (1999): 693–713.

Guillemot, François. "Autopsy of a Massacre on a Political Purge in the Early Days of the Indochina War." *European Journal of East Asian Studies* 9, no. 2 (2010): 225–65.

———. "'Be Men!' Fighting and Dying for the State of Vietnam (1951–54)." *War and Society* 31, no. 2 (2012): 184–210.

———. "The Lessons of Yên Bái, or the 'Fascist' Temptation: How the Đại Việt Parties Rethought Anticolonial Nationalist Revolutionary Action, 1932–1945." *Journal of Vietnamese Studies* 14, no. 3 (2019): 43–79.

Gunn, Geoffrey. *Rice Wars in Colonial Vietnam: The Great Famine and the Việt Minh Road to Power.* Lanham, MD: Rowman and Littlefield, 2014.

Gustafsson, Mai Lan. *War and Shadows: The Haunting of Vietnam.* Ithaca, NY: Cornell University Press, 2009.

Habermas, Jürgen. "Further Reflections on the Public Sphere." In *Habermas and the Public Sphere,* edited by Craig Calhoun, 421–61. Cambridge, MA: MIT Press, 1991.

———. *The Structural Transformation of the Public Sphere: An Inquiry into a Category of Bourgeois Society.* Translated by Thomas Burger. Cambridge, MA: MIT Press, 1991.

Hà Mai Việt. *Thép và Máu: Thiết-giáp trong chiến-tranh Việt-Nam* [Steel and blood: armor in the Vietnam War]. N.p. [US]: n.p., 2015.

Hannah, Joseph. "Local Non-Government Organizations in Vietnam: Development, Civil Society, and State-Society Relations." PhD dissertation, University of Washington, 2007.

Hansen, Peter. "Bắc Di Cư: Catholic Refugees from the North of Vietnam, and Their Role in the Southern Republic, 1954–1959." *Journal of Vietnamese Studies* 4, no. 3 (Fall 2009): 173–211.

Hardy, Andrew. *Red Hills: Migrants and the State in the Highlands of Vietnam.* Copenhagen, Denmark: NIAS Press, 2003.

Herring, George. *America's Longest War.* 4th ed. New York: McGraw-Hill Education, 2002.

———. "'Peoples Quite Apart': Americans, South Vietnamese, and the War in Vietnam." *Diplomatic History* 14, no. 1 (1990): 1–23.

Hess, David. "The Educated Vietnamese Middle Class of Metropolitan Saigon and Their Legacy of Confucian Authority, 1954–75." PhD dissertation, New York University, 1977.

Hoang, Tuan. "Ideology in Urban South Vietnam, 1950–1975." PhD dissertation, University of Notre Dame, 2013.

Hội Sinh Viên Việt Nam [University Student Union of Vietnam]. *Sơ Thảo Lịch Sử Phong Trào Học Sinh Sinh Viên và Hội Sinh Viên Việt Nam (1945–1998)* [A historical sketch of the pupil and university student movement in Vietnam (1945–1998)]. Hanoi: Thanh Niên, 1999.

Holcombe, Alec. *Mass Mobilization in the Democratic Republic of Vietnam, 1945–1960.* Honolulu: University of Hawaii Press, 2020.

Hồ Ngọc Nhuận. *Đời Hồi Ký* [Life, a memoir]. 2010. https://app.box.com/s/z1mrnn33uv bd7bqrshqaj8d0mpgehxwg.

Hợp Phố. "Trung Tâm Cứu Trợ 4 Duy Tân" [Relief center, 4 Duy Tan]. In *Tuổi Trẻ Sài Gòn Mậu Thân* [Saigon youth in the Tet Offensive], 202–6. Ho Chi Minh City: Trẻ, 2013.

Huff, Gregg. "Causes and Consequences of the Great Vietnam Famine, 1945–5." *Economic History Review* 72, no. 1 (2019): 286–316.

Hunt, David. *Vietnam's Southern Revolution: From Peasant Insurrection to Total War.* Amherst: University of Massachusetts Press, 2008.

Huỳnh Văn Lang. *Ký Ức Huỳnh Văn Lang* [Huynh Van Lang's memoir]. Vol. 1 (1928–1955). Published by the author, 2011.

———. "Món nợ văn hóa bình dân và sứ mạng văn hóa dân tộc" [The debt of popular culture and the mission of people's culture]. Nam Kỳ Lục Tỉnh.org, December 6, 2008. http://namkyluctinh.org/hvlang/hvlang-vanhoa.htm.

Immerwahr, Daniel. *Thinking Small.* Cambridge, MA: Harvard University Press, 2015.

Isaacs, Arnold. *Without Honor: Defeat in Vietnam and Cambodia.* Baltimore: Johns Hopkins University Press, 1983.

Jacobs, Seth. *Cold War Mandarin: Ngo Dinh Diem and the Origins of America's War in Vietnam, 1950–1968.* Lanham, MD: Rowman and Littlefield, 2006.

Jamieson, Neil. *Understanding Vietnam.* Berkeley: University of California Press, 1995.

Jammes, Jérémy. "Caodaism in Times of War." *Sojourn: Journal of Social Issues in Southeast Asia* 31, no. 1 (2016): 247–94.

Keith, Charles. *Catholic Vietnam: A Church from Empire to Nation.* Honolulu: University of Hawaii Press, 2012.

Kelly, Gail Paradise. *French Colonial Education.* Ann Arbor, MI: AMS Press, 2000.

Kerkvliet, Benedict J. Tria. "An Approach for Analysing State-Society Relations in Vietnam." *Sojourn: Journal of Social Issues in Southeast Asia* 33, no. S (2018): S156–98.

———. "Governance, Development, and the Responsive-Repressive State in Vietnam." *Forum for Development Studies* 37, no. 1 (2010): 33–59.

———. "Workers' Protests in Contemporary Vietnam (with Some Comparisons to Those in the Pre-1975 South)." *Journal of Vietnamese Studies* 5, no. 1 (2010): 162–204.

Kirk, Donald. "The Thieu Presidential Campaign: Background and Consequences of the Single-Candidacy Phenomenon." *Asian Survey* 12, no. 7 (July 1972): 609–24.

Klimke, Martin. *The Other Alliance: Student Protest in West Germany and the United States in the Global Sixties.* Princeton, NJ: Princeton University Press, 2010.

Kocher, Matthew A., Thomas B. Pepinsky, and Stathis N. Kalyvas. "Aerial Bombing and Counterinsurgency in the Vietnam War." *American Journal of Political Science* 55, no. 2 (2011): 201–18.

Kohn, Margaret. "Panacea or Privilege? New Approaches to Democracy and Association [Review Essay]." *Political Theory* 30, no. 2 (April 2002): 289–98.

Koo, Jeong-Woo. "The Origins of the Public Sphere and Civil Society: Private Academies and Petitions in Korea, 1506–1800." *Social Science History* 31, no. 3 (Fall 2007): 381–401.

Koven, Seth, and Sonya Michel. "Womanly Duties: Maternalist Politics and the Origins of Welfare States in France, Germany, Great Britain, and the United States, 1880–1920." *American Historical Review* 95, no. 4 (October 1990): 1076–108.

Kwon, Heonik. *After the Massacre: Commemoration and Consolation in Ha My and My Lai.* Berkeley: University of California Press, 2006.

——. *Ghosts of War in Vietnam.* Cambridge: Cambridge University Press, 2008.

Landau, Ingrid. "Law and Civil Society in Cambodia and Vietnam: A Gramscian Perspective." *Journal of Contemporary Asia* 38, no. 2 (May 2008): 244–58.

Lê Cung, and Trần Thanh Thủy. "Sinh Viên, Học Sinh các Đô Thị Miền Nam Việt Nam Trong Phong Trào Phật Giáo Năm 1966" [University students and pupils in the Buddhist movement in South Vietnamese cities, 1966]. *Nghiên Cứu Lịch Sử* 7 (2018): 47–59.

Le Hoang Anh Thu. "Doing Bodhisattva's Work: Charity, Class, and Selfhood of Petty Traders in Hồ Chí Minh City." *Journal of Vietnamese Studies* 15, no. 4 (2020): 4–32.

Lê Huy Ruất. "Những 'hội tương trợ' ở thôn quê" [Mutual-aid societies in rural villages]. *Thanh Nghi* (April 1942): 16–19.

Lessard, Micheline. "The Colony Writ Small: Vietnamese Women and Political Activism in Colonial Schools during the 1920s." *Journal of the Canadian Historical Association* 18, no. 2 (January 2007): 3–23.

Lê Thị Bạch Vân. *Hồi ký bà Tùng Long: Viết là niềm vui muôn thuở của tôi* [Memoir of Mrs. Tùng Long: writing is my eternal happiness]. Ho Chi Minh City: Trẻ, 2003.

Lê Thị Sâm. "Các tổ chức từ thiện tôn giáo tại Đô Thành" [Religious charitable organizations in the capital]. Graduating thesis, National Institute of Administration, Saigon, 1970.

Lê Trong Lộc. "Người đi trong 'Đại Lộ Kinh Hoàng'" [People who traveled on the Highway of Horror]. In *Quê Ngoại: Những bài viết về Quảng Trị* [Maternal homeland: essays about Quang Tri], edited by Hoàng Long Hải, 407–58. Gardena, CA: Van Moi, 2009.

Lê Văn Nuôi. *Sài Gòn Dậy Mà Đi* [Get up and go, Saigon]. Ho Chi Minh City: Tuổi Trẻ, 2000.

Levene, Mark. Introduction to *The Massacre in History,* edited by Mark Levene and Penny Roberts, 1–38. New York: Berghahn Books, 1999.

Li, Kevin. "Partisan to Sovereign: The Making of the Bình Xuyên in Southern Vietnam, 1945–1948." *Journal of Vietnamese Studies* 11, no. 3/4 (2016): 140–87.

Li Tana. "An Alternative Vietnam? The Nguyen Kingdom in the Seventeenth and Eighteenth Centuries." *Journal of Southeast Asian Studies* 29, no. 1 (March 1998): 111–21.

Luong, Hy Van. "Social Capital Configuration Variation and the Contemporary Transformation of Rural Vietnam." *Pacific Affairs* 91, no. 2 (June 2018): 283–307.

——. "The State, Local Associations, and Alternate Civilities in Rural Northern Vietnam." In *Civil Society, Globalization, and Political Change in Asia,* edited by Robert Weller, 123–47. New York: Routledge, 2005.

Luong, Nhi Ky. "The Chinese in Vietnam: A Study of Vietnamese-Chinese Relations with Special Attention to the Period 1862–1961." PhD dissertation, University of Michigan–Ann Arbor, 1963.

Lý Quí Chung. *Hồi Ký Không Tên* [Untitled memoir]. Ho Chi Minh City: Trẻ, 2004.

Madsen, Richard. "The Public Sphere, Civil Society and Moral Community: A Research Agenda for Contemporary China Studies." *Modern China* 19, no. 2 (April 1993): 183–98.

Malarney, Shaun Kingsley. *Culture, Ritual and Revolution in Vietnam.* Honolulu: University of Hawaii Press, 2002.

——. "'The Fatherland Remembers Your Sacrifice': Commemorating War Dead in North Vietnam." In *The Country of Memory: Remaking the Past in Late Socialist Vietnam*, edited by Hue-Tam Ho Tai, 46–76. Berkeley: University of California Press, 2001.

Mann, David. *The 1972 Invasion of Military Region I: Fall of Quang Tri and Defense of Hue*. Project CHECO Report (Contemporary Historical Examination of Current Operations), Directorate of Operations Analysis, Declassified. Reprint. Christiansburg, VA: Dalley Books Service, 1973.

Marr, David. "A Passion for Modernity: Intellectuals and the Media." In *Postwar Vietnam: Dynamics of a Transforming Society*, edited by Hy Van Luong, 257–95. Singapore: ISEAS and Rowman and Littlefield, 2003.

——. "Political Attitudes and Activities of Young Urban Intellectuals in South Viet-Nam." *Asian Survey* 6, no. 5 (1966): 249–63.

——. "A Study of Political Attitudes and Activities among Young Urban Intellectuals in South Viet-Nam." MA thesis, University of California–Berkeley, 1965.

——. *Vietnamese Anticolonialism 1885–1925*. Berkeley: University of California Press, 1971.

——. *Vietnamese Tradition on Trial*. Berkeley: University of California Press, 1981.

Marston, Hunter. "Bauxite Mining in Vietnam's Central Highlands: An Arena for Expanding Civil Society?" *Contemporary Southeast Asia* 34, no. 2 (2012): 173–96.

Masur, Matthew. "Exhibiting Signs of Resistance: South Vietnam's Struggle for Legitimacy, 1954–1960." *Diplomatic History* 33, no. 4 (2009): 293–313.

McAllister, James. "'A Fiasco of Noble Proportions': The Johnson Administration and the South Vietnamese Elections of 1967." *Pacific Historical Review* 73, no. 4 (November 2004): 619–52.

——. "The Lost Revolution: Edward Lansdale and the American Defeat in Vietnam." *Small Wars and Insurgencies* 14, no. 2 (2003): 1–26.

——. "'Only Religions Count in Vietnam': Thich Tri Quang and the Vietnam War." *Modern Asian Studies* 42, no. 4 (2008): 751–82.

McGarr, Paul. "'Quiet Americans in India': The CIA and the Politics of Intelligence in Cold War South Asia." *Diplomatic History* 38, no. 5 (2004): 1046–82.

McHale, Shawn. *Print and Power: Confucianism, Communism, and Buddhism in the Making of Modern Vietnam*. Honolulu: University of Hawaii Press, 2004.

——. "Understanding the Fanatic Mind? The Việt Minh and Race Hatred in the First Indochina War (1945–1954)." *Journal of Vietnamese Studies* 4, no. 3 (2009): 98–138.

Military History Institute of Vietnam. *Victory in Vietnam: The Official History of the People's Army of Vietnam, 1954–1975*. Translated by Merle Pribbenow. Lawrence: University Press of Kansas, 2002.

Miller, Edward. *Misalliance: Ngo Dinh Diem, the United States, and the Fate of South Vietnam*. Cambridge, MA: Harvard University Press, 2013.

——. "Religious Revival and the Politics of Nation Building: Reinterpreting the 1963 'Buddhist Crisis' in South Vietnam." *Modern Asian Studies* 49, no. 6 (2015): 1903–62.

——. "Vision, Power and Agency: The Ascent of Ngô Đình Diệm, 1945–54." *Journal of Southeast Asian Studies* 35, no. 3 (2004): 433–58.

Miller, Edward, and Tuong Vu. "The Vietnam War as a Vietnamese War: Agency and Society in the Study of the Second Indochina War." *Journal of Vietnamese Studies* 4, no. 3 (2009): 1–16.

Minh Đức. "Bộ Xã Hội Chương Trình Cô Nhi Viện" [Orphanage program of the Ministry of Social Welfare]. *Nguyệt San Xã Hội* [Society month review, published by the School of Social Work] 4 (1972): 17–32.

Morgan, Simon. "'A Sort of Land Debatable': Female Influence, Civic Virtue and Middle-Class Identity, c 1830–c 1860." *Women's Historical Review* 13, no. 2 (2004): 183–209.

Morris, R. J. "Voluntary Societies and British Urban Elites, 1780–1850: An Analysis." *Historical Journal* 26, no. 1 (1983): 95–118.

Morton, Berry. "Education in Viet Nam." *Contemporary Education* 45, no. 3 (Spring 1974): 201–8.

Munck, Ronaldo. "Mutual Benefit Societies in Argentina: Workers, Nationality, Social Security, and Trade Unionism." *Journal of Latin American Studies* 30 (1998): 573–90.

Ngo Quang Truong. *The Easter Offensive*. Indochina Monograph Series. Washington, DC: US Army Center of Military History, [1979].

Nguễn Thị Điều. "'A Day in the Life': Nation-building the Republic of Ngô Đình Diệm, 26 October 1956, Symbolically." *Modern Asian Studies* 53, no. 2 (2019): 718–53.

Nguyễn Cao Kỳ. *Buddha's Child: My Fight to Save Vietnam*. New York: St. Martin's Press, 2002.

Nguyễn Huy Quí. "Nguyên Nhân và Sự Đóng Góp Của Các Tôn Giáo Trong Lãnh Vực Xã Hội" [The causes and contributions of religious groups in society]. Graduating thesis, National Institute of Administration, Saigon, 1973.

Nguyễn Kinh Châu. "Bảy tháng giữa những xác người" [Seven months in the midst of human corpses]. *Thời Báo* (Toronto), November 20, 2009, 107–9.

Nguyễn Lang. *Việt Nam Phật Giáo Sử Luận* [Historical discussion of Vietnamese Buddhism]. Saigon: Lá Bối, 1974. https://langmai.org/tang-kinh-cac/vien-sach/giang-kinh/viet-nam-phat-giao-su-luan/chuong-40-chinh-quyen-ngo-dinh-diem-sup-do/.

Nguyen, Lien-Hang. *Hanoi's War: An International History of the War for Peace in Vietnam*. Chapel Hill: University of North Carolina Press, 2012.

Nguyen, Martina Thuc Nhi. "French Colonial State, Vietnamese Civil Society: The League of Light [Đoàn Ánh Sáng] and Housing Reform in Hà Nội, 1937–1941." *Journal of Vietnamese Studies* 11, no. 3/4 (2016): 17–57.

Nguyễn Ngọc Linh, ed. *Niên Lịch Công Đàn* [Public forum almanac]. Saigon: Công Đàn, 1961.

Nguyễn Ngọc Ngạn. *The Will of Heaven: A Story of One Vietnamese and the End of His World*. Toronto: Van Lang, 1982.

Nguyen, Phi Vân. "Fighting the First Indochina War Again? Catholic Refugees in South Vietnam, 1954–59." *Journal of Social Issues in Southeast Asia* 31, no. 1 (2016): 207–46.

Nguyen Tai Thu et al. *The History of Vietnamese Buddhism*. Washington, DC: Council for Research in Values and Philosophy: Institute of Philosophy, Vietnamese Academy of Social Sciences, 2008.

Nguyen, Thanh V. "Vietnamese Buddhist Movement for Peace and Social Transformation, 1963–66." PhD dissertation, Saybrook Graduate School and Research, San Francisco, 2006.

Nguyen The Anh. "Japanese Food Policies and the 1945 Great Famine in Indochina." In *Food Supplies and the Japanese Occupation in South-East Asia*, edited by Paul Kratoska, 208–26. New York: St. Martin's Press, 1998.

Nguyễn Thị Oanh. *Hồi ký công tác xã hội* [Memoir of social work]. Unpublished memoir, 2003.

———. "School of Social Work." *Bulletin of the Council of Voluntary Agencies in Vietnam* 1 (Fall 1969): 41–42.

———. "Historical Development and Characteristics of Social Work in Today's Vietnam." *International Journal of Social Welfare* 11 (2002): 84–91.

——. *Viên Trợ Nhân Đạo của Mỹ tại miện Nam Việt Nam* [American humanitarian aid in South Vietnam]. Saigon: Ủy Ban Đoàn Kết Công Giáo Yêu Nước Việt Nam [Committee of Patriotic Catholics], ca. 1975.

Nguyễn Thị Thương. "Hội bạn trẻ em và nữ nạn nhân chiến cuộc" [Society for friends of children and women war victims]. *Nguyệt San Xã Hội* [Society month review, published by the School of Social Work] 3 (1972): 46–55.

Nguyen, Thuy-Phuong. "The Rivalry of the French and American Educational Missions during the Vietnam War." *Paedagogica Historica* 50, nos. 1–2 (2014): 27–41.

Nguyễn Trần Quý. "Hiện trạng các tập thể thanh-niên Việt Nam" [The present situation of youth organizations]. Graduating thesis, National Institute of Administration, Saigon, 1969.

Nguyễn Từ Chi. "The Traditional Viet Village in Bac Bo: Its Organizational Structure and Problems." In *The Traditional Village in Vietnam*, edited by Phạm Huy Lê, 44–142. Hanoi: The Gioi Publishers, 1993.

Nguyễn Tường Cẩm. "Vài nét về hoạt động của đời tôi" [Some notes about my life's activities]. Unpublished essay shared by the author, October 2, 2011.

Nguyễn Văn Vẽ. "Sinh viên và hoạt động chính trị" [University students and political activities]. Graduating thesis, National Institute of Administration, Saigon, 1971.

Nguyễn Việt Chước. *Lược sử báo chí Vietnam* [A brief history of newspapers in Vietnam]. Saigon: Nam Sơn, 1974.

Nguyen, Viet Thanh. *Nothing Ever Dies*. Cambridge, MA: Harvard University Press, 2016.

Nguyen-Marshall, Van. "The Ethics of Benevolence in French Colonial Vietnam." In *The Chinese State at the Border*, edited by Diana Lary, 162–80. Vancouver: University of British Columbia Press, 2007.

——. *In Search of Moral Authority*. New York: Peter Lang, 2008.

Nguyen-Vo, Thu Huong. "Forking Paths: How Shall We Mourn the Dead?" *Amerasia Journal* 31, no. 2 (2005): 157–75.

Ngy Thanh. "Đại Lộ Kinh Hoàng" [Highway of Horror]. *Thời Báo*, November 20, 2009, 57–59.

Ninh, Kim. *A World Transformed: The Politics of Culture in Revolutionary Vietnam, 1945–1965*. Ann Arbor, MI: University of Michigan Press, 2002.

Paget, Karen. *Patriotic Betrayal: The Inside Story of the CIA's Secret Campaigns to Enroll American Students in the Crusade against Communism*. New Haven, CT: Yale University Press, 2015.

Pettus, Ashley. *Between Sacrifice and Desire: National Identity and the Governing of Femininity in Vietnam*. New York: Routledge, 2003.

Peycam, Philippe. *The Birth of Vietnamese Political Journalism*. New York: Columbia University Press, 2012.

Phạm Ngọc Thanh. "Phong trào Hướng Đạo Việt Nam" [The Scout movement of Vietnam]. Graduating thesis, National Institute of Administration, Saigon, 1972.

Phạm Trần. "Life and Work of a Journalist." In *The Republic of Vietnam, 1955–1975. Vietnamese Perspectives on Nation Building*, edited by Tuong Vu and Sean Fear, 117–25. Ithaca, NY: Cornell Southeast Asia Program Publications, 2019.

Pham, Van Minh. "Socio-political Philosophy of Vietnamese Buddhism: A Case Study of the Buddhist Movement of 1963 and 1966." Master's thesis, University of Western Sydney, 2001.

Phan Phát Huồn. *Việt-Nam Giáo-Sử* [History of religion in Vietnam]. Vol. 2, *1933–1950*. Saigon: Cứu Thế Tùng-Thư, 1962.

Phúc Tiến. "Các Điểm Hẹn" [Rendezvous points]. In *Từ xếp bút nghiên lên đàng đến xuống đường dậy mà đi* [From putting down our pens to taking to the streets], 263–99. Ho Chi Minh City: Trẻ, 2010.

Phung Thi Hanh. *South Vietnam's Women in Uniform* [pamphlet]. Saigon: Vietnam Council on Foreign Relations, [1970].

Picard, Jason A. "'Renegades': The Story of South Vietnam's First National Opposition Newspapers, 1955–1958." *Journal of Vietnamese Studies* 10, no. 4 (2015): 1–29.

Pike, Douglas. *Viet Cong: The Organization and Techniques of the National Liberation Front of South Vietnam.* Cambridge, MA: MIT Press, 1966.

Purcell, Victor. *The Chinese in Southeast Asia.* London: Oxford University Press, 1965.

Putnam, Robert. "Bowling Alone: America's Declining Social Capital." *Journal of Democracy* 6, no. 1 (1995): 65–78.

———. *Making Democracy Work: Civic Traditions in Modern Italy.* Princeton, NJ: Princeton University Press, 1993.

Quinn-Judge, Sophie. "Giving Peace a Chance: National Reconciliation and a Neutral South Vietnam, 1954–1964." *Peace and Change* 38, no. 4 (2013): 385–410.

———. *The Third Force in the Vietnam War.* London: IB Tauris, 2017.

Ramsay, Jacob. *Mandarins and Martyrs: The Church and the Nguyen Dynasty in Early Nineteenth-Century Vietnam.* Stanford, CA: Stanford University Press, 2008.

Reilly, Brett. "The Sovereign States of Vietnam, 1945–1955." *Journal of Vietnamese Studies* 11, no. 3–4 (2016): 103–39.

Republic of Vietnam. *Cuộc Di Cư Lịch Sử Tại Việt Nam* [Historic Migration in Vietnam]. Sài Gòn: Phủ tổng ủy di cư tị nạn, [1958?].

———. *Pháp Lý Tập San* [Legal review]. Saigon: Ministry of Justice, 1956.

———. *Quy Chế Báo Chí* [Press regulations]. Saigon: Ministry of Information, 1969.

———. *Quy Chế Báo Chí. Sửa đổi bờ sắc luật 007-TT/SLu ngày 4-8-1972 của Tổng Thống Vietnam Cộng Hoà* [Press regulations: revised according to Decree 007-TT/SLu of the president of the Republic of Vietnam]. Saigon: Ministry of Information, 1972.

Rettig, Tobias. "French Military Policies in the Aftermath of the Yên Bay Mutiny, 1930: Old Security Dilemmas Return to the Surface." *South East Asia Research* 10, no. 3 (November 2002): 309–31.

Rodell, Paul. "International Voluntary Services in Vietnam: War and the Birth of Activism." *Peace and Change* 27, no. 2 (2002): 225–44.

Rodima-Taylor, Daivi. "Passageways of Cooperation: Mutuality in Post-Socialist Tanzania." *Africa* 84, no. 4 (2014): 553–75.

Ryan, Mary. "Civil Society as Democratic Practice: North American Cities during the Nineteenth Century." *Journal of Interdisciplinary History* 29, no. 4 (Spring 1999): 559–84.

———. "Gender and Public Access: Women's Politics in Nineteenth-Century America." In *Habermas and the Public Sphere*, edited by Craig Calhoun, 259–88. Cambridge, MA: MIT Press, 1991.

Schwenkel, Christina. *The American War in Contemporary Vietnam: Transnational Remembrance and Representation.* Bloomington: Indiana University Press, 2009.

Sémelin, Jacques. "From Massacre to the Genocidal Process." *International Social Science Journal* 54, no. 174 (December 2002): 233–42.

Sleezer, Karen. "Atrocities and War Crimes." In *The Vietnam War Handbook of the Literature and Research*, edited by James Olson, 193–230. Westport, CT: Greenwood Press, 1993.

Smith, Harvey, et al. *Area Handbook for South Vietnam.* Washington, DC: US Government Printing Office, 1967.

Stewart, Geoffrey C. *Vietnam's Lost Revolution: Ngo Dinh Diem's Failure to Build an Independent Nation, 1955–1963.* Cambridge: Cambridge University Press, 2017.

Stroup, Robert H., and Michael B. Hargrove. "Earnings and Education in Rural South Vietnam." *Journal of Human Resources* 4, no. 2 (1969): 215–25.

Stur, Heather. "Blurred Lines: The Home Front, the Battlefront, and the Wartime Relationship between Citizens and Government of the Republic of Vietnam." *War and Society* 38, no. 1 (February 2019): 57–79.

———. *Saigon at War: South Vietnam and the Global Sixties.* Cambridge: Cambridge University Press, 2020.

———. "'To Do Nothing Would Be to Dig Our Own Graves': Student Activism in the Republic of Vietnam." *Journal of American–East Asian Relations* 26 (2019): 285–317.

Sutherland, David. "Voluntary Societies and the Process of Middle-Class Formation in Early Victorian Halifax, Nova Scotia." *Journal of the Canadian Historical Association/ Revue de la Société historique du Canada* 5, no. 1 (1994): 237–63.

Swenson, Sara. "The Affective Politics of Karma among Buddhist Cancer Charities in Vietnam." *Journal of Vietnamese Studies* 15, no. 4 (2020): 33–62.

Tai, Hue-Tam Ho. "Faces of Remembrance and Forgetting." In *In the Country of Memory: Remaking the Past in Late Socialist Vietnam*, edited by Hue-Tam Ho Tai, 167–95. Berkeley: University of California Press, 2001.

———. *Radicalism and the Origins of the Vietnamese Revolution.* Cambridge, MA: Harvard University Press, 1992.

Tait, Janice. *The Devil's Snare: A Memoir of Saigon.* Toronto: McGilligan Books, 2005.

Talentino, Andrea Kathryn. "The Two Faces of Nation-Building: Developing Function and Identity." *Cambridge Review of International Affairs* 17, no. 3 (2004): 557–75.

Tan, Mitchell. "Spiritual Fraternities: The Transnational Networks of Ngô Đình Diệm's Personalist Revolution and the Republic of Vietnam, 1955–1963." *Journal of Vietnamese Studies* 14, no. 2 (2019): 1–67.

Taylor, Keith. *A History of the Vietnamese.* Cambridge: Cambridge University Press, 2013.

Thayer, Thomas. *War without Fronts: The American Experience.* Annapolis, MD: Naval Institute Press, 2016.

Thích Nhất Hạnh. *Basic Concepts of Policy and Method: Movement of Youth for Social Service.* Saigon: University of Vạn Hạnh, [1966].

———. *Fragrant Palm Leaves, Journals 1962–1966.* Translated by Mobi Warren. New York: Riverhead Books, 1999.

Thích Thanh Văn. "The School of Youth for Social Service and Its Concepts on Rural Social Activities." *Bulletin of the Council of Voluntary Agencies in Vietnam* (Spring 1970): 34–36.

Thiện Mộc Lan. *Phụ-nữ Tân-văn Phấn Son Tô Điểm Sơn Hà* [Women's news: powder and lipstick to adorn the homeland]. Ho Chi Minh City: Văn Hóa Sài Gòn & Công Ty Sách Thời Đại, [2004].

Thompson, Michele. "Setting the Stage: Ancient Medical History of the Geographic Space that Is Now Vietnam." In *Southern Medicine for Southern People: Vietnamese Medicine in the Making*, edited by Laurence Monnais, C. Michele Thompson, and Ayo Wahlberg, 21–60. Cambridge: Cambridge University Press, 2011.

Tisdale, Betty. "Helping and Loving Orphans." In *Chicken Soup for the Adopted Soul*, edited by Jack Canfield, Mark Victor Hansen, and LeAnn Thieman, 332–36. Deerfield Beach, FL: Health Communications, 2008.

Tôn Thất Manh Tuong. "Chân Tín: A Non-Violent Struggle for Human Rights in Viet Nam." *Viet Nam Generation Big Book* 5, no. 1–4 (March 1994). http://www2.iath.virginia.edu/sixties/HTML_docs/Texts/Scholarly/Tuong_Chan_Tin_bio.html.

Toner, Simon. "The Life and Death of Our Republic: Modernization, Agricultural Development, and the Peasantry in the Mekong Delta in the Long 1970s." In *Decolonization and the Cold War: Negotiating Independence*, edited by Leslie James and Elisabeth Leake, 43–62. London: Bloomsbury Academic, 2015.

———. "'The Paradise of the Latrine': American Toilet-Building and the Continuities of Colonial and Post-Colonial Development." *Modern American History* 2, no. 3 (2019): 299–320.

Tonnesson, Stein. *Vietnam 1946: How the War Began.* Berkeley: University of California Press, 2010.

Topmiller, Robert. *The Lotus Unleashed: The Buddhist Peace Movement in South Vietnam, 1964–1966.* Lexington: University Press of Kentucky, 2002.

———. "A Missed Opportunity for Peace in Vietnam—1966." *Peace and Change* 27, no.1 (2002): 59–96.

Trần Angie Ngọc. *Ties that Bind: Cultural Identity, Class, and Law in Vietnam's Labor Resistance.* Ithaca, NY: Cornell Southeast Asia Program Publications, 2013.

Tran, My-Van. "Beneath the Japanese Umbrella: Vietnam's Hòa Hà during and after the Pacific War." *Crossroads: An Interdisciplinary Journal of Southeast Asian Studies* 17, no. 1 (2003): 60–107.

Trần Nhật Vy. *Ba Nhà Báo Sàigòn.* Ho Chi Minh City: Văn Hóa-Văn Nghệ, 2015.

Tran, Nu-Anh. *Disunion: Anticommunist Nationalism and the Making of the Republic of Vietnam.* Honolulu: University of Hawaii Press, 2022.

———. "'Let History Render Judgment on My Life': The Suicide of Nhất Linh (Nguyễn Tường Tam) and the Making of a Martyr in the Republic of Vietnam." *Journal of Vietnamese Studies* 15, no. 3 (2020): 79–118.

Trần Thị Liên. "The Challenge for Peace within South Vietnam's Catholic Community: A History of Peace Activism." *Peace and Change* 38, no. 4 (October 2013): 446–73.

Trần Thị Ngọc Hảo. "Tay Nắm Tay Che" [Hand held, hand covered]. In *Tuổi Trẻ Sài Gòn Mậu Thân* [Saigon youth in the Tet Offensive], 194–201. Ho Chi Minh City: Trẻ 2013.

Trùng Dương. "Hốt Xác Đồng Bào Tử Nạn trên Đại Lộ Kinh Hoàng" [Collecting corpses of compatriots on the Highway of Horror]. *Thời Báo*, November 20, 2009, 59, 104–7.

———. "Sóng Thần's Campaign for Press Freedom." In *The Republic of Vietnam, 1955–1975: Vietnamese Perspectives on Nation Building*, edited by Tuong Vu and Sean Fear, 139–54. Ithaca, NY: Cornell Southeast Asia Program Publications, 2019.

Trương Bá Cần. *50 năm nhìn lại* [50 years of looking back]. Ho Chi Minh: Ho Chi Minh City Publishing, 2008.

Truong Chinh and Vo Nguyen Giap. *The Peasant Question, 1937–1938.* Translated by Christine Pelzer White. Ithaca, NY: Cornell Southeast Asia Program, 1974.

Trương Nhu Tang. *Viet Cong Memoir.* New York: Vintage, 1986.

Tsai, Maw-Kuey. *Les Chinois au Sud-Vietnam.* Paris: Bibliothèque Nationale, 1968.

Turley, G. H. *The Easter Offensive: The Last American Advisors, Viet Nam.* Novato, CA: Presidio, 1985.

Turley, William. *The Second Indochina War.* 2nd ed. Lanham, MD: Rowman and Littlefield, 2009.

US Department of Labor. *Labor Law and Practice in the Republic of Vietnam (South Vietnam).* Washington, DC: US Department of Labor, Bureau of Labor Statistics, 1968.

Uyên Thao. "Giấy bút làm than" [Paper and pen turned to coal]. *Cỏ Thơm Magazine*, December 2001. http://cothommagazine.com/index.php?option=com_content&task=view&id=549&Itemid=1.

Veith, George. *Black April: The Fall of South Vietnam.* New York: Encounter Books, 2012.

Vickers, George R. "U.S. Military Strategy and the Vietnam War." In *The Vietnam War: Vietnamese and American Perspectives*, edited by Jayne Wener and Luu Doan Huynh, 113–29. Armonk, NY: M. E. Sharpe, 1993.

Vo, Alex-Thai. "Nguyễn Thị Năm and the Land Reform in North Vietnam, 1953." *Journal of Vietnamese Studies* 10, no. 1 (Winter 2015): 1–62.

Võ Long Triều, *Hồi Ký* [Memoir]. Vol. 1. Westminster, CA: Người Việt, 2009.

Võ Phiến. *Văn Học Miền Nam tổng quan* [Comprehensive Vietnamese literature]. Reprint. N.p.: Người Việt Books, 2014.

Vũ Công Hùng. "Phong trào tranh đấu của sinh viên, 1970" [The struggle movement of university students, 1970]. Graduating thesis, National Institute of Administration, Saigon, 1972.

Vu, Ngu Chieu. "The Other Side of the 1945 Vietnamese Revolution: The Empire of Viet-Nam (March–August 1945)." *Journal of Asian Studies* 45, no. 2 (February 1986): 293–328.

Vũ Thị Thu Thanh. "Tạp chí Bách Khoa và đời sống xã hội Sài Gòn" [Bách Khoa journal and social life in Saigon]. In *Nam Bộ Đất và Người* [Land and people], Vol. 9, edited by Võ Văn Sen, 209–21. Ho Chi Minh City: Đại Học Quốc Gia, 2013. http://www.sachhay.org/cao-thom/ChiTiet/2800/tap-chi-bach-khoa-va-doi-song-xa-hoi-sai-gon.

Vu, Tuong. "'It's Time for the Indochinese Revolution to Show Its True Colours': The Radical Turn of Vietnamese Politics in 1948." *Journal of Southeast Asian Studies* 40, no. 3 (2009): 519–42.

Vu, Tuong, and Sean Fear, eds. *The Republic of Vietnam, 1955–1975: Vietnamese Perspectives on Nation Building*. Ithaca, NY: Cornell Southeast Asia Program Publications, 2019.

Walkowitz, Daniel. *Working with Class: Social Workers and the Politics of Middle-Class Identity*. Chapel Hill: University of North Carolina Press, 1999.

Walzer, Michael. *Arguing about War*. New Haven, CT: Yale University Press, 2004.

Wehrle, Edmund. "'Awakening the Conscience of the Masses': The Vietnamese Confederation of Labour, 1947–75." In *Labour in Vietnam*, edited by Anita Chan, 13–45. Singapore: Institute of Southeast Asian Studies, 2003.

———. *Between a River and a Mountain: The AFL-CIO and the Vietnam War*. Ann Arbor: University of Michigan Press, 2003.

Weller, Robert. *Alternate Civilities: Democracy and Culture in China and Taiwan*. Boulder, CO: Westview, 1999.

Whitmore, John K., and Brian Zottoli. "The Emergence of the State in Vietnam." In *The Cambridge History of China*, vol. 9, edited by Willard Peterson, 197–233. Cambridge: Cambridge University Press, 2016.

Wiesner, Louis. *Victims and Survivors*. New York: Greenwood Press, 1988.

Wiest, Andrew. *Vietnam's Forgotten Army: Heroism and Betrayal in the ARVN*. New York: NYU Press, 2009.

Wiktorowicz, Qintain. "Civil Society as Social Control: State Power in Jordan." *Comparative Politics* 33, no. 1 (October 2000): 43–61.

Wischermann, Joerg. "Vietnam in the Era of Doi Moi: Issue-Oriented Organizations and Their Relationship to the Government." *Asian Survey* 43, no. 6 (November–December 2003): 867–89.

Woodside, Alexander. *Community and Revolution in Modern Vietnam*. Boston: Houghton Mifflin, 1976.

———. "The Development of Social Organizations in Vietnamese Cities in the Late Colonial Period." *Pacific Affairs* 44, no. 1 (1971): 39–64.

———. *Vietnam and the Chinese Model*. Cambridge, MA: Harvard University Press, 1971.

Zinoman, Peter. "Nhân-Văn-Giai Phẩm and Vietnamese 'Reform Communism' in the 1950s." *Journal of Cold War Studies* 13, no. 1 (Winter 2011): 60–100.

———. *Vietnamese Colonial Republican: The Political Vision of Vũ Trọng Phụng*. Berkeley: University of California Press, 2014.

# Index

Adenauer Foundation, New Life Development Project and, 93

adult literacy and education programs, 83–84, 96

AFL-CIO (American Federation of Labor–Congress of Industrial Organizations), Vietnam Confederation of Workers and, 51, 52

Ái Lan, 71

Alliance of National, Democratic, and Peace Forces, 118, 161

alternative civility, mutual-aid and friendly societies and, 31

alumni associations, 37, 43–46

American Council of Voluntary Agencies, aid to Vietnamese organizations, 108

American Friends of Vietnam, 49, 85

American Friends Service Committee, Voluntary Youth Association and, 105

American Wives Club, 62

Amnesty International, 143

Ana Lê Văn Cang, 72

ancestral veneration ceremonies, lineage societies and, 40

Anderson, Marian, 82–83

An Lạc orphanage, 55, 61–62

Annam, 10; rebellion in, 12

Ấn Quang Buddhist group, 45, 46

Ấn Quang Buddhist Welfare Organization, 129

anti-American sentiments. *See also* antiwar movement: aid to private organizations and distrust of motives, 93–94, 96, 97; Vietnamese youth distrust of, 109–10, 114

anticolonial critique of French, 11–13

anticommunist student groups, 115–16

anticorruption movement, 153–59

anti-Diệm protests, 43, 45, 102, 111–12

antiwar movement: prison reform and right to live campaigns and, 143, 144–45; student, 113, 114, 118–19, 139

Argentina, mutual-aid and friendly societies in, 34

Army of Vietnam (ARVN): conscription of young men, 99; invasion of Cambodia, 28;

Quảng Trị killing and, 122–24; support for burial project, 134; Vietnamization of, 139

arts and culture organizations, 1

Asia Foundation: aid to summer youth program, 108–9; Library Association and, 48, 49, 50; Popular Culture Association and, 84, 85; Popular Polytechnic Institute and, 82; School of Youth for Social Service and, 88; Voluntary Youth Association and, 105

Asian Christian Services, New Life Development Project and, 93

Associated State of Vietnam (ASVN), 15; encouraging migration to the south, 17; nation building in, 17, 18–22

Associated States of Cambodia and Laos, 15

associational life: civil society, public sphere, and, 3–6; in contemporary Vietnam, 163–64; in Democratic Republic of Vietnam, 162–63; under French colonial rule, 162

Association for Health Engineers and Hygiene Specialists (Hội kỹ sư y tế và chuyên-viên vệ sinh), 47

Association for the Protection of Servicemen's Families (Hội bảo trợ gia đình binh sĩ), 66–67

Association of Buddhist University Students, 111

Association of History and Geography Professors (Hội giáo sư sử-địa), 36

Association of Newspaper Owners (Hội chủ báo), 152

Association of Periodical Publishers (Hội báo định kỳ), 151

Association of Technical School Graduates (Hội ái hữu cựu sinh viên các trường kỹ thuật), 38

Association of the Industrial and Commercial Employees of the Tonkin (Bắc-kỳ công-thương đồng-nghiệp hội), 34

Association of US University Graduates, 38

associations fees, mutual-aid and friendly societies, 36, 38

authoritarian governments, relationship to associational life, 6, 161–64

World War II, disruption of French colonialism and, 13–14

Writers Union, 162

*Xây Dựng* (To Build) (newspaper), 149, 156

*Ý Hướng* (Intention) (periodical), 98, 114

Young Catholic Workers, 58

Young Christian Workers (YCW) (Thanh Lao Công), 92, 104–5

youth organizations, 8, 102–3; Catholic, 58

youth participation in social organizations. *See also under* students: as distraction and source of fun, 110–11; motivations for, 110

Youth Union, 162

youth work camps, 105